"Our practices of Christian public worship every part of our lives and are shaped by the bring with us as we gather. This book offers dynamic, with particular attention to Christian discipleship in the workplace. It is ideal for any believer who longs for deeper connections between worship and daily life, and for any pastor or worship leader who shapes public worship. It is a book that promises to spark generative ideas and to prompt deeper engagement with public prayer, preaching, and other central practices of worship."

—**John D. Witvliet**, Calvin Institute of Christian Worship, Calvin University, and Calvin Theological Seminary

"This book is for bridge builders who desire to put into practice what it can mean to live a fully integrated life. There is so much truth in this book that it made my heart ache for our current reality and, at the same time, soar with hope for what could be by simply understanding that the church can provide so much more for its community of laborers. Kaemingk and Wilson approach this topic with great self-awareness and humility, offering readers many resources to bring work and worship together."

—**Julie Chung**, connections minister, Saddleback Church

"Both honest and hopeful, *Work and Worship* explores the gap between Christian worship and Christians' work lives, offering a clarion call to challenge what is broken and celebrate what is promising about human labor in light of God's own work. With probing theological reflection and vivid examples drawn from worshiping communities around the world, Kaemingk and Willson's efforts are historically contextualized and faithfully grounded, making this book a practical, pastoral addition to any shelf. *Work and Worship* is a gift to the whole Christian community—drawing from diverse traditions for the faithful within each congregation who are aching to hear a good word about their work."

—**Laura Kelly Fanucci**, author of *To Bless Our Callings: Prayers, Poems, and Hymns to Celebrate Vocation*

"In *Work and Worship* Kaemingk and Willson offer us a profound exploration into worship practiced in light of the daily grind. This is a reconciliatory vision for Christian leaders and laypeople who wonder how worship on Sunday and work on Monday are interconnected. The range of materials here—both biblical and historical—lay deep foundations that I want to see my students engage as they move from their classrooms to worship to the table and then out into their wider vocations."

—**Bruce Benedict**, chaplain of worship arts, Hope College campus ministries

"Nothing is more important for the local church today than to reconnect our Sunday services with our work on Monday so our whole lives can be an act of worship. This wise, accessible, and learned book is a magnificent gift to all who seek insight—theological and practical—on how to do that well. I'll be recommending this book for years to come."

—**Greg Forster**, director, Oikonomia Network

WORK
AND
WORSHIP

WORK
AND
WORSHIP

Reconnecting Our Labor and Liturgy

Matthew Kaemingk and Cory B. Willson

Foreword by Nicholas Wolterstorff

ℬ
Baker Academic
a division of Baker Publishing Group
Grand Rapids, Michigan

Published by Baker Academic
a division of Baker Publishing Group
PO Box 6287, Grand Rapids, MI 49516-6287
www.bakeracademic.com

Printed in the United States of America

Library of Congress Cataloging-in-Publication Data
Names: Kaemingk, Matthew, 1981– author. | Willson, Cory B., 1977– author.
Title: Work and worship : reconnecting our labor and liturgy / Matthew Kaemingk and Cory B. Willson.
Description: Grand Rapids, Michigan : Baker Academic, a division of Baker Publishing Group, 2020. | Includes bibliographical references and index.
Identifiers: LCCN 2020012750 | ISBN 9781540961983 (paperback) | ISBN 9781540963550 (casebound)
Subjects: LCSH: Work—Religious aspects—Christianity. | Worship.
Classification: LCC BT738.5 .K27 2020 | DDC 261.8/5—dc23
LC record available at https://lccn.loc.gov/2020012750

21 22 23 24 25 26   7 6 5 4 3

For
Uli Chi, Bill Hoehn,
and all those for whom work is worship

Contents

Foreword

Nicholas Wolterstorff

Many are the writers who lament the breach between the faith and the work of Christians in the modern world. Some go beyond lament and seek to contribute to healing the breach. Their typical strategy is to develop a theology of work—supplemented, now and then, with a theologically informed ethic of work. Their assumption is that if Christians acquire the right theological thoughts about work by reading their writings, the breach between faith and work will be healed and integration will ensue.

The authors of this book join the crowd of those who lament the breach, but they stand out from the crowd in a way that is of fundamental importance. They remark that they, too, once assumed that teaching the laity a theology of work was the path to integration. No longer. They became "*convinced that theologies of work need to be practiced, embedded, and embodied in communities of worship.*" Furthermore, "daily work should 'show up' in the community's prayers and sermons, its songs and benedictions, its testimonies and sacraments. Theologies of work matter, but they need to be sung and prayed. We need to find ways for our theologies of work to inhabit more than our brains—they need to enter our bones. . . . An integrated life is not an intellectual achievement, an all-of-a-sudden eureka moment of theological discovery. . . . *The fabric of faith and work needs to be slowly and intentionally woven back together over a lifetime of prayer and worship.*"

Lest mistaken conclusions be drawn, the writers go on to declare that "The mind of the worker still matters. What workers think about theology, vocation, and work is still important." But the question that concerns them is this: "How does a theological idea about work actually embed itself deeply in the life of a worker? Put another way, how does an *intellectual* theology of work become a *lived* theology of work? Some Christians have a theology of work floating about in their brains; others have it embedded in their bones. We want the latter."

The authors observe that they have found nothing quite like the book they have written. "As far as we can tell," they say, "the academic fields of 'workplace theology' and 'worship studies' have never been brought together in sustained conversation." Liturgical studies "almost never mention work or workers," nor are there "any books on workplace theology that seek to learn from the field of worship studies." I, too, know of nothing quite like this book. It is a trailblazing achievement!

After an opening section that the authors call "Foundations," in which they develop the case for their approach, there is a section of six chapters called "Resources" in which they describe, in considerable detail, how work was integrated with worship in ancient Israel and in the early church. The section is truly remarkable, both in the skill with which it brings to life those ancient worship practices and in the breadth of scholarship that it displays.

In the final section on "Practices," the authors consider ways in which the worship of the church today can become what they call "vocationally conversant worship." Though they offer concrete examples of such worship, they emphasize that theirs is not a how-to-do-it manual. Christian worship is too diverse, and work in the modern world is likewise too diverse for any one-size-fits-all list of suggestions. The examples are not meant to be copied but to stir the imagination of worship leaders to craft vocationally conversant worship that fits their particular worshipers and their particular workers.

Though the scholarship is remarkable in its breadth, it is presented in a way that makes it readily accessible to those who are neither theologians nor liturgical scholars—lucid and blessedly free of scholarly jargon. Take and read!

Introduction

How beautiful will be the day when all the baptized understand their work, their job, is a priestly work . . . [that] each metal worker, each professional, each doctor with the scalpel, the market woman at her stand, is performing a priestly office!

—Oscar Romero, *The Violence of Love*

There exists a profound separation between work and worship in the lives of many Christians today. Their gathered worship in the sanctuary and their scattered work in the world often feel as if they are a million miles apart.

Monday after Monday, people engage in a variety of workplace rituals: driving to work, walking across the factory floor, quickly scanning email, checking equipment, meeting with staff around the conference table. Work—be it white collar or blue—has some predictable rhythms to it. Standing at a register or sitting at a desk, mopping or designing, typing words or picking fruit. All workers have rituals, things they "just do" every Monday morning—often without thinking.

Sunday after Sunday, people engage in a variety of worship rituals: driving to church, walking down the aisle, singing hymns, saying prayers, listening to Scripture readings, confessing, and participating in Communion around the Lord's Table. Christian worship—be it ancient or contemporary—often has a predictable rhythm to it. Standing in song or sitting in a pew, praying or praising, eating bread or drinking from the cup. All worshipers have rituals, things they "just do" every Sunday morning—often without thinking.

What do these activities we label "worship" and "work" have to do with one another? Should they intersect or inform each other? Some workers do their best to keep their worship and work separate. Others attempt to connect them in all sorts of fascinating and creative ways. By and large, most pastors and worship leaders deeply desire for Sunday morning worship to meaningfully connect with the Monday morning lives of their people. But does it?

Walking into a sanctuary, many workers feel like they're visiting another world, a world quite detached from their world of work. Sitting in their pews, workers feel as if an increasingly wide chasm has opened up between the rituals they're being asked to perform in the liturgy[1] and the rituals they perform in their daily work. This chasm between work and worship is not new. Nearly one hundred years ago G. A. Studdert-Kennedy noted,

> A very large number of the people who attend our services and partake of the sacrament are disassociated personalities. They are one person on Sunday and another on Monday. They have one mind for the sanctuary and another for the street. They have one conscience for the church and another for the cotton factory. Their worship conflicts with their work, but they will not acknowledge the conflict. I want to press home what seems to me to be obvious, that while this unfaced conflict exists, the soul is not on the road to salvation.[2]

Some contemporary workers have completely resigned themselves to this growing chasm. Some have even grown to appreciate it. They're grateful for a liturgical escape, a chance to forget about the pressures and pains of work—even if just for a moment. In the sanctuary they find a spiritual haven from the cares of work and the world.

Other workers are deeply bothered by the growing chasm, haunted by a gnawing sense that the sanctuary is completely irrelevant—incapable of responding to the raw struggles, questions, and issues they face in the workplace. The chasm eats at them. They long for things to connect.

1. Some readers will be given pause at the word "liturgy." Nicholas Wolterstorff offers a helpful description of this term and its usefulness to discussions of corporate worship: "Whenever Christians assemble on Sundays they enact a liturgy. There may be nothing printed out, the cues may consist entirely of 'audibles' voiced by one or more leaders, and the participants may be strongly opposed to the claim that they have a liturgy; the term suggests to them the 'ritualism' they abhor. They speak instead of 'the order of worship.' But . . . their order of worship is an example of what I call a 'liturgy.'" He continues, "There will be actions that are to be performed and, usually, an order in which they are to be performed; and that is their liturgy. This is true even for the meetings of Quakers on the Eastern seaboard of the United States. Each person is to meditate in silence until he or she feels moved by the Spirit to say or sing something; the others are then to listen attentively." What a liturgy provides is a form of "scripted activity" that guides the bodily movements and speech patterns of participants. Wolterstorff, *Acting Liturgically*, 8, 12, 13.

2. In *Report of the Anglican-Catholic Congress* (London: Society of Saints Peter and Paul, 1923), quoted in Leech, *Eye of the Storm*, 2.

Some workers make valiant attempts to forget about daily work during worship. They do their level best to psychologically check their work at the church door. With no dedicated time or space to spiritually reflect on their "work stuff," it piles up inside their souls. The emotional plaque of vocational stress and anxiety is something they will "deal with" themselves. Perhaps, at some point in their lives, these workers were told that when they go to church they need to "focus on God" and "put the stresses of the week out of their minds." Whatever the case, these workers imagine that a sacred sanctuary is not the place to wrestle with the mundane issues of secular work.

The next step comes rather quickly: if the sanctuary is not really interested in work, perhaps it is not really interested in workers either. Left to their own devices, workers try to "handle it" themselves—through exercise or alcohol, vacations or yoga, medication or entertainment. Whatever it is, workers are on their own.

This is a problem worth tackling. The integrity of our work and our worship is at stake. Separated from one another, their relationship can quickly become distorted. We can easily begin to "worship our work, work at our play, and play at our worship."[3]

This contemporary divorce is a pervasive and devastating fact of life in the modern West. There is no need for a laundry list of surveys, stories, or statistics to substantiate it. Those of us who live in this culture know intuitively that the divorce is real. We see it with our eyes. We feel it in our bones. Modern Christians are living their lives in pieces—and the pieces are dying.

The purpose of this book is not to argue that a divorce exists between worship and work. That much is obvious. Our goal is to explore how these separated worlds of labor and liturgy might actually come to be reconciled.

Integrating Faith and Work *through* Worship

> If all of life is going to be worship, the sanctuary is the place where we learn how.
>
> —James K. A. Smith, "Sanctification for Ordinary Life"

Theologians, of course, value theology. And, rather predictably, theologians believe that good theology can be profoundly helpful for just about everything that ails humanity. Whenever theologians come across a problem, be it political or psychological, artistic or economic, you can be assured that a theologian will prescribe *more theology*. It should be no surprise,

3. Dahl, *Work, Play, and Worship*, 12.

therefore, that when theologians come across an issue like the separation of faith and work, their first reaction is to prescribe more theological education. After all, when you're a theological hammer, everything looks like a theological nail.

Why do people struggle to connect their faith to their work? How can they integrate these two disparate parts of their lives? Well, the answer is quite simple. They need to be theologically trained.

The theological line of thinking continues. If workers would only read more books about theology, work, and vocation; if they would only hear a good theological lecture about business and economics; if they would only study a biblical worldview of labor and industry; if they would only join a class to help them think Christianly about nursing or marketing or accounting—*then* these workers would be intellectually equipped to connect their faith and their work. Their faith and their work will be held together through the sheer power of their theological minds. Simply put, if workers were more like theologians, everything would be better.

Our task in this book is not to dismiss theology. We *are* theologians. We love theology. Nor is our task to belittle the importance of theological education. We have dedicated our lives to its cause. We believe in the power of theological ideas. We certainly would not write a book filled with them if we didn't. Christian workers absolutely need some level of theological training.

However, through our research and experience working alongside pastors, professionals, and congregations on this issue of faith and work, we've become increasingly convinced that *theologies of work need to be practiced, embedded and embodied in communities of worship.* Theologies of work will never be sustainable if they remain theoretical. If my work truly matters to God, that theological assertion needs to be reflected in my community's worship. Daily work should "show up" in the community's prayers and sermons, its songs and benedictions, its testimonies and sacraments. Theologies of work matter, but they need to be sung and prayed. We need to find ways for our theologies of work to inhabit more than our brains—they need to enter our bones.

In the past, the two of us followed a common path. We believed that faith and work "integration" was an intellectual problem that needed to be intellectually grasped. A worker either "got it" or didn't. Today we believe that "integration" is not so much an intellectual concept that you grasp; it's more like a craft or a skill that you practice. An integrated life is not an intellectual achievement, an all-of-a-sudden eureka moment of theological discovery. *It is more like a fabric that's been torn into pieces. The fabric of faith and work needs to be slowly and intentionally woven back together over a lifetime of prayer and worship.* In short, integration is more a habit to be practiced than an idea to be learned.

Our wager here is that gathered worship in the sanctuary can offer workers the time and space they desperately need to begin the long process of mending the torn fabric of "faith" and "work." Week after week a worker can practice bringing her daily work before her Lord in worship. Through prayer and petition, thanksgiving and lament, she practices laying down her work before the larger work of God. The torn cloth of her faith and her work can be mended *in and through her worship*.

The mind of the worker still matters. What workers think about theology, vocation, and work is still important. The question is, in part, one of pedagogical method and formation. How does a theological idea about work actually embed itself deeply in the life of a worker? Put another way, how does *intellectual* theology of work become *lived* theology of work? Some Christians have a theology of work floating about in their brains; others have it embedded in their bones. We want the latter.

Our wager here is simple: if we want to cultivate this deeper way of knowing, we will need the practices of worship. Studying biblical and theological concepts about faith and work will always matter. However, if these ideas are not constantly reinforced and remembered in and through the practices of communal worship, they will fail to put down sustainable roots.

Two Nurses, Two Pastors

Imagine, if you will, two nurses and two pastors. The first nurse comes to her pastor and shares stories of the highs and lows from her past year of work at the local hospital. She talks about her struggles with anxiety regarding her patients. She shares her workplace joys of accomplishment, healing, and blessing. She asks some difficult theological questions about illness, disability, and death. She shares some laments about the health-care system.

The first pastor responds by making a valiant attempt to answer her many difficult theological questions. He falters a bit (he's never worked in health care). Running out of things to say, he gives the nurse a book about faith and work and looks up another on theology and health care. Finally, he lets her know that he will be leading a book club on faith and work in the spring. Perhaps she could invite her fellow nurses to come and hear him teach.

The second nurse goes to his pastor and offers the same reflections. He receives a very different response from her. Hearing him out, the second pastor makes no attempt to teach him about faith, work, or health care. This pastor offers no theological answers about death or disability. Instead, she listens and asks probing questions about the nurse's work and his workplace joys and heartbreaks.

In closing, the pastor asks if she could meet with him and the five other nurses from their congregation for lunch at the hospital. Sitting around a small table in the hospital cafeteria, the pastor asks the nurses even more questions about their work. She wants to hear more about their victories and failures with their patients. She wants to hear more about their prayers for their colleagues and doctors, their challenges and frustrations of work on their specific floors. The pastor takes notes. She commends them, prays for them, and closes by inviting them to worship on Sunday morning rather than to a class.

That Sunday, during worship, the pastor asks the nurses to come forward. She asks the elders to lay their hands on them and she prays—not a generic prayer but one that she's composed specifically for them. The prayer articulates the nurses' vocational struggles, longings, praises, and pains to God— all those things they shared in the hospital cafeteria. The prayer asks for the Holy Spirit's protection and power to go with the nurses as they return to the hospital the next day. Following the prayer, the congregation stands together and commissions the nurses. The pastor sends the nurses out with a blessing and a charge for their ministry to their patients.

Two nurses and two different pastoral responses. In the first encounter, church is largely understood as a place you go for theological "answers" about work. It is a place of theological training. However, in the second interaction, we find a different understanding of the church. It is not, first and foremost, a place for theological training or answers; instead, it is a place where workers can carry their workplace questions, pains, and praises to God in community. The church won't always have answers for work, but it can provide a set of practices and a group of fellow workers who can bear the weight of work together—week after week.

There was nothing inherently wrong with the first pastor or his response. There is a chance that the nurse will remember (and perhaps even appreciate) the pastor's class and his attempts to answer her theological questions about death and disability. There is even a chance that she might read and remember a few of the ideas from his books on faith, work, and health care.

But the second nurse? There is no possibility whatsoever that he will ever forget the day his entire church surrounded him, placed their hands on him, and prayed for his work. He will never forget that they carried the joys and the heartbreaks of his hospital, that they—as one—offered his career up to God's sovereign grace. This is the power of worship.

A Modern, Western, and Urban Problem

The one who sows hoping in you will harvest the richness of your grace.

—Ethiopian prayer, in Mebratu Kiros Gebru,
"Liturgical Cosmology"

In many ways, the divorce between work and worship is a universal malady of the human condition. In Genesis 3, the deep connections between worship and work were distorted and severed. No longer directed toward God, work and worship took their own idolatrous paths. After Genesis 3, all children of Adam and Eve universally experience this cataclysmic divorce between worship and work. Every culture, every time, and every individual fails to worship and work faithfully. East of Eden, the divorce is universal.

While this is a universal affliction, one specific culture has grown particularly adept at exacerbating the division. We are speaking, of course, about the modern and urban West. Over the past four centuries, Western modernity has erected a wide array of conceptual and cultural barriers between "reason and religion," "facts and values," "public and private," "material and spiritual," "work and worship." These formidable walls make any effort to practice an integrated life extremely difficult.

There is an urban element to this division as well. In many modern cities an individual's place of worship is often far removed from their work. As they commute, their modern lives, labors, and liturgies are being geographically stretched to the breaking point by the city itself. Take, for example, an executive who works downtown but lives and worships in the suburbs. Attending a suburban church led by a suburban pastor, he most likely will experience *suburban* sermons, *suburban* prayers, *suburban* confessions that are specifically relevant for his *suburban* life. His work downtown, however, will rarely make an appearance in the worship service designed by and for the suburbs. This is just one example (of many) of how the disparate geography of urban life can exacerbate the divorce between work and worship.

Compare this to life in a medieval European village. There a worker's labor and liturgy were all geographically centered around the intimacy of the town square and its surrounding fields. A farmer could likely see the church steeple while he worked in the fields. Merchants bartered within the steeple's shadow. Likewise, a parish priest was intimately aware of droughts in the local fields or corruption in the central market. The actual geography of the village bound the life, labor, and liturgy of the people together. The urban geography of the modern West, however, can actively pull apart pastors and professionals, worship and work.

In light of the modern West's struggles with worship and work, our research project intentionally looks to other times and other cultures for wisdom. To this end, *we primarily draw insight from premodern, non-Western, and nonurban contexts to learn from their collective wisdom.* This is the main reason why ancient Israel, early Christianity, and the global and rural church serve as our primary guides throughout this text. We do not wish to idealize or romanticize these communities. Nor do we wish to say that nothing good is happening within the modern West; that is certainly not the case. Our hope, rather, is to highlight specific ways in which our premodern and non-Western sisters and brothers might inform our efforts to bring worship and work together.

The Authors

One might rightly say that we, the authors, are a part of the problem—not the solution. The two of us are modern Western urbanites. To complicate matters further, we both are systematic theologians who are white, male, and Reformed. This means that we are academically trained to slice and dice life into the neat little theological categories called "faith," "work," and "worship."

Everything we write is contextual; our eyesight is limited by our cultural privilege and the unique worship communities that we call home. Rather than take on the audacious role of speaking for all cultures and all worshiping communities, our desire is to do the hard work of focusing our critical eye on our own community and majority culture context. We invite our diverse readers to do the same with theirs.

We've tackled this topic not from a feeling of personal mastery but out of a sense of urgent need. We knew that our culture and tradition alone could not offer us a path out of this mess, and so we needed to learn from other communities whose worship looks quite different from our own. This book, therefore, constitutes an expedition of sorts into some strange and illuminating worlds of ancient and global worship. As Reformed scholars, we've worked hard to highlight important insights from Catholics, Pentecostals, Anglicans, Baptists, and Eastern Orthodox. We've also sought to learn from racially and culturally diverse worshiping communities across the United States and around the world.

Both of us have spent more than a decade investigating the divorce between faith and work in a variety of urban American contexts. We've either researched or served in faith and work organizations in New York, Los Angeles,

Phoenix, Seattle, and San Francisco. Today we live in Houston, Texas, and Grand Rapids, Michigan, where we teach at Fuller and Calvin Theological Seminaries. We spend much of our time training Christian leaders on issues surrounding faith and public life, theology and culture, missiology, and marketplace ministry. Over the years we've had the privilege to interview and work alongside a wide variety of working professionals and marketplace leaders. Their careers and callings were ever before us throughout this long research project.

Furthermore, we are the sons of hardworking parents. As children, we watched our mothers and fathers leave early and stay late for jobs in nursing and carpentry, waitressing and teaching, auto repair and home construction. Many years were a grind for our parents. Our grandparents, children of the Great Depression, had raised them with the no-nonsense maxim of the age: "If you don't work, you don't eat." As young boys, we worked alongside our fathers as they built our family homes. Today, our scholarly hands are far softer than theirs, but our fathers' patterns of work (healthy and not) have left their mark on us. Over the years we watched our parents worship their God in and through their daily work. Their labors inspired this book.

One final, and more painful, memory informs this research project. Throughout our childhoods we went to church. Sunday after Sunday we gathered for worship with our parents. Sunday after Sunday we watched our parents pray for missionaries and nonprofit leaders to go and "do God's work." We listened to pastors pray for Christian ministries all over the city and all around the world. *But never once did we see our parents' labors in the fields of the Lord recognized or blessed during gathered worship.* Never once did the pastor mention our fathers' construction sites or auto shops. Never once did they mention our mothers' hospitals or restaurants. Never once were the countless students, employees, patients, and customers whom our parents blessed and served ever mentioned. The silence of the sanctuary still rings in our ears. It informs and energizes this book.

The Readers

We had three specific types of readers in mind for this book: workers in the marketplace, worship leaders in the sanctuary, and scholars and students in the academy.

Working professionals who read this book may be challenged by some of its academic terminology. However, if they stick with it, they will encounter a variety of ways in which they can bring their working lives before God in gathered worship. Herein workers can explore how their vocational struggles and praises, questions and thanksgivings can (and must) be brought into worship.

Pastors and worship leaders who read this book will discover a variety of illuminating resources and paradigms for leading worship that deeply engages work and workers. The concepts and models provided in the book will enable them to create worship services that speak directly to workers in deeper and more transformative ways.

Scholars and students will discover what we believe to be several fascinating theological intersections between labor and liturgy in both Scripture and history. Academic readers will encounter an array of theological resources and rabbit trails in the notes begging for further research and investigation (see the bibliography for an extensive list of resources). There is much more to be done. Finally, as scholars, we've done our best to keep this book accessible for thoughtful lay readers. To this end, we've relegated many of our more technical discussions and academic references to the footnotes.

Overview of the Book

The purpose of this book is to explore how faith and work can be reconciled through gathered worship. Informed by the wisdom of ancient Israel, early Christianity, and the rural and global church, this book aims to articulate a vision for worship that is "vocationally conversant." By "vocationally conversant" we mean forms of worship that engage work and workers in a divine dialogue. Worship that is vocationally conversant facilitates an honest exchange between workers and their God. Herein workers are invited to communicate openly with God about their daily work. They are invited to carry their vocational failures and frustrations, their praises and their requests, directly into worship. Workers are also invited to listen and learn about God's work in the world and the city. In and through vocationally conversant worship, workers discover the patterns of God's work, creativity, and service. In this, they are invited to make God's patterns of work their own.

This book is divided into three distinct sections. The first lays the conceptual foundations for the project and explores the contemporary divorce between worship and work. We examine the failure of worship today to engage that divorce. The chapter titled "Workers in the Pews" offers a theological and pastoral examination of modern workers and the working lives they bring with them into worship.

The second section of the book is the scholarly heart of the research project. There we explore the interwoven nature of work and worship in the Old Testament and the early church. Insights from global and rural worship communities are inserted throughout in the form of brief but illuminating vignettes.

In the third and final section we address the question of practice. What difference does this make for the church today? Here we offer principles and practices for reconciling faith and work through communal worship.

What This Book Is Not

This book is academic, but it is not written exclusively for academics. We draw on a variety of academic disciplines to make our case. While we hope that this book contributes to academic discourse, our primary concern is that it remains accessible to the church. Moreover, while this is an academic work of theology, it does not subscribe to the traditional theory-praxis method (theology first, application second). Instead, it takes the work of the people, their lives and labors, as its starting point for biblical and theological investigation and reflection.

This book is designed to serve worship leaders, but it is not a "how-to" manual. There are no five easy steps to developing "worship for workers." Every worshiping community is different (different music and prayers, liturgical styles and traditions). Likewise, every economic community is different (blue- and white-collar communities bring different concerns into worship). Rather than dictating a one-size-fits-all solution, this book provides readers with a diverse array of Scriptures, resources, and paradigms through which diverse *worship* leaders can imagine their own ways forward.

As we complete this book, COVID-19 is circling the globe. Millions have lost their jobs. Millions more are experiencing profound professional exhaustion, frustration, anxiety, and fear. To make matters worse, these workers cannot physically gather to cry out to God in worship. Pastors and worship leaders are being forced to improvise, imagine, and create something new. This unique historical moment highlights two critical themes that run throughout the book. First, congregational worship needs to be attentive and responsive to the vocational challenges facing Christians in the world. Second, societal challenges that impact people's working lives often require creative liturgical responses. Our task in this book is not to prescribe a universal plan for tying worship and work together that is applicable to every time and place. Our task is to provide a set of enduring biblical, theological, and liturgical resources that diverse leaders can use to imagine and create deeper connections between worship and work—come what may.

This book occasionally engages in critique and deconstruction. However, on the whole, it's designed to serve as a positive and constructive resource on the issue of work and worship. We occasionally will criticize trends in pastoral and worship leadership. Both the church and the marketplace will sustain critical hits—so will seminaries, for that matter. When we consider the mess of work and worship in the modern world, there is plenty of blame to go around. Christianity and capitalism, pastors and professionals—all have a share in the guilt. That said, writing a book filled with nothing but critical deconstruction is not terribly interesting or helpful. We grow weary of the dark and defeatist cynicism surrounding the church and the marketplace. We want this book to serve as a constructive contribution for all parties involved. As theologians, we see ourselves primarily as servants called to build up the church, the pastorate, and the priesthood of all believers.

This book celebrates the creational goodness of human work and industry. However, it will not romanticize the raw challenges that real workers face in a sometimes brutal global marketplace. In our experience, Christian discussions of faith and work tend to be overly cheery and positive. "God cares about your work!" "Your work can be worship!" "You can find God at work!" "You can change the world through work!" While these sunny declarations might inspire us for a moment, the hard and simple truth is that work—for a lot of people—is often horrible. Work in a fallen world can be degrading, boring, unjust, stressful, and ugly. This book will not idealize or romanticize the current state of work; it will not paper over its broken or sinful nature. It will never suggest that Sunday morning worship should try to ignore the injustice and ugliness of work or blindly pretend that everything is okay. Christian worship should never instruct a suffering worker to "whistle while you work."

This book is focused on paid work. It rarely discusses unpaid vocations like parenting, marriage, volunteering, or political activism. These vocations are all deeply important to God, and their absence from this book is not meant to communicate otherwise. In the interest of space and time, we decided to remain laser-focused on paid work. We fully expect volunteers, stay-at-home parents, students, and active retirees to find useful information and insights within these pages. We trust that this book will help them carry their vocations into gathered worship as well.[4]

---

4. Our discussion of "parish" in chap. 3 will be of particular interest to those readers seeking to understand how to put their creative, culture-making gifts to use outside the workplace.

In this book we often label human beings "workers." Human beings are clearly more than just workers. They're also called to serve as parents, friends, neighbors, and citizens as well. We call them "workers" not to reduce their humanity but rather to highlight and carefully examine an important aspect *of* their humanity—their work.

We make the case that gathered worship can have a (trans)formative impact on work and workers. We believe that worship can help workers lead more integrated lives. However, the primary purpose of worship is not to solve the problem of faith and work; the ultimate purpose of worship is to glorify God. Gathered worship should not be instrumentalized or reduced to a pedagogical tool. The formative benefits of worship are a secondary by-product of liturgies that are primarily concerned with God's glory and honor.

This book is primarily focused on reexamining Sunday worship in the sanctuary. Readers should keep in mind, however, that worship can happen anytime and anywhere. Moreover, as we will see, *our daily work can be a form of worship to God.* With that clearly stated, our primary goal is to explore how gathered worship on Sunday can help reconcile the modern divorce between faith and work.

Finally, while we believe that gathered worship can powerfully contribute to the reconciliation of faith and work, *worship is not a cure-all.* It is not a panacea. The modern chasm between faith and work is deep and wide. Western modernity is an extremely powerful and divisive cultural force. It is a gusting wind that is constantly endeavoring to pull faith, work, and worship apart. Against the prevailing winds of culture, a single hour of gathered worship on Sunday cannot possibly hold these disparate aspects of our lives together on its own.

An Invitation

After four years of research we could not find a single book quite like this one. As far as we can tell, the academic fields of "workplace theology" and "worship studies" have never been brought together in sustained conversation. Seminary textbooks on worship almost never mention work or workers at all. (We're not entirely certain who these textbooks imagine worship is for—if not for workers.) Likewise, we've never found any books on workplace theology that seek to learn from the field of worship studies. (If they had, they might have discovered that corporate worship was a primary way ancient Israel and the early church weaved together their faith with their public lives.)

While academics have never put liturgy and labor into sustained conversation, those serving on the ground (workers and worship leaders) have been wrestling with these questions for centuries. Therefore, our references and footnotes will point to many historical and contemporary voices that shed important light on this matter. Because of the significant academic silence on the issue, there is no established academic method or road map for this project. We—authors and readers alike—are on an uncharted journey together. This is the beginning of a conversation, not its end.

PART 1
FOUNDATIONS

1

Worship That Forms Workers

We do not go into liturgy in order to escape the world, we go there to learn how to do it the correct way.

—David Fagerberg, *Consecrating the World*

Worship as a Heartbeat

A healthy heart constantly pumps and pulsates. It beats with a predictable and consistent rhythm. It will draw blood in. It will send blood out. This systolic and diastolic movement, this gathering and scattering, is how the entire body receives life-giving oxygen. At specific moments the heart valves must tighten and release. This opening and closing movement draws blood in and propels it out. Without this rhythm, the blood stagnates. It becomes static and stale. Without the heart's dynamic force—pull and push, gather and scatter—the blood, the heart, and the entire body begin to decay and ultimately die.

The liturgical theologian J.-J. von Allmen asserts that worship is the heartbeat of the church. Like a heartbeat, Christian worship has a life-giving rhythm. Like a heartbeat, it has a systolic and diastolic function. Worship welcomes and gathers people in. Worship sends and scatters people out. In and out. Pull and push. Von Allmen argues that the regularity of worship's systolic-diastolic rhythm matters a great deal. One day in and six days out.

Like the valves of a healthy heart, the doors of worship must regularly open and close to draw people in and send people out.

Like a healthy heart, worship has no interest in holding people statically inside the sanctuary. Worship is concerned with the rhythmic *movement* of the people. This movement of souls is essential to the health of both the worship and the worshiper. Like a heartbeat, if worship stalls, worshipers struggle to access the life-giving oxygen of the Holy Spirit. Everything begins to decay—the worship, the worshipers, and the community itself. Like a heartbeat, worship must be constantly gathering and scattering people in and out.

Healthy worship, von Allmen writes, is "a pump which sends into circulation and draws in again, it claims and it sanctifies."[1] Worship scatters God's people into "the world to mingle with it like leaven in the dough, to give it savor like salt, to irradiate like light." Similarly, worship gathers people in "from the world like a fisherman gathering up his nets or a farmer harvesting his grain."[2] On their way into the sanctuary, they carry their whole lives—their fish and their grain—into the presence of the Lord. On their way back out to the city, worshipers carry the grace of Christ, the law of God, and the power of the Holy Spirit into the world. Gathered and scattered. Welcomed and sent. This is the heartbeat of healthy Christian worship.[3]

In its *diastolic* function, worship gathers workers in from a wide variety of careers and callings. From all over the city they come. Worship gathers workers so that they might offer their working lives to God and so that God might offer his work to them. In its *systolic* function, worship does the opposite. It sends them out with a great work that must be extended into the city. Worship scatters workers, transformed by the work and Word of the Lord, throughout the city to be salt and light wherever they have been called. Worship blesses and commissions workers so that they may go (with systolic force) out into their various careers and callings. Worship scatters workers so that they can extend Sunday worship into Monday work.

Worship does not cease come Monday. Disciples continue to worship God in a new way through their daily work. As Clayton Schmit asserts, "The sending forth of gathered worshipers is the pivotal moment when worship turns from adoration to action. . . . In the sending, worship redirects its focus from the liturgy of assembly to become the living liturgy of discipleship."[4]

Charles Price and Louis Weil echo these sentiments but add an additional insight. They argue that Christ is the only leader of the church's whole life

1. Von Allmen, *Worship*, 55.
2. Von Allmen, *Worship*, 56.
3. Wolterstorff, "More on Vocation."
4. Schmit, *Sent and Gathered*, 155.

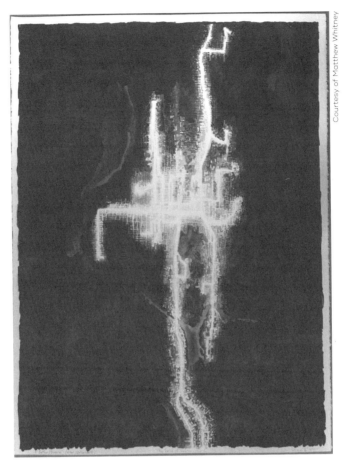

Courtesy of Matthew Whitney

Figure 1.1. *Gather and Disperse* by Matthew Whitney

Matthew Whitney is a visual artist whose work focuses on the spaces that urban citizens navigate on a daily basis. This piece depicts the gathering and scattering of a church as it goes about its life and labor within the city of Seattle, like a heart that gathers and scatters blood throughout the body. See the artist's website, www.matthewwhitney.com, and his discussion of the poetics of walking at www.matthewwhitney .com/writing-in-the-urban-grid.

of worship. The worship that Christ leads has two movements: intensive and extensive. In Christ's *intensive* worship, the church is gathered to receive assurance, pardon, and renewal. In Christ's *extensive* worship, the church is scattered into the world to love and serve the Lord. These two distinct forms of worship, intensive and extensive, are one in Christ.[5]

5. Price and Weil, *Liturgy for Living*, 14.

Pastors and worship leaders have a responsibility to encourage both intensive and extensive worship, in the sanctuary and in the world. Worship must facilitate this systolic and diastolic movement of work and worship. Worship must generously draw work and workers into the presence of the Lord, and it should also send them out the door with some systolic force. Workers who remain stagnant, whether in the sanctuary or in the workplace, begin to decay. Movement in the Spirit is life—it is oxygen.

Worship Gathers

> Let me tell you what he has done for me.
> —Psalm 66:16

Nicholas Wolterstorff extends von Allmen's heartbeat metaphor even further. He argues that corporate worship not only gathers our *souls* but gathers our *stories* as well. When the doors of the sanctuary open, worshipers enter carrying their stories with them from all over the city. These are stories from their week—stories that they need to share with God. Wolterstorff argues that faithfully designed worship will welcome three specific types of stories: stories of thanksgiving and praise, stories of sin and rebellion, and stories of heartbreak and lament.[6]

While worshipers need to communicate their weekly stories to God, they don't always know how to articulate them. Some feel awkward, others unsure. Good worship, Wolterstorff maintains, provides worshipers with three helpful mediums to articulate their various stories to God. Wolterstorff calls them trumpets, ashes, and tears. Through *trumpets*, a worshiper is empowered to communicate their praise and thanksgiving—their happy stories of the beauty, goodness, and abundance they've experienced throughout the week. Through *ashes*, worshipers can confess and honestly carry their weekly stories of rebellion and sin to God. Through *tears*, worshipers are graciously given some time and space to openly share their weekly stories of sadness, confusion, and even anger with God.

For our purposes of worship and work, these images of trumpets, ashes, and tears are profoundly helpful. They enable everyday workers to honestly carry their workplace thanksgivings, confessions, and laments to God. Here worship can cultivate a candid conversation between God and workers, faith and work, the sanctuary and the workplace. Worship that is vocationally conversant will make space for all three.

6. See Wolterstorff, *Hearing the Call*, chap. 1.

This book will make two additions to Wolterstorff's list: petitions and fruits. Workers need to regularly carry their workplace petitions and requests before God. As members of the priesthood of all believers, workers need to practice the ministry of priestly intercession. They need to intercede before God on behalf of their workplace. As priests, they must petition God with urgency to move on behalf of their coworkers, clients, customers, and entire industries. All workers have a priestly responsibility to carry their workplace petitions to God, to intercede for divine action and transformation in their industries. Gathered worship is a place where workers can begin to practice their own sacred calling to the priesthood of all believers.

The final element that workers need to carry with them into worship is fruit. Healthy worship regularly calls workers to carry the fruits of their labor to God's table. In the sanctuary, workers can practice offering their first fruits, the best work of their hands in a holy and pleasing act of worship. Healthy and formative worship will find ways to welcome the diverse fruits of workers as a holy offering of praise.[7] As we will see, carrying workplace fruits into worship is far more involved than simply dropping cash into an offering plate or directing an electronic transfer of funds. There are many reasons the Bible clearly instructs workers not to come before the Lord empty-handed (Deut. 16:16).

What does this look like in practice? How might Sunday worship gather a worker's trumpets, ashes, tears, petitions, and fruits? These critical questions will be explored in the book's final section in dialogue with Scripture, history, and rural and global practice. There we will give practical examples and models, but for now we're simply laying the conceptual groundwork for developing worship that is vocationally conversant.

Worship that is vocationally conversant is able to gather workers and their work openly and honestly before God. It gives workers the space and time, and the language and practices, to offer their whole lives and their whole work to God as a living sacrifice of praise, holy and pleasing to God (Rom. 12:1).

Some workers will come into worship with bright and shining faces, excited to offer their vocational trumpets of praise and their first fruits of thanksgiving. Some workers will come to worship with faces that are weary and broken; they will come with nothing but ashes, petitions, and tears. Worship

---

7. Evelyn Underhill writes, "Here, the human creature presents his little offering, the raw material of his concrete and yet symbolic sacrifice; and with this small gesture of generosity he moves out towards the Supernatural, goes up to the Altar of God, becomes a part of the great spiritual action of the Church in Christ her Head, and is subdued to the movement of the whole. 'In the oblation the Church, that poor widow, casts all her life into the treasury of God,' says St. Irenaeus." Underhill, *The Mystery of Sacrifice*, 14.

that is vocationally conversant will welcome these diverse workplace stories into the presence of Christ and the transformative power of the Holy Spirit.

After Jesus's crucifixion, two disciples are walking to Emmaus. Along the road they discuss the past week (Luke 24:13–35); their stories from the week are both painful and beautiful. Jesus interrupts them on the road to Emmaus. He inserts himself into the conversation and wants to hear their stories. Of course, Jesus already knows—quite intimately—all the things that have occurred in the city. And yet still he asks, "What things?" In the divine encounter, Jesus wants to hear about our week.

Worship Dialogues

But gathered worship is not a one-way conversation. God is not mute. God does not sit back and passively absorb our weekly trumpets, ashes, tears, petitions, and fruits. God is not inert. In worship, God has a story to tell, a Word to proclaim, fruits to offer, and a work to accomplish. Worship is not a monologue; it's a dialogue. Workers who enter the sanctuary are entering into a conversation—a dialogical exchange that may very well challenge, disrupt, and transform the stories they tell themselves about their work.

In the sanctuary, workers offer their stories to God. God does the same. Workers tell God about their work. God does the same. This great dialogue, this dynamic and gracious exchange between workers and God, reaches its zenith at the Lord's Table. Here workers offer their whole lives to God, and God does the same. Both sides have a story to tell. Both sides offer their work, their bodies, and their lives. Both sides receive the work of the other. In the worship dialogue, nothing is held back.

Returning to the Emmaus encounter, Constance Cherry's reflections are instructive. We, the disciples, share our stories with Christ, and Christ shares his disruptive presence and story with us. In corporate worship, "we are approached by his presence, instructed in his presence, fed by his presence, and we depart with his presence . . . a journey with Jesus together."[8]

In worship that is vocationally conversant, both God and workers take turns speaking and listening, offering and receiving, acting and waiting. By engaging in this dialogue, workers slowly and clumsily begin to practice putting their *faith* in God and their *work* in the world into conversation.

When describing worship as a "dialogue," we need to make one thing perfectly clear. This dialogue between God and worker in the sanctuary is not, in

8. Cherry, *The Worship Architect*, 48.

any way, equal. A worker's story from the past week comes under God's story for the whole world—not the other way around. A worker's fruits offered to God are a mere pittance compared to the fruits God offers to the worker. A worker's body offered to God in worship is nothing compared to God's body offered to the worker at the Lord's Table.

Moreover, without God's *primary* work on their behalf, workers would have no standing whatsoever to enter into his holy presence and offer their work as worship. God made the workers, gave them gifts, gave them fruits to offer, called them into worship. Yes, worship is a gracious exchange between God and workers. Yes, it is mutual dialogue and a vocational conversation. Both sides have something to say, and both have something to offer. However, the origin, essence, and end of this vocational conversation is not the worker; it is God.

Worship (Trans)forms

O Jesus, Master Carpenter of Nazareth, who on the cross through wood and nails didst work man's whole salvation; wield well thy tools in this workshop, that we who come to thee rough-hewn may, by Thy hand, be fashioned to a truer beauty and a greater usefulness. . . . Lord in your Mercy—hear our prayer.

—Congregational prayer in Cameron Butland, *Work in Worship*

While the primary purpose of worship is the glory of God, it has a secondary purpose, a by-product, so to speak: the (trans)formation and sanctification of the church. Worship that is vocationally conversant will *both* glorify the work of God and (trans)form the work of the church.

Sometimes the sanctuary can impact workers by offering them comfort and assurance. It can remind workers who are either oppressed or downtrodden where their true value lies. It can remind them of their true master—the one who wills their liberation. As we will see in the psalms, the sanctuary can assure workers that the Lord establishes their work and that their daily labors are not in vain. It can remind workers that God is with them and works at their side.

While worship can sometimes offer comfort to workers, it can be a source of discomfort as well. Sometimes worship can be downright confrontational to workers. Sanctuary practices of kneeling, bowing, listening, submitting, and confessing can disrupt the self-assured worker. Worship practices can directly confront vocational postures of greed, dominance, pride, and grasping. Sanctuary stories of relationships that are covenantal, communal, and

gracious can confront marketplace stories of relationships that are contractual, competitive, and utilitarian. A worship experience of silence, rest, and
waiting can disrupt a working experience of noise, busyness, and personal
initiative. A sanctuary's encouragement to freely offer and freely receive can
run up against a market's encouragement to seize and exploit. The economy
of God and the economy of this world are not always the same thing. Good
worship can expose this dissonance. Workers moving back and forth between
these two economies, these two patterns of exchange, will not always feel
comfortable or self-assured. Discomfort in the sanctuary can be a good thing.
It can even be a (trans)formative thing.

In this book we argue that *gathered worship can be a (trans)formational
space for workers and their work*. This space can be a place where workers
learn about the unique patterns of God's economy. More than that, it can be
a place where workers learn to slowly mimic and practice God's patterns of
work in their own working lives. Through worship, little by little, workers are
invited to sing and pray about the works of God. Little by little, workers sing
and pray about God's craftsmanship and creativity, God's sacrifice and service, God's liberation and beauty. Little by little, workers begin to make God's
patterns of work their own. In and through worship, they begin to inhabit this
alternative economy of God. The lawyer can pray prayers for God's justice.
The construction worker can read texts about God's craftsmanship. The oppressed field laborer can sing songs about God's liberation. The therapist can
hear prophecies about God's coming restoration and healing. In and through
worship, workers encounter the work of God, the economy of God. In this,
they are invited to make God's patterns and practices of work their own. The
sanctuary poses a question to the worker: If God is working in the world for
beauty, justice, craftsmanship, abundance, and healing, how might you join
that work? As Rodney Clapp notes, "Christians do not stop being Christians
after they participate in the Sunday liturgy. They depart to live the liturgy."[9]

How might the humble practice of footwashing on a Sunday impact a
powerful CEO's practices on Monday? How might it impact the way she
treats her employees, partners, and clients? In generous sharing of the bread
and wine on Sunday, how might she begin sharing with others on Monday?
As she waits humbly to take Communion on Sunday in a long line behind
children, the unemployed, and the disabled, how might she reflect on her
business's treatment of these people on Monday?

Here the sanctuary is potentially a dangerous place for a worker. Here the
economy of God is revealing certain unseemly things about the economy of

---

9. Clapp, *A Peculiar People*, 117.

the world. Through worship, the work of God threatens to invade workers and transform their work. In worship that is vocationally conversant, our work is made open to God's work. As we move forward in this book, we will explore through Scripture, history, and global Christianity precisely how worship can transform workers; we will show how it can slowly habituate the work of God into the work of the church. The leading desire will be to develop an understanding and a practice of vocationally conversant worship.

The Present Challenge

Before we can chart a course for the future, we must honestly acknowledge the present challenge. Gathered worship today, by and large, is not "vocationally conversant." Many Christians today do not enter the sanctuary expecting to dialogue with God about their work. Some choose to withhold their daily work from God. Others try to bring their work into worship, but they feel as if the doors are closed on them. For a wide variety of complex reasons, gathered worship is not often a place where faith and work come together. Even churches that profess to a great theology of work rarely mention work in their congregational prayers, blessings, confessions, sermons, and songs. Why is that? What's going wrong? This is the focus of the next chapter.

2

Worship That Fails Workers

In nothing has the Church so lost her hold on reality as in Her failure to understand and respect the secular vocation. She has allowed work and religion to become separate departments, and is astonished to find that, as a result, the secular work of the world is turned to purely selfish and destructive ends, and that the greater part of the world's intelligent workers have become irreligious, or at least, uninterested in religion.

—Dorothy Sayers, *Creed or Chaos?*

Connecting faith and work in the modern world is hard. Bad worship can make it even harder. Before we develop a constructive account of how gathered worship can positively contribute to the integration of faith and work, we must first take a hard look at the ways in which our worship can actively pull faith and work apart.

Sadly, it turns out that there are a wide variety of ways in which worship can fail workers. Poorly worded songs, prayers, and sermons can all divide a worker's life into a series of compartments and competitions: church versus world, private versus public, spiritual versus material, faith versus work. Congregations will never develop vocationally conversant worship until they take a hard and honest look at the ways in which their existing forms of worship actively inhibit and obstruct conversations between workers and their God. In essence, before we can understand how good worship can integrate our lives we need to examine how bad worship can *disintegrate* them. To that end, this chapter explores some of the ways in which gathered worship can fail workers and widen the modern gap between faith and work.

A note of caution: our discussion of worship failures is brief, incomplete, and specific to our context.[1] Its purpose is to provide an initial mapping from our vantage point. Readers from other cultural contexts and worship traditions will likely relate to some but not all the liturgical problems discussed below. Our hope is that our catalog will constitute an invitation for readers to critically examine their own worship practices and the ways they fail workers in their own contexts. Our goal is to initiate a hard but necessary conversation about the multiplicity of ways in which worship can fail our workers.

How Worship Can Fail Workers

Vocationally conversant worship deeply engages the lives and labors of everyday workers. The following is a brief accounting of seven ways we have seen worship fail to live up to this vision. Here we explore the specific ways in which bad worship can actively discourage vocational conversations between workers and God. We also outline some of the negative consequences that can emanate from these liturgical failures.

Institutional Worship

Institutional worship will often highlight the work of the gathered church and ignore the work of the scattered church. The "institutional" church is the church formally organized. It includes the work of pastors, elders, volunteers, and all the official programs and nonprofits that the church officially supports. The "organic" church, on the other hand, is the people of God scattered throughout the city, working and serving in a wide variety of capacities throughout the week.

Institutional worship recognizes and blesses the hard work of official church staff and volunteers. It prays for sponsored missionaries and shares stories about nonprofit leaders and activists that the institution supports. *These* are the people who truly do the work of God. *These* are the people at the center of

---

1. This catalog is neither globally comprehensive nor universally applicable. Diverse worshiping communities have their own unique challenges in connecting faith and work through worship. The problem of connecting labor and liturgy is global, impacting every worker, church, and culture. Every worship style falls short: modern or traditional, high church or low church, Catholic or Pentecostal, European or African. There is no single problem of worship and work, and no single solution. On both counts there are many.

the kingdom of God. But the organic church—the people working in medicine, business, agriculture, and manufacturing—they are never mentioned or prayed for. These workers are never invited to the front to share their vocational stories on the stage. After all, other than money, what does a dentist contribute to the institution? As a result, institutional worship does not commission or send the organic church into the world. Through sermons, songs, and prayers, the message of institutional worship is clear: the work of the institutional church contributes to God's kingdom; the organic church does not.

Workers who participate in institutional worship for long periods of time begin to suspect that their only purpose in life is to pray for (and pay for) the *institutional* church. If they want to actively participate in the mission and work of God, they have a number of options: become a pastor, volunteer at church, or start working for a Christian nonprofit. Those are the only vocations that mean something to the institution, the only ones that participate in the mission of God. If workers can't do these things, they are instructed to send money and prayers. Immersed in this world of institutional worship, workers find it increasingly difficult to imagine that their work participates in the mission of God at all.

Spiritualized Worship

Spiritualized worship cultivates an unbiblical competition between a Christian's material and spiritual life. It accomplishes this in two specific ways. First, the songs, prayers, and sermons in spiritualized worship cultivate a destructive hierarchy in which "spiritual" things matter and "material" things do not. Second, spiritualized worship encourages workers to think about the sanctuary as a sacred place (something that is close to God) and the world as a secular place (something far from God). Here the sanctuary begins to feel like a bubble, a spiritual safe haven, hermetically sealed off from the material tensions and secular tasks of their work outside. Sunday morning is a time of spiritual escape from the material world. Christianity is portrayed as a spiritual rescue mission from the material matters of the flesh. Materiality and the things of this world weigh Christians down; Christ offers a spiritual ascent above and out of the material world. On Sunday, workers can pretend that their material world and work are not real, or at least they don't truly matter. Entering into this spiritual space, workers are encouraged to check their material baggage at the door and enter a time of spiritual ascent and material denial.

Immersed in spiritualized worship for long periods of time, workers find it difficult to imagine that their material work has any place whatsoever in the worship of God. Some workers begin to see their material work as irrelevant to God, while other workers begin to see God as irrelevant to their material work. Over time, spiritualized worship has a shrinking effect. Work is shrunk down to a bare material action that is spiritually insignificant. Faith is shrunk down to a bare spiritual feeling that is materially irrelevant in the workplace. The size and scope of God and worship are reduced as well. Worship is shrunk to one "spiritual" hour a week. God is shrunk to a god of spiritual things. Both worship and God are made fundamentally irrelevant to the raw material realities of a worker's life. Here workers gather in the sanctuary to engage in an hour of spiritual pretend. They pretend, through song, prayer, and sermon, that their material work is barely real and barely matters.

Individualistic Worship

Individualistic worship will seek to cultivate a personal encounter between an individual worshiper and God. Here worship is understood as an isolated and autonomous experience, a moment between "me and Jesus." Within this form of worship, individualistic songs, prayers, and sermons rely heavily on "I" language. These practices cultivate in the worker a mistaken belief that it is both possible and good to follow Jesus alone.

Christian workers often feel like they are on their own in the workplace. Some greatly enjoy the feeling of freedom, independence, and self-sufficiency; others are burdened by feelings of isolation and loneliness. Individualistic worship does nothing to combat these feelings. It fails to remind workers that, when they go to work, they are neither autonomous nor alone. Through the prayer and song, bread and wine, workers are deeply connected to both God and a great communion of saints. The fellowship gathered around the Lord's Table goes with them into the workplace. They are never alone. Individualistic worship fails to remind workers of the covenantal ties that bind them to God, the church, and their coworkers in the marketplace.

If a worker is immersed in individualistic worship for a long period of time, their sense of isolation within the sanctuary and the workplace will only grow. If faith is a private and personal journey, the task of integrating faith and work is going to be a lonely one. Strong individuals might walk this lonely road for a time, but not forever.

Saccharine Worship

Saccharine worship attempts to paint a sweet, rosy, and dishonest picture about God, the world, and the worker's calling within it. The songs, sermons, and prayers of saccharine worship do not acknowledge the raw frustrations, boredom, and injustice that workers confront in their daily labors. The deep brokenness and the rebellion of the world are ignored. The sentimental sweetness and positivity of saccharine worship send a clear message to downtrodden workers: your sadness, frustration, and laments about work are not welcome here. This is a happy place. Check your negative baggage at the door.

Surrounded by saccharine worship, workers may begin to suspect that their pastors and worship leaders are either mendacious or woefully out of touch with the suffering of the world. Other workers might begin to suspect that the flaw rests within *themselves*: Why can't I be happy like my worship leaders? Why can't I sustain their sugary sweetness throughout my workweek? What is wrong with me?

Passive Worship

Passive worship encourages workers to sit back and submissively consume a "worship experience." Worship is done for them—on their behalf. The worker's responsibility is to recline, listen, and absorb. They're not actively learning to walk in the ways of the Lord. Worship is not an active training ground where disciples practice and participate in the patterns of God's grace. In passive worship, the worship leader's responsibility is to provide an excellent worship performance for workers to passively consume. The worker takes in the experience and either enjoys or critiques it from a safe distance. Having no active participation in the worship of God on Sunday, workers struggle to actively participate in the work of God on Monday. They have practiced the patterns of passivity on Sunday, and they continue those patterns on Monday.

Christian workers are called to be active members of the priesthood of all believers. As priests, they must actively worship God throughout their week. As priests, they must actively pray for their workplace and intercede on its behalf. *A worker who does not practice being an active and responsible priest in the sanctuary will find it difficult to actively assume this role in the workplace.* The priesthood of all believers needs opportunities on Sunday to train and practice their priestly calling for Monday. Passive worship robs them of this opportunity to practice. When a worker is reduced to a passive consumer, a liturgical slouch, the worker's muscles for faithful work and worship begin to atrophy. Eventually they will die.

Fueling Worship

In fueling worship, the sanctuary is treated like a religious "pit stop" of encouragement, energy, and emotional enthusiasm for the week ahead. Such worship reinforces a devastating misconception that the workplace is a spiritual desert, a wasteland far from God, a purgatorial existence that the worker must endure. All week at work they long for God's oasis. God's nourishing presence can be experienced only in the sanctuary. This myopic and limited understanding of God's presence and power is reinforced in a multiplicity of ways—through sermons, songs, prayers. One can hear it ring in pastoral phrases like "We return to you today, Lord" and "We come back into your presence today, God."

Workers who regularly engage in this sort of worship struggle to connect with God in their workplaces. Their work is understood as having a vampire-like quality. Throughout the workweek the disciple is slowly being drained of spiritual life and power. On Sunday the worker must run to the sanctuary in order to refuel for the week ahead. Fueling worship convinces workers that the sanctuary is the only place where Christ can truly be Emmanuel—God with us.

Privatized Worship

Private worship ignores the economic and political realities happening in the public square. Is the economy booming or in shambles? One would never know in private worship. Are the principalities and powers in the local marketplace enabling workers to flourish or are they crushing them underfoot? In privatized worship, one would never know. If an economic disaster happens in a community (e.g., a recession, a drought, an exhausted mine), privatized worship offers no response but rather keeps marching on undeterred. Moreover, though economic or political suffering might be all around, privatized worship will not offer workers any space or language to cry out to God for economic help or political restoration.

Likewise, in times of public and economic flourishing, privatized worship offers no language for praise and thanksgiving. If a new factory brings thousands of jobs to the community, privatized worship will make no mention of it. No words of praise and thanksgiving will be offered to God for the economic prosperity the factory will bring, for the families it will feed and the lives it will change. In contrast, if a local industry is publicly exposed for widespread corruption, privatized worship will offer no word of prophetic rebuke, no call to confession or repentance.

Individual workers regularly deal with the public misuse of power in their working lives. They wrestle with the principalities and powers of this world every day. They deal with cheating and harassment, sexism and racism, unfair pay and unhealthy working conditions, and more. Privatized worship pretends that these public struggles don't exist. No matter what is happening in the marketplace, the prayers, songs, and sermons in the privatized sanctuary don't change in the slightest. This world of worship has nothing to say to the world of work.

Workers who spend extended periods of time in privatized worship can begin to build higher and higher walls separating their private faith from their public work. These workers can begin to imagine that their city's economic flourishing or poverty, or its political honesty or corruption, are of no real concern to God. Over time, workers come to believe that the misuse of power in the workplace is outside God's interest or influence. The public work of humanity is beyond the privatized work of God. In the public square, workers are—by and large—on their own.

Shifting Our Worship Mind-Set

This catalog of worship failures is certainly incomplete, insufficient, and more than a little hyperbolic. But it represents a start, an open invitation to readers to reflect on their own worship context and the ways in which their liturgies might be inhibiting a vocational conversation between faith and work, God and the worker. The necessary shifts in worship are captured briefly in the list below. This brief list will grow in depth and breadth as our argument develops throughout the book. While the vocabulary and visual representation of this figure are limited, it signals the sorts of shifts we hope to encourage throughout this book.

Institutional	→	Organic
Spiritual	→	Material
Individualistic	→	Covenantal
Saccharine	→	Truth-telling
Passive	→	Active
Fueling	→	Formative
Privatized	→	Public

There are, of course, many complex theological and cultural reasons why diverse denominations continue to design worship services that fail workers. We cannot and will not investigate all of them.

However, in the next chapter we will investigate one of the largest (if not *the* largest) contributing factors to this significant liturgical failure. Simply put, *those who lead worship rarely consider fully what it means that worshipers are also workers.* It is *workers* who are sitting in the pews, *workers* who are raising their hands, *workers* who are bowing their heads and shedding their tears. It is *workers* who are being blessed, prayed for, and sent out. When planning worship, church leaders rarely ask themselves: Who are these workers? What workplace questions, pains, and praises are they carrying with them into the sanctuary? How might worship this Sunday better equip them to glorify God on Monday?

3

Workers in the Pews

Work is about a search for daily meaning as well as daily bread, for recognition as well as cash, for astonishment rather than torpor, in short, for a sort of life rather than a Monday through Friday sort of dying.

—Studs Terkel, *Working*

Deliah and Daniel have been married for ten years. Raising their children, ages five and three, is a full-time calling that they try to manage on top of their careers. Deliah works three twelve-hour shifts every week as a charge nurse. Daniel works four ten-hour shifts as a builder. Fortunately, Grandma lives close by and can help with childcare on days when their work schedules overlap. Juggling the roles of parent, spouse, and employee is never easy. Being a working parent, they say, means you feel like you're always short-changing someone.

To help foster spiritual vitality in the midst of these vocational pressures, Deliah has recently started to compose her own psalms. These are, in a sense, personal and devotional letters written to God about her life and work. Folding them up and sticking them in her pocket, Deliah carries the psalms with her as she does her rotations at the hospital. Even if she doesn't read them during her shift, Deliah reports that their presence serves as a reminder to her that God is present—not simply with her but also with her patients who are suffering. The psalms help her remain strong and tender toward the nurses under her supervision. This intentional practice helps Deliah cope with the emotional and physical demands of her job. In a way, this practice reminds Deliah that she is called to be a priest, called to intercede before God on behalf of her local parish—the hospital. This is the place where she has been called by God to render holy service and worship. This nurse is a priest, and this hospital is her parish.

Daniel's experience on the construction site is quite different. He believes that his work as a contractor is honorable. He believes that the worksite is a holy place where he can participate in God's mission. However, the rough and crass culture of his work crew can often direct him away from the path of Christ. To counteract the worksite's toxicity and his own lack of spiritual mindfulness, Daniel has developed a new morning ritual. Along with a coworker, Daniel arrives fifteen minutes early to walk through the worksite and pray. Slowly, the daily walk has started to change the way in which Daniel inhabits the worksite.

Daniel is now embracing his new role as a spiritual intercessor for the construction site. He prays for his own work but also for the projects, culture, and people on the construction site who work by his side. Daniel is no longer simply an employee; he's also a priest. He offers his work—and the construction site as a whole—up to God's sovereign grace and glory. With both humility and courage, Daniel stands before God and asks the Holy Spirit to move powerfully through the construction site.

Amidst the cacophony of their lives and labor, Deliah and Daniel report that Sunday morning is the only time in their week when they are able to be completely still before God. In this stillness there are moments when they can reflect back on the week—the marital conflicts they've had over coordinating their schedules, the demands for increased productivity that Daniel's foreman is placing on the crew, the grief of losing a patient on Deliah's Friday night shift. In the gracious silence of the sanctuary they experience a freedom to be still, repent, lament, or plead with God for help in the workplace. Sometimes, in these precious moments of Sunday worship, they hear the still, small voice of God whispering, "Well done, good and faithful servant."

Worship with the Worker in Mind

Sunday worship can fail workers for a variety of reasons. One significant reason is that pastors and worship leaders do not spend enough time attending to a series of simple questions about the workers sitting in the pews. What have they been working on all week? What sorts of workplace experiences are they bringing with them on Sunday morning? How might gathered worship interact with those experiences? In this chapter, we do not wish to shame church leaders, nor do we want to place all the blame for the present problems of faith, work, and worship at their feet. Instead, we hope to help them pay closer attention to the critically important role that work plays in the lives of the people sitting in the pews.

Pastors and worship leaders need to cultivate a hungry curiosity about their people's work. Learning about their careers and callings will improve the sermons they write, the prayers they pray, the benedictions they offer, and the songs they select. Church leaders must regularly wrestle with their people's vocational victories and defeats, their longings and heartbreaks. *This practice of vocational listening is the first pastoral step in developing forms of worship that can deeply engage and shape workers.*

This chapter offers ten brief answers to the critical question, "Who is the worker sitting in the pew?" Our reflections are divided into two sections. In the first section, we attempt to answer the question *as pastors* who have learned to listen carefully to workers in the pews. In the second section, we attempt to answer the question *as theologians* who have learned to reflect theologically about the workers in the pews.[1]

A Pastoral Reading of the Worker in the Pew

Workers Work

It's obvious, but it needs to be said: the people sitting in the pews *work*.[2] As they plan worship, church leaders need to reckon with the glaring fact that

---

1. We are well aware that our answers to "Who is the worker sitting in the pew?" are contextual, not universal. Our work was with a very specific demographic of workers. We've spent a significant amount of time listening to workers (like Deliah and Daniel) in congregations in Seattle, San Francisco, Los Angeles, Houston, Grand Rapids, and New York. Our sampling is, of course, not representative of all workers in all cultural contexts. Comprehensively describing all workers who fill the pews throughout North America is an impossible task. Geographic and socioeconomic contexts differ greatly, as do the ethnic and vocational makeup of worshiping communities. Speaking with a single voice on behalf of all these groups and individuals would be irresponsible and unwise. Nevertheless, our reflections should constitute an invitation to pastors and worship leaders to reflect on workers in their own contexts. What sorts of workers sit in *your* pews? What have they been working on all week? Listening to workers; discerning their felt needs, struggles, and pains; wrestling theologically with *their* work and *their* participation in the mission of God—these are the pastoral practices that this chapter aims to inspire.

2. We are very mindful of the unemployed, retired, and disabled workers in our congregations as well. Every person is an image bearer of God and has an inborn impulse to put their gifts and energies to use to shape the world in some way. Taking this dignified view of the human person and work does not have to demean those whose ability to use such gifts is impacted because of

these people are not *just* worshipers; they're also workers. As such, their work experiences, their vocational joys, sorrows, stresses, and successes are carried in their bodies every time they enter the sanctuary, sometimes consciously and sometimes totally unawares.[3] Entering the sanctuary, some worshipers want to forget about their work. They just want a place to rest or escape. However, there is a significant group of workers who, like Deliah, long for spaces to process their week with their creator.[4]

It is important for pastors and worship leaders to regularly investigate the joyful and heartbreaking vocations that workers carry into worship.[5] When pastors look into the pews, they need to see people who may have recently been transferred, or promoted, or laid off. They need to see people who may be wrestling with quarterly reports, workplace racism, the opening of a new business, or the selling of the family farm.

---

disability or job loss. It can help us attune to the pain they experience and point ways forward for meaningful use of their gifts and abilities.

3. Bessel A. van der Kolk claims that stressful experiences (trauma) leave imprints on the human mind, emotions, and body. Such stressors are inscribed in workers and cannot be simply reasoned away through disciplined thinking or talk therapy. Some form of embodied activity or ritual is needed in the healing process (van der Kolk, *The Body Keeps the Score*). While van der Kolk's research focuses on *trauma* to the mind-emotion-body connections, his research provides insights on the ways in which stress, anxiety, and emotions impact our bodies, inscribing themselves into our bodies. For our present discussion, it is enough to note that the strain of work experiences is present in the bodies of workers on Sunday mornings. Obviously, Sunday liturgies are not sufficient for healing apart from other psychological therapies, but certainly they should play some role in the process.

4. See, e.g., ethnographic research reported in Willson, "Shaping the Lenses on Everyday Work," 205–7, 251–53.

5. Pastors and worship leaders should regularly speak with their people about their working lives. The Theology of Work Project recommends that they even conduct regular workplace visits.

British Baptist Pastor David Coffey says, "In my time as a Pastor I made a regular pattern to visit church members in their place of work, whenever this was appropriate. I have sat with the defense lawyer in a court room; I have watched a farmer assist in the birth of a calf; I have spent time with a cancer consultant in his hospital; I have walked the floor of a chemical factory and sat in the office of a manager who runs a large bookshop. I have driven a tank and spent time with some senior military officers; I have shared the tears and joys of family life with homemakers; I have visited a London hostel for the homeless and walked round a regional prison with a Governor. The purpose of such visits is primarily to encourage and disciple a church member in that place where God has called them to be a worker."

Bible scholar Dale Bruner reports, "The revered Presbyterian preacher, George Buttrick, told a preaching class that the reason he gave a considerable amount of his workweek to visiting his parishioners in their homes and offices in downtown New York City was a passage from John's Gospel: 'the sheep will not listen to the voice of strangers' (John 10:4–5). I could believe that much of Dr. Buttrick's effectiveness as a preacher was this care for and time with his parishioners." (Theology of Work Project and Mackenzie, "The Equipping Church")

Having wrestled with their workers' experiences, the next step for pastors will be to ask a simple but challenging question: *How will their workplace joys and heartbreaks intersect with the prayers, songs, confessions, sermons, and offertories that I lead on Sunday?* Is my congregation populated with industrial workers undergoing layoffs and retraining? Space may be needed for voicing lament and loss in worship. How should a recession inform your community's observance of Advent or Lent? Perhaps you have a lot of students and educators in your community. How might your church's prayers in August prepare them for the academic year ahead? During the busy Christmas shopping season, might the retail workers be mentioned in some way? What about the accountants during tax season? Farm laborers during the harvest?

The more that pastors and worship leaders immerse themselves in the working lives of their people, the more responsive and conversant worship can become. The people in the pews work. Investigating that reality with pastoral curiosity is a critical first step. Responding with liturgical creativity and sensitivity is the next.

Workers Worry That Work Isn't Welcome

Many workers sitting in the pews honestly believe that the cares and concerns of their working lives are not welcome in the sanctuary. They do their level best to suppress thoughts of work while they sit there. This is a sacred place where they need to focus on spiritual things. Workplace thoughts constitute an unwanted "interruption"; vocational concerns are a "distraction" from the pure and spiritual activity of holy worship.[6]

In subtle and not-so-subtle ways the people in the pews are trained to check their work at the door. There are habits of pastoral speech, strange forms of "worship leader talk," that communicate that work is not welcome in the sanctuary. Gathering prayers often declare, "Thank you, God, that we get to gather here, free from the worries and cares of the week; free from the distractions, noise, and busyness of our lives; free to sit in silence and focus on you, and you alone." Deliah and Daniel report that one Sunday their worship leader encouraged them to take some time to clear their minds and hearts of all "worldly distractions" so that they could "focus" on God.

Within this paradigm, workers expect pastors and worship leaders to effectively distract them from work—to keep their focus exclusively on God. Intrusive thoughts about work while worshiping are a collective failure. The

6. See, e.g., an excerpt from an interview with a worker in Willson, "Shaping the Lenses on Everyday Work," 232–33.

worker has failed to remain exclusively focused on God. The pastor or worship leader has failed to keep their attention. The underlying theological assumption of all of this is that one can either wrestle with God or with work, but *never both at the same time*. God speaks only when we ignore our lives and labors and focus on God alone. This is all a very far cry from John Calvin's vision of the symbiotic relationship between knowing God and knowing self.[7]

A worshiper who catches herself thinking about work during worship will (predictably) feel guilty. She'll believe that she has failed to focus on God. She has sullied a holy place with her worldly cares. How dare she? After all, she focused on work for five straight days, why can't she focus on God for one? God doesn't want to hear about her work; God wants her to hear about God.

Congregations that wish to reconnect worship and work need to recognize that they are not working with a blank slate. Both pastors and professionals have inherited some bad theology and some bad worship habits. Both sides have contributed to this destructive belief that work is not welcome in worship.

Thoughts of work will always interrupt Deliah's and Daniel's worship. But these "interruptions" need not be seen as problems that either they or their pastor need to overcome. As we will explore in future chapters, the presence of work in worship is actually a gift, a profound opportunity. Workplace questions, ideas, victories, and failures need not carry us away from God's presence in worship. They might actually draw us closer. In fact, the Holy Spirit may actually be the initiator of these interruptions. A workplace intrusion in worship may be God's way of drawing the worshiper into a redemptive vocational conversation. "Deliah and Daniel, you don't need to carry this work alone. Bring this to me."

Workers Can't Always See a Liturgical Connection

The faith and work movement has grown dramatically in North America over the past fifty years. Because of the movement's tremendous influence, a growing number of Christian workers theologically understand that their daily work matters to God.[8] And yet, while they intellectually grasp the *theo-*

---

7. Calvin, *Institutes of the Christian Religion* 1.1.1.

8. Made to Flourish network has done much to spread this vision of "all of life worship" through its conferences, publications, and resources to the rank-and-file workers in many evangelical churches (www.madetoflourish.org). See also the Barna Group's "Is the Gap Between Pulpit & Pew Narrowing?," a report on research for the Center for Faith and Work at LeTourneau University.

In his book *You Are What You Love*, James K. A. Smith offers a wonderful distillation of this vision of loving and worshiping God in our vocations (see esp. chap. 7, "You Are What

logical connection between faith and work, they don't yet understand the *liturgical* connection. Put another way, they don't see what difference all of these Sunday songs, prayers, sacraments, and rituals actually make for their working lives.[9]

What is the link between the Lord's Supper and Daniel's construction project? How is the benediction related to Deliah's administration of IVs or dressing of wounds? Christian professionals today increasingly know their work matters to God. This is a wonderful development. But they don't know how their work intersects with their corporate worship.

Deliah's and Daniel's experience of corporate worship stands out in contrast to many workers in this regard. Quite on their own, these two have found their own creative ways of making connections between the workplace and the sanctuary. But for many workers, the idea that the sanctuary would provide space to lift up prayers from their workplace is a new—and revolutionary—idea.

What if Deliah and Daniel did not stand out as abnormal or eccentric worshipers? What if their stories provided a clue to a more integrated approach to work and worship on Sunday? Here pastors might learn from workers. Drawing inspiration from Deliah and Daniel, worship leaders might develop forms of worship that could help other workers carry the hopes and heartaches from their week into worship. There are pastoral strategies for framing benedictions, offerings, and Communion that can help workers bridge the gap between the particular liturgy and their daily labor.

Workers Already Have Workplace Rituals

Work shapes our body, fills our thoughts and speech, stamps our character. The accountant bears the imprint from decades of vouchers as surely as the carpenter bears the weight of tons of lumber and the jolt from thousands of hammer swings. The plumber's forearms are speckled with burns from molten solder, and the banker's face bears a crease for every foreclosure. Whatever else we make through our labor, we also make ourselves.

—Scott Russell Sanders, *Writing from the Center*

Rituals and liturgies are not limited to cloistered or ancient religious communities. Our twenty-first-century working lives are positively shot through

---

You Want: Vocational Liturgies," 171–88). Smith writes, "So the love that attracts us to God is something that grows through practice and repetition, and if we want to pursue God in our vocations, we need to immerse ourselves in rituals and rhythms and practices whereby the love of God seeps into our very character and is woven into not just how we think but *who we are*" (187).

9. Willson, "Shaping the Lenses on Everyday Work," 233.

with liturgies and rituals. Think about it: quarterly performance reviews, weekly meetings, morning traffic, rounds in the hospital, mopping the floor, cold-calling prospects, arguing with a judge, cleaning the equipment, reporting to shareholders, washing the dishes.[10]

Each industry and vocation has its own set rituals and liturgies. And there is good reason for this. A set of common workplace rituals provides structure and predictability. Patterns create order. They can enable companies to organize and orient their workers toward specific corporate goals. While some workplace rituals are life-giving, others are degrading and destructive. Some rituals are relatively neutral and inert, having little formative power (a morning cup of coffee or a walk down the hallway). Others contain a great deal of intentionality and formative power.

For example, many companies engage in quarterly performance reviews, and some even rank their employees. This regular corporate liturgy trains employees to desire, imagine, and strive for specific goals that the company values. Quarterly performance liturgies like these can form and redirect employees to seek after specific corporate values like production, efficiency, growth, teamwork, improved client relations, and more. Over time these corporate rituals coalesce into liturgies that can effectively shape individual workers and a corporate culture into a coherent way of life. Independent workers are habituated and trained to pull together in one collective direction.[11] Workplace rituals and liturgies like these can sometimes train workers to desire and behave in ways that are beautiful and life-giving. But this is not always the case.

Throughout a workweek, countless rituals contend for a worker's heart. Should the worker sacrifice her time, health, or family on the altar of success and power? Should she offer her all for the respect and praise of her colleagues or to achieve the next promotion? Should her family be denied the gift of her physical presence in exchange for a bigger house, better vacation, or lavish Christmas gifts? Should she go along with the norms of hoarding of power and information to secure her own competitive advantage or engage in backbiting of coworkers to get ahead? The world of work can surround a worker with powerful idols, each fully equipped with its own formative rituals and liturgies. The world of work can accomplish this through corporate policies and rituals, models and vision statements. In many ways the workplace can function like a sanctuary—only more powerful. As such, workplace liturgies can direct workers toward their vision of the true, the good, and the beautiful.

10. Smith, *You Are What You Love*, 185.
11. Smith, *You Are What You Love*, 180.

For workers who are disempowered or oppressed, workplace rituals can be extremely degrading and destructive. Participating in them day after day, the worker can begin to absorb and even accept a dehumanized sense of self-worth. Workplace systems of injustice, harassment, and discrimination habitually train marginalized workers to see themselves as the rightful objects of manipulation. Within this degrading liturgical world of work it becomes increasingly difficult for oppressed workers to see themselves as endowed with value, creativity, and purpose. The *imago Dei*—which never left—becomes harder and harder to see. Writing about African Americans working in the Jim Crow South, James Cone notes,

> After being told six days of the week that they were nothings by the rulers of white society, on the Sabbath, the first day of the week, black people went to church in order to experience another definition of their humanity. . . . Those six days of wheeling and dealing with white people always raised the anxious question of whether life was worth living. But when blacks went to church . . . they realized that [Jesus] had bestowed a meaning upon their lives that could not be taken away by white folks. . . . That affirmation enabled black people to meet "the Man" on Monday morning.[12]

Another major way workplace rituals form workers concerns their orientation toward time. It is important for pastors to remember that while they live within the church's liturgical calendar, workers live within their industry's liturgical calendar. A worker's temporal orientation is marked by things like annual reports, harvest time, quarterly earnings, project deadlines, seasonal tourism, Black Friday, and the end of the fiscal year. The high holy days of the marketplace contain their own habit-forming rituals designed to shape the temporal orientation of the worker.

During the Middle Ages, some marketplaces were disrupted by a church bell rung at specific intervals throughout the day. This sonic interruption reminded merchants that God's time was paramount. Merchants needed to cease their work to meditate on Christ's work. Workers, it was assumed, needed to reorient their time and work around God's time and work.[13] "St. Robert Bellarmine

---

12. Cone, *God of the Oppressed*, 12.
13. Edward Muir writes of the loss of this convention over time:
     Although the notion that some days were holy survived the Reformation and industrialization, the grand liturgical passage of the seasons did not, and the modern world has lost a sensitivity to a calendar defined by mysteries rather than by the demands of work. The loss was useful for industry, discipline, and social control, but the result has been the rigidification of human lives in accord with the mechanics of production and clocks. Despite the many legacies of church time, merchant time has been relentlessly

. . . gives the rule as follows: In the morning call to mind the memory of the Incarnation, at noon the memory of the Passion, and in the evening the memory of the Resurrection."[14]

Twenty-first-century workers no longer experience these temporal and ecclesiastical interruptions in their workplace. Modern workers will speed up or slow down, relax or toil according to the liturgical calendar of their industry—not the church. Our rhetorical use of "Sunday" and "Monday" language in this book is increasingly irrelevant for many workers who are now accessible 24/7 via their phones. For them, there are no hard-and-fast temporal boundaries. Work can be done anywhere and anytime. Sabbath is assimilated. We can learn two things from this. First, how workers inhabit time in the marketplace will shape their minds and hearts. Second, their relationship to time—be it healthy or not—will always be brought into the sanctuary. A soul that is rushed all week long will have a hard time slowing down and being still. The marketplace calendar—and its monetized relationship with time—will impact the way a worker inhabits worship.

In summation, workers are being liturgically formed (and deformed) all week long. Let's return to Daniel and Deliah to illustrate the positive (and negative) effects of workplace liturgies. Daniel works for a construction company with one bottom line (profit). Deliah works for a hospital with a triple bottom line (profit, people, planet). Both workplaces have developed a liturgical world that intentionally directs workers to serve these bottom lines. On the construction site, Daniel encounters constant reminders and practices designed to increase worker speed, efficiency, and production. Working within this liturgical world of construction, Daniel feels constant external and internal pressure to cut corners and serve the single bottom line of profit. These practices form Daniel into a specific sort of person. He carries this formation home with him. He also carries it to church. Deliah's hospital, on the other hand, has developed a whole series of intentional processes and practices to undergird its commitment to a triple bottom line. Day after day, Deliah is ritualistically reminded and trained to value not simply profit but also people and the planet. Through these institutional rituals the hospital is training Deliah to embody these three values. The hospital has done more than simply teach Deliah ideas. *It has formed the way her hands, head, and heart move through the hospital. She too carries this liturgical formation with her to her home and her church.*

---

victorious: the modern holidays now celebrate important historical events for the state or work itself, as in the European May Day or the American Labor Day. (Muir, *Ritual in Early Modern Europe*, 76)

14. Jungmann, *The Early Liturgy*, 105.

Pastors and worship leaders need to recognize that workplace rituals are forming and deforming their people all week long. Here is where Sunday morning worship comes in. Deformed workers need *counter*-liturgies or subversive rituals that can actively contest the ways in which they've been deformed in the marketplace. *Pastors and worship leaders have a responsibility to develop Sunday liturgies that can confront and respond to marketplace malformations.*[15]

They also have a responsibility to understand and respond to the liturgical seasons of the marketplace around them. As we will see, the liturgical seasons of ancient Israel and the church in the Middle Ages were deeply conversant with and responsive to the agricultural seasons of the workers in the surrounding community.[16] When the workers were harvesting and planting in ancient Israel and the medieval church, worship leaders were preparing services to frame that agricultural work within the economy of God. We will discuss these issues in greater depth later on. For now, the simple point stands: *workers sitting in the pews are engaged in formative rituals and liturgies all week long.*

Workers Miss God

Many worshipers intellectually understand that God is with them in the workplace. And yet, while they theologically comprehend God's omnipresence in the workplace, *they don't feel it*. They feel alone and disconnected. Sitting in the pews on Sunday, workers sometimes feel like this is their only shot—their only chance to feel God's hand on their back.[17] Workers need pastors and worship leaders who are aware of this weekly experience of spiritual loneliness. But more than that, workers need leaders who can actively help them address this deep sense of spiritual isolation.

15. Smith explains how worship trains our imagination that in turn shapes how we inhabit our workweek: "[Sunday] worship is not some escape from 'the work week.' To the contrary, our worship rituals train our hearts and aim our desires toward God and his kingdom so that, when we are sent from worship to take up our work, we do so with a habituated orientation toward the Lover of our souls. This is also why we need to think about habit-shaping practices— 'vocational liturgies,' we might call them—that can sustain this love throughout the week." Smith, *You Are What You Love*, 187.

16. Lester Grabbe observes, "Cultic activity took place on a daily basis, but the focus tended to be on certain regular festivals: the weekly sabbath and the seven annual festivals. The annual festivals grew out of the agricultural year and celebrated significant points within it (beginning of the barley harvest; end of the wheat harvest; grape harvest). Special sacrifices were designated for the weekly sabbath, the monthly new moon, and especially for the main festivals." Grabbe, *Judaic Religion in the Second Temple Period*, 141. See also Armerding, "Festivals and Feasts," 311.

17. See a summary of interview findings in Willson, "Shaping the Lenses on Everyday Work," 246–47.

How can the spiritual intimacy of Sunday worship begin to reverberate out into Monday work? How might this sense of divine connection and presence last? These are complex and critically important questions that pastors and worship leaders need to wrestle with.

Part of the answer, as we will discover later, is to help workers practice a critical skill while they are in the sanctuary: the skill of bringing their work to God and dialoguing with him about it. As Daniel carries his frustrations from the construction site into the sanctuary, he begins to inhabit worship differently. He hears God use a lyric from a song, an image from a prayer, or an illustration from a sermon that speaks directly to his struggles on the worksite. Then, when he returns to the construction site, Daniel begins to inhabit that space differently as well. Having spoken with God about the worksite in the sanctuary, Daniel begins to move through the site with a sense of courage and awareness of God's imminent presence and power. This connection—forged in the sanctuary—provides Daniel with an assurance and expectation that he will find the Holy Spirit's presence in the midst of his trials at work. As we will discuss later, *intimacy with God at work can begin when a worker learns to bring their work to God in worship.*

A second part to the pastoral response is to see Monday work as an extension of Sunday worship. Sunday morning is not a "moment" of worship; it is the beginning of a whole week of worship. A more appropriate title for worship leaders might be "worship starters." It is their responsibility to launch workers into a whole week of worship.

Denise Daniels and Shannon Vandewarker write persuasively, "How we enter our work sets the tone for our awareness of God's presence throughout the workday and week." For, in "paying attention to the way you begin your work, you begin the habit of paying attention to where God might be at work throughout your day."[18] As we mentioned earlier, Daniel begins his day at the construction site walking and praying his way around and through the construction space. The regularity of Daniel's entrance ritual had a direct impact on his awareness of God's presence and power at the construction site. Note that Daniel's morning ritual does not magically conjure or convince God to show up at work; rather, it awakens Daniel to a divine presence and power that, on his own, he is prone to forget (see Gen. 28:16).

In our interviews with workers, many of them specifically mentioned the power of what we call "entrance rituals" (personal prayers during the commute, the walk to the office, the first five minutes at the desk). One worker prays as she swipes her key card upon entry. Another removes his shoes for a

---

18. Daniels and Vandewarker, *Working in the Presence of God*, 15.

morning prayer at his desk. Each of their entrance rituals attests to the claim of Daniels and Vandewarker: intimacy with God at work is directly connected to *how* we enter the workplace.

Workers miss God at work. They often feel spiritually disconnected and lonely. As pastors and worship leaders look out into the pews, they need to recognize that many workers come hungry and longing for connection with God. While connecting with God in the sanctuary is critical, *the manner in which* workers connect with God on Sunday is going to impact their connection with God on Monday. Workers need to participate in Sunday liturgies that awaken them to God's presence and power in all of life—not simply in the sanctuary. This will be a critical theme throughout our study.

A Theological Reading of the Worker in the Pew

In the first section of this chapter we answered the question, "Who is the worker in the pew?" from a more *pastoral* position. In this second section we want to answer the question from a more *theological* position. This very brief and truncated "theology of the laity" will be biblically and theologically unpacked in future chapters.

Workers Are People Who Are Integral to the Mission of God

When you find a man who is a Christian praising God by the excellence of his work—do not distract him and take him away from his proper vocation to address religious meetings. . . . Let him serve God in the way to which God has called him. . . . [Do] not take him away from it, so that he may do ecclesiastical work for you. But, if you have any power, see that he is set free to do his own work as well as it may be done. He is not there to serve you; he is there to serve God by serving his work.

—Dorothy Sayers, *Creed or Chaos?*

From a theological perspective, pastors and worship leaders do not invite workers into the mission of God. The workers in the pews have been laboring within the *missio Dei* all week long.[19] Gathered worship should not only acknowledge the worker's participation in God's mission but also bless it. The work of the people is integral to the mission of God, not incidental.[20] When

19. Kraemer, *A Theology of the Laity*, 114, 118.
20. Garber, "Vocation as Integral, Not Incidental."

addressing workers, pastors and worship leaders should keep their status of workers in mind, and they should speak about workers and their mission with an accordant honor and respect. Gathered worship must honor—and never belittle—the worker's centrality within the mission of God.

In the middle of the twentieth century, a group of Protestant and Catholic theologians recovered a robust theological understanding of the priesthood of all believers. They argued that the laity were at the leading edge of God's mission in the world.[21] The mission of God in the world is both larger and more complex than pulpit ministry, overseas missions, nonprofit service, or political activism on behalf of the marginalized. While these are important vocations, they don't exhaust the complex and kaleidoscopic work of God in the world. The mission of God cannot be limited to the narrow goals of either soul-saving or social justice.[22]

Instead, the mission of God includes the renewal, restoration, and reformation of all things. All Christian workers, in all industries, are invited to participate in the multifaceted mission of God. Vocations in business and medicine, poetry and engineering, counseling and chemistry, marketing and finance all have a role to play in Christ's cosmic work of reconciling *all things*.[23] As the apostle Paul writes,

> For in him all things were created: things in heaven and on earth, visible and invisible, whether thrones or powers or rulers or authorities; all things have been created through him and for him. He is before all things, and in him all things hold together. . . . For God was pleased to have all his fullness dwell in him, and through him to reconcile to himself all things, whether things on earth or things in heaven, by making peace through his blood, shed on the cross. (Col. 1:16–17, 19–20)

Here we must address the tragedy of narrow and myopic conceptions of the *missio Dei*. This can be seen particularly in the assumption that the Christian calling can be limited to either the Great Commission (Matt. 28:18–20) or the Great Commandment (Matt. 22:36–40). To be sure, the mission of God includes both, but it is not limited to them.

Long before giving humanity the Great Commandment and the Great Commission, God commanded human beings to explore, name, develop,

21. Kraemer, *A Theology of the Laity*, 114, 118; Newbigin, *Unfinished Agenda*, 203; Goheen, "The Missional Calling of Believers," 40.

22. Goheen, *Introducing Christian Mission Today*, 26.

23. Mouw, *When the Kings Come Marching In*. See especially chap. 1, "What Are the Ships of Tarshish Doing Here?," 17–42.

and cultivate the creation (Gen. 1:28). The Great Commission and the Great Commandment do not replace this original command to work within God's creation. The astronomer who explores, the scientist who names, the artist who develops, and the farmer who cultivates all participate in the creational purposes of God. The Great Commission and the Great Commandment do not remove or lessen the value of their work. Instead, these later commands elucidate important dimensions of their holy vocations that are grounded in creation.[24]

Put another way, God's mission in the world did not begin with Christ's commands to love one's neighbor and to make disciples. God's mission begins with and is grounded in the creation itself. At the fall, God did not give up on the world, its restoration or its development. The command to work and to care for creation did not cease. *Loving one's neighbor, sharing the gospel, and working in the garden are all part of God's mission in the world.* The laity's work in God's world has always been—and will always be—integral to the mission of God in Christ through the Spirit.

Furthermore, the laity's work in creation makes the church's fulfillment of the Great Commandment and the Great Commission possible. The workplace is, in many ways, the primary medium through which the laity will either obey or reject Christ's commands. The workplace is a critical (if not *the* critical) space in which workers will either learn to follow Christ faithfully or walk away from him.[25]

God has called the laity in unique contexts—places where pastors and missionaries may never go. God has called them into those spaces to cultivate the creation, love their neighbor, and share the good news through their words and their work. The mission of God encompasses it all.

Deliah's position in the hospital can illustrate the point. As a charge nurse, Deliah regularly evaluates the performance of other nurses working in her particular unit. This practice is not tangential to God's mission at the hospital; it's integral. Embedded within the hospital's evaluation criteria is a tacit vision of what it means to be human and what human flourishing entails.[26] How Deliah conducts her performance reviews fosters within her nurses a particular way of being human. It cultivates a distinct culture on her wing of the hospital. *If Deliah's evaluations contribute to the flourishing of nurses and the hospital in a way that honors Christ, then her work on these evaluations is how she faithfully participates in the mission of God.*

24. Smith, *You Are What You Love*, 178–79.
25. Newbigin, *Sign of the Kingdom*, 66.
26. Dyrness, *Poetic Theology*, 84–85. See also Smith, *Desiring the Kingdom*, 39, 53, 62.

When pastors and worship leaders look out into the pews, they must see a people who—aware of it or not—are already on mission. The pastor's liturgical task is not to give these people a mission. Nor is it to invite them into a church-centered mission. Instead, their liturgical task is to *awaken* and *remind* the people of their integral role within the mission of God *through their daily vocations.*[27]

Workers Are Integral to the Mission of the Local Church

Through its laity the Church is present in every area of human activity. It is in offices, in schools and universities, in hospitals, in stores, in factories and hotels.

—Anne Rowthorn, *The Liberation of the Laity*

Deliah's and Daniel's work is integral not only to God's mission but to their local church's mission as well. Workers (not pastors) are the primary agents of a church's mission in the community. Likewise, the workplace (not the church building) is the primary locale of a church's local mission. This theological truth profoundly challenges existing models of local mission that are pastor-centric, program-centric, building-centric, and neighborhood-centric.[28]

In America, church-based staff and volunteers often expend a great deal of time and energy trying to develop outreach programs and missions to surrounding neighborhoods. Programs often include community gardens, neighborhood picnics, ministries to local homeless, after-school programs for neighborhood kids, food drives, and door-to-door visitations. Once these programs are established, a lot of energy is expended trying to recruit volunteers to "participate" in the mission of the local church—as if they weren't already.

Make no mistake, these outreach programs are often vital and important. However, if churches begin to recognize that the daily *work* of their people is central to their mission, their thinking about what counts as "outreach" and "mission" begins to dramatically change. Suddenly the church is already on mission in workplaces across the city.

Some church leaders will be familiar with the concept of a special Mission Sunday, an evangelical tradition in which a missionary visits a church and presents stories of all the things God is doing on "the mission field." Typically, the pastor takes the week off from preaching, and the songs, prayers, and sanctuary decorations are oriented around the theme of the Great Commission. The

27. Newbigin, *The Good Shepherd*, 77–80.
28. Boff, *Church, Charism and Power*, 142.

worship trains the people to see this one missionary as serving the mission of the local church *on their behalf.*

A more holistic theology of the church's mission would see every worker in the pews as a missionary and each of their workplaces as a strategic outpost of the local mission.[29] The city will be renewed not by five church planters and five nonprofit leaders; it will be renewed by the complex callings and careers of the five hundred other people sitting in the pews. With this theological vision in hand, pastors and worship leaders need to reimagine the place of the worker in the worship service. If worship services can be completely redesigned to highlight the missionary's work, they can be redesigned to highlight the people's work as well. The mission of the local church is not limited to a single outreach program; it is not limited to a single missionary. It is pluriform, complex, and all-inclusive. The church's mission is embodied in the diverse work of the people all over the city—and the church's worship should name and reflect this.

Workers Are Priests

There is no such thing as a nonordained person in the Church.

—John Zizioulas, *Being as Communion*

This spade work—this vocation—in the garden is priestly work.

—Uche Anizor and Hank Voss, *Representing Christ*

Workers sitting in the pews are members of the priesthood of all believers. A "priest" here is understood as a person who has a sacred calling, a divine ordination to offer holy worship directly to God. Priests have been set apart. They've been called. They've been given a priestly authority to intercede on behalf of others and the world before the face of God. *All work*, when done in faithful service to both God and neighbor, is a priestly act of worship.[30] Therefore, as we will demonstrate, when workers enter the sanctuary, they don't arrive for a moment of worship; they've been engaged in priestly worship all week long.

The gathered worship of the church must recognize and reflect the priesthood of all believers sitting in the pews.[31] Faithful workers are living sacrifices holy and pleasing to God. Their skillful and worn hands praise God. Their priestly bodies, in the sanctuary and on the factory floor, glorify God.

29. Willson, "Putting Business on the Mission Map."
30. Kuyper, *The Exalted Nature of Christ's Kingship*, 474.
31. Newbigin, *The Good Shepherd*, 79–80.

But what do we mean when we make the audacious claim that "workers are priests" and "all work can be priestly worship"? This needs some unpacking. A helpful place to begin is the doctrine of the *munus triplex*. In this historic formulation we are told that Jesus Christ serves as humanity's prophet, priest, and king.[32] Called to be a prophet, Christ reveals and speaks God's truth. Called to be a priest, Christ intercedes for a broken world and mediates God's grace. Called to be a king, Christ reigns in power and executes God's justice.

Those who follow Christ are called to follow this threefold calling. What does this mean for workers? Called to be prophets, workers have a responsibility to speak up and advocate for God's truth and justice in their daily work. Called to be priests, workers have a responsibility to engage in the ministry of reconciliation and intercession in their workplace. Called to be kings and queens, workers have a royal responsibly to steward their power well and execute justice in the workplace. As workers grow in Christ,[33] they increasingly live out this threefold calling to be prophets, priests, and kings in the workplace.

Contemporary workplace theologies often lean heavily on the "royal" calling of workers while they largely ignore the priestly and prophetic callings of workers. A royal framing of workers goes like this: Adam and Eve were the king and queen of creation. They were given royal power to steward God's creation wisely.

This royal framing of Adam and Eve produces a particular sort of workplace theology, one that concerns itself primarily with the responsible execution of creative power within the workplace. Here, to be a "good worker," Deliah and Daniel must become aware of one's God-given responsibility to faithfully work and steward creation. This model can be conducive for workers who have power, but it can also be quite alienating for workers who do not. This may explain why royal theologies of work have flourished in white-collar communities in the West and largely languished in more blue-collar communities.

The doctrine of the *munus triplex* alerts us to the fact that Adam and Eve were given more than a royal calling in the garden: *they were given a priestly*

---

32. Bavinck, *Sin and Salvation in Christ*, 367.

33. Rowan Williams makes clear that humanity's priesthood is found as they participate in Christ's priesthood. "Christians are priests entirely in a derivative sense: They 'offer,' which is the characteristic priestly act, but only because they are being offered by the eternal high priest, and because they have been made a worthy offering by the atonement achieved epha-pax in the cross." They are not priests "in virtue of their own faithfulness, but because of the faithfulness . . . of the sole authentic priest, the one who cannot be anything other than priest, whose priestly life and death constitute the ground of all subsequent offering." R. D. Williams, *Eucharistic Sacrifice*, 16.

calling as well.[34] According to recent scholarship, the garden of Eden can and should be understood as God's first temple. Moreover, Adam and Eve were God's first priests.[35] As the "garden priests," Adam and Eve were called to guard and to keep this primordial temple holy.[36] Whenever these two priests worked the temple's soil, they were engaging in worship as well. God took delight in their priestly labor and received their work as worship. When Adam and Eve lifted the fruits of the garden up to God and gave thanks, they were acting not simply as royal stewards but also as priestly worshipers.[37] These were garden priests, leading a garden worship service.[38]

According to this theological framing, Eden was the original site of fully integrated work and worship. The garden functioned as both a workplace and a temple. Adam and Eve's "royal" and "priestly" callings were one within the garden.[39] Their work and worship were one and the same.[40] Their diverse acts of material cultivation and spiritual adoration were a seamless collection of movements that all processed toward the glory and worship of God.[41] "To subdue the earth was to extend God's garden sanctuary throughout the earth and thus prepare the way for the presence of Yahweh to permeate the world in its entirety."[42]

In Scripture we learn that creation itself is constantly praising God. The hills and mountains, plants and trees, sun, moon, and stars all produce songs of holy praise (Ps. 148). God delights in the worship creation offers. When Adam and Eve enter into creation, they are walking through a garden that is *already* offering worship. Their acts of human cultivation *join* creation's preexisting state of praise.

34. Anizor and Voss, *Representing Christ*, 29.

35. Beale, *The Temple and the Church's Mission*, 66; Walton, *The Lost World of Genesis One*, 86–88.

36. Kline, *Kingdom Prologue*, 55; Beale, *The Temple and the Church's Mission*, 68.

37. N. T. Wright, *After You Believe*, 79–81.

38. Zizioulas, "Proprietors or Priests of Creation?"

39. Meredith Kline notes that in the creation story, the "unity of the royal-cultural and the priestly-cultic functions as alike in covenantal service rendered to the heavenly Suzerain prohibits any dichotomizing of man's life into religious and nonreligious areas. . . . Within the creation-theocracy (and in any redemptive reestablishment of that theocratic order) the cultural dimension is . . . cult-oriented; it is itself holy." Kline, *Kingdom Prologue*, 67. G. K. Beale comments, "Adam should always best be referred to as a 'priest-king,' since it is only after the 'fall' that priesthood is separated from kingship." Beale, *The Temple and the Church's Mission*, 70.

40. Beale writes, "While it is likely that a large part of Adam's task was to 'cultivate' and be a gardener as well as 'guarding' the garden, that all of his activities are to be understood primarily as priestly activity is suggested not only from the exclusive use of the two words in contexts of worship elsewhere but also because the garden was a sanctuary." Beale, *The Temple and the Church's Mission*, 68.

41. Morrow, "Work as Worship in the Garden and the Workshop," 161–62.

42. Anizor and Voss, *Representing Christ*, 30.

Consider a heuristic example. A tree gives glory and praise to God simply by being a beautiful and healthy tree. A tree can "clap its hands" to worship God without any human help (Isa. 55:12). However, if a worker carefully shapes that tree into a beautiful violin, that tree's worship is not silenced; instead, the tree's worship is actually extended and amplified. God takes delight in this new articulation of the tree's worship. Workers, therefore, can worship God in and through their work in creation. As the theologian Jeremy Begbie argues, humans are called to articulate creation's praise.[43]

Deliah's and Daniel's work is more than a royal act of obedient steward-ship: *it is also a priestly act of holy worship*. Here an anthropomorphic distinction between God's "eyes" and God's "nostrils" may prove momentarily helpful. God does not simply look down on his royal stewards with his eyes to ensure that they are obeying his cultural mandate. God is also hovering over his priests breathing into his nostrils the pleasing aroma of their worshipful work (cf. Lev. 2:9; 3:5, 16). God does not simply mandate human work; God delights in human work. God accepts it with joy, not as mere obedience but as worship.

But priests do more than offer worship. They also engage in the priestly ministry of reconciliation and intercession. As members of the priesthood of all believers, Deliah and Daniel are called to prayerfully intercede before God on behalf of their places of work, coworkers, clients, and entire industry. When priestly workers enter the sanctuary, they need to carry their coworkers and workplaces before the Lord and intercede on their behalf.[44] Likewise, when priestly workers enter the workplace, they have a priestly calling to reconciliation, healing, care, and restoration. These priestly acts of intercession and reconciliation are worship.

Labeling Deliah and Daniel as "priests" does not diminish the importance of their pastors and worship leaders in any way. If anything, it increases their importance. Similarly, claiming that their "work is worship" does not diminish the importance of gathered worship on Sunday. If anything, it increases Sunday's importance.[45] As we will discuss later on, the priesthood of all believers desperately needs to be reminded of its high and holy calling to worshipful work.

In summation, if the pews are filled with priests, *pastors and worship leaders need to consider how Sunday worship can remind these workers of their priestly callings to the ministries of intercession, reconciliation, and worship*

---

43. Begbie, *Resounding Truth*, 212.
44. Wolterstorff, "More on Vocation," 20–21; Newbigin, *The Good Shepherd*, 88.
45. Newbigin, "Ministry and Laity," 481.

in the workplace. As this book proceeds, we will explore how gathered worship can awaken workers to their membership in the holy priesthood.

Workers Already Have a Parish

Every priest has a parish, and the priests sitting in the pews are no different. Their parish, Monday through Friday, is their workplace. This is the place to which they have been called to live out their priestly calling. Most pastors, when asked to describe their people's "parish," would begin by drawing a line around the neighborhood that immediately surrounds their church building. We intend to theologically challenge this understanding of the people's parish.

Adam and Eve were placed in the garden of Eden, not the garden of Gethsemane. Israel was called to the land of Canaan, not the land of Cush. Exiled Jews were called to seek the shalom of Babylon, not Jerusalem. Early Christians were called to be salt and light in the Roman Empire, not the Greek. God calls specific people to specific spaces. Every priest has a parish, a bounded space to serve and worship the Lord. The pews of the church are filled with priests who are called to work in a wide variety of diverse places and spaces. Deliah offers her priestly worship at the hospital, not the bank. Daniel's priestly offering comes from the construction site, not the university.

The word "parish" evokes the image of a medieval Catholic village. Here all of the villagers worked and worshiped under the same steeple; they all served in a unified and singular parish. The world has changed a great deal since then. In the global marketplace, Christian workers often travel long distances for work—across vast cities, countries, and even around the world. In the digital world, workers can interact with multiple countries in a single day. A Christian's daily work can extend thousands of miles away from the neighborhood surrounding the building where their church gathers. For these reasons (and many more), when twenty-first-century workers file into a sanctuary, they represent many diverse parishes, not simply the one immediately surrounding the church building.

A local church no longer has one parish; it has many. Therefore, when pastors and worship leaders prepare for Sunday morning, they need to understand the multiplicity of parishes that are represented in the pews. The local church should not call workers to come and serve God in its parish; instead, it should equip them to serve God in *their own* parish.[46]

If the people sitting in the pews represent a multiplicity of parishes, three liturgical questions follow: First, how can worship leaders acknowledge these

---

46. Newbigin, *The Good Shepherd*, 88.

parishes during worship? Second, how can leaders encourage workers to pray for their parishes? Third, how can leaders effectively send workers back to their parishes with a sense of priestly purpose?

Workers Need Sunday

The liturgy cannot be lived at each moment . . . unless it is celebrated at certain moments.

—Jean Corbon, *The Wellspring of Worship*

Worship grounds me again in the real world of God's creation, dislodging me from whatever world I have imagined for myself.

—Kathleen Norris, *The Quotidian Mysteries*

If work is worship, why gather for worship on Sunday? If workers are "priests" in the workplace, what is the significance of gathering around professional priests in the sanctuary?

Here we will draw on Clayton Schmit's helpful distinction. The priesthood of all believers is called to worship God through daily action; it is also called to worship God through weekly adoration.[47] Both adoration and action matter. Neither can replace the other; both are necessary. Gathered worship in the sanctuary offers workers a number of elements that scattered worship in the world does not. These distinctions are captured well in parts of Puritan thought and practice. The Puritans believed that a whole week of faithful work was worshipful to God. Some even viewed the Sabbath as the culmination of the workweek—the vantage point from which God's glory throughout the week could be seen and understood. There was something different about Sunday, something critical in the week's design and makeup—six days out for work and one day in for rest. One Puritan preacher, Lewis Bayly, helped merchants and business leaders see the beauty and richness of the Sabbath through the imagery of local marketplace. Here is a modern paraphrase of Bayly's older English: "The Sabbath day is God's market day for the week's provision wherein God will have us come to him and buy of him, without silver or money, the bread of angels, and water of life, the wine of the sacrament, and milk of the Word to feed our souls; tried gold to enrich our faith; precious eye-salve to heal our spiritual blindness; and the white clothing of Christ's righteousness to cover our filthy nakedness."[48]

---

47. Schmit, *Sent and Gathered*, 155.
48. You can read the original in Bayly, *The Practice of Piety*, 170.

On God's market day, workers need to cease their serving so they can be served. They need to cease their grasping so they can reflect on what they've been given. There's no need to fight for their clothing in the sanctuary; here they are clothed in Christ. In the sanctuary they are immersed in God's strange and upside-down economy in which the currency of the world has no value. Bayly says that, on Sunday, workers must "cease in thy calling to do thy work, that the Lord by his calling may do his work in thee."[49]

James K. A. Smith captures the idea poignantly when he writes, "If all of life is going to be worship, the sanctuary is the place where we learn how."[50] In other words, gathered worship equips workers for their scattered worship in the world. The sanctuary practices workers into the gracious work of God. Here the sanctuary functions like a training ground, a spiritual gymnasium for the worker's soul.

David Fagerberg, a liturgical theologian, echoes Smith's point when he asks rhetorically, Why do we need a sanctuary liturgy when all of life is liturgy? Why have sanctuary sacraments if the whole "profane world is a sacrament"? The answer is, "we come [into the sanctuary] for eye surgery. We cannot return to [the world] until our priesthood has been repaired. . . . [The leader] in the sanctuary ministers to the men and women in the nave so they can resume beyond the narthex the career that Adam and Eve had forfeited."[51]

Engaging in holy and worshipful work in today's global marketplace is not simple or straightforward. Priestly postures in the workplace do not come naturally; they must be practiced. Worker-priests need to be taught and trained, shaped and formed into the image of their high priest, Jesus Christ. Gathered worship must play a central role in the preparation and formation of priestly workers. As the Holy Spirit moves through song and sacrament, prayer and benediction, workers can slowly be trained to walk in the ways of the Lord.

Smith's writings about the formative power of gathered worship are a timely gift to the discipling efforts of the church. This book, however, will not simply repeat his argument. In fact, it will flip his statement over and explore it from another angle. Throughout the book we will make this argument: *if sanctuary worship is going to be formative for workers, their working lives will need to be brought into it.*

Let's explore that statement. Workers sitting in the pews need the formative power of worship—Smith makes this much clear. However, worship cannot impact workers if they fail to honestly bring their work forward for

49. Bayly, *The Practice of Piety*, 188.
50. Smith, "Sanctification for Ordinary Life."
51. Fagerberg, *Consecrating the World*, 91.

transformation. When worshipers hold their working lives back, when they "check their work" at the sanctuary door, the sanctuary cannot really challenge or transform their work at all. The transformative power of the Holy Spirit demands that we carry our *whole* lives, the work of our hands, before God in worship. We will say it again: *if sanctuary worship is going to be formative for workers, their working lives will need to be brought into it.*

The pews are filled with workers like Deliah and Daniel who need Sunday. They need to carry their labors forward and have a candid dialogue with God about work. If Sunday is going to be transformative, *it cannot be a monologue in which God and pastors speak at the worker.* The people in the pews need to actively and honestly participate in the liturgical dialogue. Deliah needs to bring her anxiety over her patients forward if God is going to bring peace and healing. Daniel needs to bring his sinful habits from the construction site forward if God is going to break and transform them. Leaving these vocational concerns outside the sanctuary will accomplish nothing. Workers need the sanctuary, and they need to bring their work with them when they come.

Conclusion

Who are these people sitting in these pews? Pastors and worship leaders need to cultivate a deeper pastoral and theological understanding of the holy priesthood to whom they've been called to minister. Listening to workers is a great start. Visiting workplaces is another. Learning about workplace rituals, liturgies, and seasons is important. Hearing about vocational hopes and heartaches enables worship leaders to better appreciate the emotional and spiritual weight that workers carry with them into worship. What we're looking for here is a pastoral curiosity in understanding both work and workers. This pastoral practice of listening and learning is the starting point for those who wish to design and lead worship that is responsive to workers. This is the first step in developing worship that is "vocationally conversant."

The pastoral practice of listening is critical, but so is the theological practice of reflection. Worship leaders need to theologically wrestle with the priestly status and calling of workers. They need to theologically grasp that the work can be worship and that it is integral to the mission of God and the church. Having engaged in these two practices of pastoral listening and theological reflection on the workers in their pews, worship leaders and pastors will be far better equipped to lead worship that truly engages workers and their working lives.

Having laid the conceptual foundations for the project, we now begin to explore a wealth of biblical, historical, and liturgical resources for pressing forward. In ancient Israel, early Christianity, and the rural and global church, we find a variety of insights for gathered worship that truly engages both work and workers.

PART 2
RESOURCES

4

The Old Testament

The Integrity of Work and Worship

> Give me an undivided heart.
> —Psalm 86:11 NRSV

Worship and work, two activities grounded in creation, receive careful attention throughout the Old Testament. Shot through Israel's history, its poetry, its laws and prophecy, the nation's practices of labor and liturgy are constantly being interwoven in a variety of surprising ways. And while the various books are diverse in their context and purpose, their attention to the interplay between worship and work is consistent—and revealing.

Throughout the next few chapters we will explore the connection between Israel's gathered worship and its scattered work; we will also investigate how these activities were intended to directly engage and impact each other. On one side of the equation, we will explore how Israel's practices of gathered worship were intended to bless, convict, and transform Israel's practices of work. On the other side, we will explore how the fruits and failures of Israel's daily labors were meant to be gathered up and brought into the nation's various liturgies.

We will see that Israel's worlds of worship and work were intentionally designed to intermingle. The walls between them were intended to be porous. Their labors and liturgy were designed to be in constant conversation, always informing each other. In the end we will see that, according to the Old Testament, a holy life is a life of deep integrity—a life in which holy work and holy worship are one.

As stated earlier, the problem of faith and work is often framed in the modern world as an intellectual problem demanding an intellectual solution. In an attempt to intellectually bridge the divide, we are instructed to read books and listen to lectures about a "theology of work." The assumption is simple: once a worker *intellectually* grasps the theological connection between faith and work, the task of "integration" is all but finished. With the mental furniture in order, the worker will naturally live the theology of work they've studied.

The Old Testament, however, does not prescribe this approach. Israelite workers, as far as we can tell, never published or prescribed a systematic "theology of work." How did they manage to connect their transcendent faith in Yahweh with their mundane work in the fields without a systematic theology book?

By and large, the connection between faith and work was forged through Israel's practices of worship. The ancient Israelites did not *think* their way into the integrated life; *they worshiped their way into it.* Through a variety of songs and sacrifices, harvest festivals, feasts, and prayers, ancient Israelite workers praised and practiced their way into integrated lives of holy worship and holy work.

A brief word should be offered on what we are *not* arguing. Nowhere will we assert that ancient Israelites were perfect. Nor will we claim that they "solved" the issue of faith, work, and worship. Constructing a romantic or imagined past in which worship and work were perfectly united will do us no good. In fact, Israel's numerous and sundry failures to connect the temple to the marketplace will offer many of our most important lessons. Finally, we do not claim to offer an exhaustive historical summary of either worship or work in ancient Israel. That is far beyond the scope of this project. Instead, we focus on a select number of illuminating moments in which Israel's gathered worship directly engages its daily work.

A Whole and Holy Life

> Holy times of worship are marked and observed so that the daily routines of life may remain constantly connected to the sacred rhythms of creation's ordering.
>
> —Samuel Balentine, *The Torah's Vision of Worship*

Old Testament scholars greatly enjoy debating nearly every aspect of Israelite history. Their academic journals are filled with scholarly squabbles—both fascinating and dull. That said, despite all of their academic disagreements about ancient Israel's history, theology, and culture, one thing they widely agree on is the deep conviction that—within ancient Israel—the holy life was an integrated one.

A "righteous" Israelite lived a life of deep integrity and integration. They walked in the ways of the Lord consistently—in the temple, the home, and the marketplace. To be a person of integrity, every aspect of one's life needed to be marked by "holiness." The concept of holiness in Israel encompassed the spiritual and material, private and public, liturgical and economic. The holy law called the Israelite workers to lives of holy integrity in private and public, at the altar and in the market. All of life was meant to be holy, faithfully lived out before the face of Yahweh.

Countless Old Testament scholars, theologians, and ethicists attest in their own unique ways to Israel's desire and design for a national life of holy integrity between labor and liturgy.[1] Walter Brueggemann argues repeatedly that gathered worship in Israel was not designed to serve as a spiritual escape from the marketplace, the fields, or the public square.[2] Instead, temple worship was meant to directly engage and challenge the economic, cultural, and political behaviors of the Israelites. To worship in the temple was to make public declaration that Yahweh alone was sovereign over Israel's political and economic life. Yahweh alone was Lord over Israel's families and fields, money and markets, armies and kings, and even its weather. When Israel's workers prayed or sang, they were engaged in a "festive act of enthroning." Yahweh was declared king over their private *and* public lives. Singing together, worshipers were engaged in a liturgical "act of submitting more and more areas of life to [the Lord's] newly wrought sovereignty."[3]

Waldemar Janzen suggests that public holiness was meant to "flow" out from Israel's "sanctuary, into the network of interhuman activity." For a worker to "live rightly . . . means first and foremost to orient all of life, and not only [sanctuary] activity, toward the presence of God."[4] Within this ancient worldview, to "live life in constant and zealous attention to Yahweh's holy presence constitutes the first great ethical imperative."[5] Any hard-and-fast

---

1. While there are many scholars who could be referenced, this section has been deeply enriched by and will occasionally reference the work of the following scholars: Walter Brueggemann, Ellen Davis, Christopher Wright, Waldemar Janzen, Jacob Milgrom, Peter Altmann, Walter Kaiser, Rick Marrs, Jacob Milgrom, and John Goldingay.

2. Brueggemann, *Israel's Praise*, 6–7.

3. Brueggemann, *Israel's Praise*, 10.

4. Janzen, *Old Testament Ethics*, 107.

5. Janzen, *Old Testament Ethics*, 107.

separation between private worship and public ethics, or what we might call "'horizontal' and 'vertical' behavior," is, according to Janzen, "foreign to the Old Testament. Both are called 'service' [avodah] in Hebrew and are intertwined in the law codes."[6]

Another scholar, Walter Kaiser, argues that "holiness" in Israel was meant to be "a way of life." Holiness, he says, was expected to permeate "the whole tenor and fiber of Israel's life, whether it involved worship of the living God or their day to day employment. The whole of life involved a constant dedication and consecration of all its components as a holy people who set themselves apart to live in communion with a holy God."[7] Holy workers do not run from the "worldliness" of the marketplace; they see holiness as a way to labor *within the marketplace.*

Christopher Wright adds that any dissonance between a worker's behavior in the marketplace and in the sanctuary was understood to be a serious issue with potentially devastating consequences. "Israel's worship," he says, "was to be marked by a deepened commitment to ethical response at the horizontal level."[8] The Old Testament cautions workers repeatedly to think twice before entering the sanctuary with hands sullied by economic dishonesty and injustice in the marketplace. "Psalms 15 and 24 make it clear that the worship of the Lord . . . is acceptable only from those who, in the everyday conduct of their lives, mirror the ethical standards of the God they presume to worship."[9] Put another way, the songs that you sing in the sanctuary about God's justice, generosity, and beauty should echo through your works in the marketplace.

Rick Marrs, looking at the prophets, remarks, "Amos, Hosea and Isaiah speak with a single voice regarding the inextricable relationship between worship, ethics and leaders." According to a prophet like Micah, "worship—apart from ethical behavior pervading every facet of life—is worthless." The prophets' many "speeches represent their attempts to reunite worship and daily life."[10]

According to John Goldingay, the prophet Isaiah repeatedly criticizes Israel because its "enthusiastic worship of Yhwh is not matched by an enthusiastic living before Yhwh in everyday life."[11] No amount of pious enthusiasm voiced in the sanctuary can overcome a worker's misconduct in the marketplace.

6. Janzen, *Old Testament Ethics,* 110 (brackets in original).
7. Kaiser, *Toward Old Testament Ethics,* 151.
8. C. Wright, *Old Testament Ethics,* 45.
9. C. Wright, *Old Testament Ethics,* 46.
10. Marrs, "Micah and a Theological Critique of Worship," 184.
11. Goldingay, *Israel's Life,* 21.

"In the absence of obedience to Yhwh in the rest of life, heartfelt worship counts for nothing."[12]

Finally, Jacob Milgrom's renowned commentary on Leviticus carries a revealing subtitle describing the ancient text: *A Book of Ritual and Ethics.* Here Milgrom explores the interplay between Israel's liturgies in the sanctuary and its various labor practices in the world. He remarks that while "the dominant view of Leviticus is that it consists only of rituals," a closer reading reveals that social and economic "values are what Leviticus is all about. They pervade every chapter and almost every verse."[13] He further observes that

> underlying the rituals, the careful reader will find an intricate web of values that purports to model how we should relate to God and to one another. Anthropology has taught us that when a society wishes to express and preserve its basic values, it ensconces them in rituals. How logical! Words fall from our lips like the dead leaves of autumn, but rituals endure with repetition. They are visual and participatory. They embed themselves in memory at a young age, reinforced with each enactment.[14]

The ancient authors of Leviticus understood something that moderns do not: "private" rituals have "public" consequences. Worship practices have the formative potential to shape economic behavior. Milgrom explains that this deep connection between ritual and ethics, faith and public life "is the quintessence and achievement of Leviticus."[15]

Porous Worlds of Worship and Work

The next three chapters will explore the strange, illuminating, and interwoven relationship between worship and work in the Old Testament. In the Pentateuch, we will explore how workers in Israel were instructed to regularly bring their working lives into worship. They carried their produce, their animals, their marketplace confessions, needs, struggles, and laments before the Lord. We will see that although the biblical texts regularly make distinctions between the temple and the marketplace, they do not separate these things. The walls between them were porous. In fact, when we come to the prophets, we will

12. Goldingay, *Israel's Life*, 23.
13. Milgrom, *Leviticus*, 1.
14. Milgrom, *Leviticus*, 1.
15. Milgrom, *Leviticus*, 4.

witness the devastating economic and liturgical consequences that inevitably come when the worlds of worship and work separate.

Like a heartbeat pumping blood in and out, Israel's life was meant to flow in and out, back and forth between the sanctuary and the square. The pumping heart of holy worship would bind their material and spiritual lives into one. Isaiah 55 beautifully captures this gathering and scattering movement of worship in its call: "Come, all who thirst" (v. 1) and "Go out with joy" (v. 12). In gathering and scattering, Israel's worship gave life, meaning, and direction to its work.

Before going further, we need to address a common pitfall for modern readers of the Old Testament. We are reading ancient texts in the hopes of addressing a modern problem. In doing so, we must not read back into the ancient texts modern questions that were alien to those times and places. In many ways, the Israelites did not have a theology of work because they did not need one. They lived in a world in which the spiritual and material were understood to be constantly intermingled. While they did not have a systematic theology of work, the ways in which they spoke about creation, labor, and worship afford us opportunities to formulate a theology and praxis for an integrated vision of work and worship.

In the next three chapters we will explore the intersections of worship and work in the Pentateuch, the psalms, and the prophets. We will examine how Israel's workers brought their working lives to God in and through worship. Be it through a shepherd's sacrifice of the best lamb or a merchant's confession of a dirty trade, a farmer's basket of fruit or a slave's lament, a prophet's rebuke of an oppressor's sacrifice or a psalmist's praise for the harvest, the Old Testament provides modern readers with a complex collection of ways in which worship brings faith and work together.

5

The Pentateuch

Bringing Work into Worship

Late one night, a group of slaves gathered their belongings and fled the brutal and oppressive economy of Egypt. Soon after, standing on the shores of the Red Sea, they watched as their taskmasters were swept under the dark waters. The liberated slaves erupted into dancing and song. They were free. Pharaoh's economy of never-ending work, greed, oppression, and exhaustion was now a relic of their past. Or so they thought.

While the Israelites had, in an overnight dash, physically left Egypt, the ravenous habits and practices of Pharaoh's economy were still deeply imprinted on their hearts. Egypt's economic patterns of overwork and rapacious acquisition were the only ones these liberated slaves knew. Extracting the Israelites out of the Egyptian economy was one thing; extracting the Egyptian economy out of the Israelites was another thing entirely.

Before entering the promised land, the freed slaves needed to develop an alternative economy, a new set of habits for work and rest, farming and trade, labor and power, possession and generosity. They needed to learn to trust their new master. They needed to learn how to rest, how to rely on their new master's provision, not their own. They needed to learn how to freely offer and freely receive, to share and celebrate. They needed to learn how to work alongside their servants, animals, and land in ways that reflected the generosity, justice, and love of their new master—Yahweh. They would learn these new economic behaviors *through* participation in worship.

Worshiping into Yahweh's Economy

The Israelites were about to enter the promised land. They were about to start working *freely*, in fields that *they* owned. They were about to become wealthy and powerful in a land flowing with milk and honey. They were about to become their own masters. This new economic reality raised important liturgical questions. How could their worship prevent them from repeating the economic patterns of Egypt? How could their worship train them to self-lessly offer their work to God and their neighbors? How could worship lead them out of the exhausting labor practices of Pharaoh and into the life-giving labor practices of Yahweh?

The rituals found in Exodus, Leviticus, and Deuteronomy are designed, in large part, to answer questions like these. What we find in their pages is not simply a set of laws about work, trade, farming, and the economy. We find festivals, offerings, sacrifices, and prayers that train Israelite workers *into* the life-giving economy of Yahweh. If the workers of Israel fail to observe these worship practices, the danger is both spiritual and economic: they will forget the economy of Yahweh[1] and go back to the economy of Pharaoh.[2]

Ellen Davis's excellent book *Scripture, Culture, and Agriculture* explores Israel's curious worship practices surrounding agricultural stewardship and cultivation, harvest, and husbandry. Davis remarks that the liturgical observance of Sabbath was meant to have a direct economic impact on the daily life and labor of the farmer. She writes that Sabbath observance was meant to mark a "definitive separation" from the oppressive economic patterns of

---

1. The importance of memory and the temptation to forget are seen clearly in Deuteronomy: Deuteronomy, as a whole, indicates the way to retain their land and freedom. The caution is that they must retain and celebrate the memory of God's acts and give thanks (i.e., understand where their true life lies). The abundant life and freedom God has given can be lost, and this is what Deuteronomy seeks to guard against. "I call heaven and earth to witness against you today that I have set before you life and death, blessings and curses. Choose life so that you and your descendants may live . . ." (30:19). What lies behind Israel's obedience to God's Torah, or teaching, is the recognition that putting trust in any other god would be the height of ingratitude. Gratitude and obedience are necessary for remembering the real source of life and for retaining possession of the land. (Christensen, "Deuteronomy 26:1–11," 60)

2. Here is a warning that speaks to this:
When you have eaten and are satisfied, praise the LORD your God for the good land he has given you. Be careful that you do not forget the LORD your God, failing to observe his commands, his laws and his decrees that I am giving you this day. Otherwise, when you eat and are satisfied, when you build fine houses and settle down, and when your herds and flocks grow large and your silver and gold increase and all you have is multiplied, then your heart will become proud and you will forget the LORD your God, who brought you out of Egypt, out of the land of slavery. . . . You may say to yourself, "My power and the strength of my hands have produced this wealth for me." (Deut. 8:10–14, 17)

Egypt. In fact, Deuteronomy mentions Egyptian slavery explicitly as a reason for the fourth commandment.

> Observe the Sabbath day by keeping it holy. . . . Six days you shall labor and do all your work, but the seventh day is a sabbath to the LORD your God. On it you shall not do any work. . . . Remember that you were slaves in Egypt and that the LORD your God brought you out of there with a mighty hand and an outstretched arm. Therefore the LORD your God has commanded you to observe the Sabbath day. (Deut. 5:12–15)

Sabbath habituated exhausted slaves into the restful economy of Yahweh. Sabbath was a liturgical reminder to workers that Israel's economy would be "a renewing economy that memorializes God's work in creation" in contrast to a rapacious Egyptian economy that "exhausts workers and material goods." Sabbath ritualistically trained workers to put down their tools and open their hands so that they might learn to rely on Yahweh's work, not their own. Israel, Davis argues, was "not to be a total-work culture, regardless of whether the compulsion [was] external or internal."[3] Without Sabbath limits workers are in danger of taking their work too seriously. As Kathleen Norris observes, without Sabbath liturgies we "come to feel too useful, so full of purpose and the necessity of fulfilling obligations that we lose sight of God's play with creation, and with ourselves."[4]

Slavery did more than simply destroy and demean the integrity of Israel's work; it inhibited Israel's worship as well. The oppression of workers destroys the worship-filled character of work.[5] The fruit of the slaves' labor was being directed to the glory of Pharaoh when those fruits should have been directed to the glory of Yahweh. If free and holy work is worship, enslaved and selfish work is idolatrous. God liberated Israelite workers in part so that they could offer their work as worship to him.

The people's collaborative construction of the tabernacle offers important insights on these matters. Ellen Davis asks us to consider the scene. Freed slaves are invited to freely offer their unique gifts, skills, craftsmanship, and aesthetic wisdom to adorn Yahweh's house. The blistered hands that built the houses of Pharaoh, hands that stacked stones to serve his imperial and

---

3. Davis, *Scripture, Culture, and Agriculture*, 143.

4. Norris, *The Quotidian Mysteries*, 26.

5. In their liberation from Egypt the slaves' *avodah* (the holy union of work, worship, and service) is restored to its proper place within Yahweh's economy. This threefold union is "symbolized in the gifts they bring as they come together to the central sanctuary. . . . The gifts that the Israelites bring to God are 'the work of [their] hands' (Ex. 16:15)." McConville, *Being Human in God's World*, 186–87.

violent glory—these hands are now invited to freely offer their vocational skill, acumen, and creative touch to the construction of Yahweh's house. Their first work project is a house of worship, decorated with color, made with hands that are rested and free. As Davis remarks, this house of worship was "meant to be the first thing that Israel makes in freedom, a project designed to counter the demeaning work of Egypt, where Israel did 'hard labor'—always a negative term in the Bible."[6]

The oppressive and rapacious patterns of Pharaoh's economy would haunt Israel for centuries. Israel would constantly be tempted to slide back into the economic patterns of Egypt. Michael Rhodes explains, "Israel's establishment in the land tempted them to return to an economy of hoarding and scarcity. Much of Israel's liturgy provided resources to resist this temptation through embodied acts of remembering."[7] Sabbath worship was an ever-present liturgical reminder for workers to reject Pharaoh's economy of grasping and walk deeper into Yahweh's economy of grace. Through the ritual observance of rest, through the regular celebration of harvests, and through public confessions of marketplace greed, Israel's workers would slowly and clumsily be brought into a new economy *through worship*.

Strange Work Requires Strange Worship

You must not live according to the customs of the nations. . . . You are to be holy to me because I, the LORD, am holy, and I have set you apart from the nations to be my own.

—Leviticus 20:23, 26

6. Davis, *Scripture, Culture, and Agriculture*, 143.
7. Rhodes, "'Follow Us as We Follow Moses,'" 183. Rhodes goes on to say,
   This liturgical shaping can be seen in the tithe-meal of Deuteronomy 26. The phrase "the land the Lord your God has given" provides the repeated theme of the liturgy. The farmer takes the first fruits and places them in a basket, declaring to the priest that the Lord has given the good gift of the land in fulfilment of the promises made to Abraham. Then, the farmer recounts the history of Israel in fairly unflattering terms. . . . Next, the farmer recites the history of the Lord's liberating of his people from Egypt before finally reiterating for the fourth time God's gift of the land. This land is a land of abundance, "flowing with milk and honey." The farmer and his family celebrate together in the third year with the "sojourners, orphans, and widows so that they may eat and be satisfied." The farmer is not to make sure he has enough for his family first, and after to give the leftovers. The farmer is to give the first fruits. This, too, is a liturgical act of hope in which the farmer purposively places himself in vulnerable dependence on God for the sake of others. . . . The liturgy reaffirms that abundance comes to humanity as sheer gift and invites the Israelites to participate in the economic sharing of this gift. (183–84)

Israel's economy was supposed to be distinct among the nations—strange, even. Their peculiar working patterns were meant to set them apart from all that surrounded Zion. The strange ways in which an Israelite worker exchanged goods, tilled the soil, paid servants, wove garments, cooked food, treated animals, and arranged for periods of rest were to be conducted according to the unique patterns of Yahweh—not the "normal" patterns of the nations.

But how, exactly, would Israelite workers maintain their economic "strangeness"? How would they sustain their unique patterns of farming, trade, labor, and rest? How would these workers guard against economic assimilation—melting into the "normal" working patterns of the nations that surrounded them?

Walter Brueggemann asserts that the unique character of Israel's economic life would be maintained not simply through teaching but through the regular and repeated practice of worship. "For," he argues, "it is in worship, and not in contextless, cerebral activity, that Israel worked out its peculiar identity and sustained its odd life in the world."[8] The strange character of Israel's work would be maintained through its strange forms of worship. For its gathered liturgies constituted "the locus of dramatic activity whereby all of life—cosmic, political, personal—was brought under the rule of Yahweh."[9] In singing together about Yahweh's sovereignty over the fields and marketplace, their daily routines of work, trade, and cultivation came under Yahweh's reign.

In the pages that follow, we examine how Israelites learned to labor within the "strange" economy of Yahweh *in and through their practices of gathered worship*. Our first example comes from a peculiar worship service designed specifically for farmers. This rather odd ritual begins with a farmer carrying a basket of his best produce directly into worship, and it ends with a strange collection of guests sitting around a harvest table.

Bringing Work to Worship

> When you have entered the land . . . take some of the firstfruits . . . and put them in a basket. . . . The priest shall take the basket from your hands and set it down in front of the altar. . . . Then you shall declare . . . "The Lord brought us out of Egypt . . . and gave us this land, a land flowing with milk and honey; and now I bring the firstfruits of the soil that you, Lord, have

8. Brueggemann, *Theology of the Old Testament*, 653.
9. Brueggemann, *Theology of the Old Testament*, 661.

given me." Place the basket before the LORD your God and bow down before him. Then you and the Levites and the foreigners residing among you shall rejoice in all the good things the LORD your God has given to you and your household.

—Deuteronomy 26:1, 2, 4, 5, 8–11

Throughout the Old Testament, workers regularly engaged in the rather strange practice of taking their daily work and lifting it up into the air. Why? *Because they believed that their deity actually cared about the little things they were working on that day*. From the Old Testament, modern readers learn how cattle herders, farmers, and shepherds habitually offered their humble offerings up to the mighty creator of all things.

Like a child holding her best drawing up to her mother, these ancient farmers believed that their terrestrial work needed to enter into celestial worship. The mother in question has, of course, provided her daughter with her paper, her crayons, her training—indeed, she has given her daughter life itself. And yet the child knows, as if by nature, that it is a good and joyous thing to offer her relatively small work back to her mother. And the mother takes great delight in seeing her work return to her. These ancient texts show us that the creator of the universe, the sovereign over all things, not only demands but also actually delights in the mundane work of his sons and daughters lifted high in worshipful return.

The pages of Exodus, Leviticus, Numbers, and Deuteronomy detail a complex variety of festive offerings, sacrifices, and harvest celebrations. As far as we can tell, these agricultural worship services constituted one of the primary ways in which Israelite workers connected the raw reality of their daily labor in the fields to their worship of Yahweh at the altar.

Consider for a moment the worker's experience in these various rituals. A worker carefully selected, gathered, and prepared the very best products of their family's labor, the most prized objects of the year's sweat and toil. The worker brought these precious products before the Lord in a material and economic act of surrender, offering, and praise. Wheat or barley, sheep or birds, fruit, honey, oil, wine, beer, cakes—the Scriptures outline a wide variety of vocational products that could be included in these offerings and meals. With a great deal of pride (and a good deal of trembling), the laborer was to bring their very best craftsmanship into the divine presence to be examined, accepted, and ultimately enjoyed.

During some offering rituals, the best and most precious work of the year was completely incinerated—consumed by the fire. Offering one's most costly cow to the flames was, no doubt, a dramatic experience for a

From Field to Altar in Zimbabwe

There is an innate human instinct to lift one's vocational harvest up to God in an act of worship. This ancient and primal desire is still cultivated in the gathered worship of many agricultural churches around the world. In Zimbabwe, the harvest season is full of rich meaning for Christians. During the two months leading up to the last Sunday of July, banners with thanksgiving poems and Scriptures are hung around the sanctuary. Members bring the finest fruits and vegetables from their farms to decorate their church and mark the harvest day. Priscilla Muzerengwa says that for the worshipers, "The decorations encourage remembering all blessings received from God. People share teachings, sermons and songs as they recall encounters with God and thank God." She goes on to describe the worship service:

> During worship, people sit in sections of about 10 households each, based on their geographic area. Each member receives an envelope in which to put a thanksgiving offering. Members of the section combine their harvest thanksgiving collection and present it as one. . . .
>
> One after the other, each section is called to present its harvest. As soon as a section is called, a song of celebration is heard from the back. Members of that section move forward—singing, whistling, ululating, clapping and dancing. The praise stirs up the entire congregation to join in celebration.
>
> A spokesperson from the section highlights the blessings received by section members. The testimonies tell of newborn babies, children who excelled in their studies, prospering businesses, opportunities received, incidents of escape from death and many other blessings. Finally, the spokesperson announces what the section has brought in cash and in-kind offerings. The collection is recorded, and a running total is kept of all collections received to be announced at the end of the service. The congregation applauds. Non-monetary gifts are sold, and the income is credited to the section that brought the goods.[a]

The service concludes with a festive lunch, with each member bringing a special dish to share with the community. Even in urban churches Zimbabweans follow similar practices and purchase produce from the market to decorate the sanctuary during the July harvest celebration season.

a. Swen et al., "Celebrating God's Bounty."

worker.[10] Learning to rest in God's provision was not an abstract theological teaching for these farmers. They saw the urgency of that theological doctrine performed before them as their cattle and crops went up in flames. The fragile and contingent nature of their work could be smelled in the smoke, heard in the crackle and pop, seen in the red, yellow, and black.[11] The command to work within God's providence was tangible, urgent, and pungent.

In a number of texts God is understood to be hovering over the farmer's offering, inhaling the aroma of the work itself. In fact, no less than thirty-eight times in Exodus, Leviticus, and Numbers, God is said to find the aroma of the work pleasing. It is common today for Christian workers to imagine a God with eyes hovering over their workplaces carefully watching their ethical behavior. The Israelites, it appears, understood their God to have nostrils as well. Yahweh, it appears, took great aromatic delight not simply in seeing the ethical correctness of their work but also in smelling its aesthetic fragrance—its excellence, care, and beauty. Holy work is not simply ethical; it is aesthetic. Holy work is well-crafted, beautiful, robust, and savory. Human culture and creativity emit a pleasing aroma that delights the creator. As the Puritan Joseph Hall said, "God loveth adverbs, and cares not how good, but how well."[12]

The modern observer of the ancient farmers should also note the important fact that they brought their work directly into the worship space. Farmers were not asked to enter into the sanctuary as disembodied souls.

---

10. Jeremy Kidwell offers this assessment of the burnt offering:

In addition to functioning in a robustly social way, there are important ethical implications of the fact that the offering is "incinerated." This is a straightforward translation of the Hebrew verb qtr, which in the *hifil* suggests, "make go up in smoke." The scope of incineration is emphasized in verse 9 with *kl* ["all of it"]. As [Jacob] Milgrom notes, "The unique distinction of the burnt offering in the sacrificial system is that all of it, except for the skin, is consumed on the altar." It is worth noting that the writer of Leviticus makes use of a different Hebrew verb to connote non-sacrificial incineration, *srp*. The contrast here seems to be that this incineration is not meant to be simply destructive. Instead, with *hqtyr*, "the offering is not destroyed but transformed, sublimated, etherealized, so that it can ascend in smoke to the heaven above, the dwelling-place of God." This represents what is the most direct material transference of the offering to YHWH at the front end of a series of other offerings . . . that involve different appropriations of economic value. The burnt offering stands in distinct contrast to those later offerings, like tithes, that are deployed into practical contexts such that the offering served either to provide for the sustenance or salaries of priestly personnel and Temple maintenance or to supply a meal for the worshippers. (Kidwell, *The Theology of Craft and the Craft of Work*, 163–64)

See also F. Hicks, *The Fullness of Sacrifice*, 15.

11. For a description of how work can be "drawn into" worship through the burnt offering, cereal offering, and peace offering, see Kidwell's discussion of Lev. 1–3 in *The Theology of Craft and the Craft of Work*, 154–55.

12. Hall, *The Works of the Right Reverend Joseph Hall*, 7:526.

They did not check their work at the door. Shepherds were not asked to become "spiritual" upon entering the worship service. They entered worship as shepherds carrying sheep. With well-worn hands Israelite workers carried the hard-won fruits of their labors directly into God's holy presence. More than that, these workers often were instructed to bring their coworkers along with them (servants, family members, laborers). Together as a working team (from the top all the way down to the lowest member) they stood as one and presented their harvest labors to God. No one came before Yahweh in worship "empty-handed."

Here we must also recognize the surprising reality that it was the worker, not the priest, who initiated and drove many of these work-oriented worship services. It was the physical work of the laborer, not the spiritual insight of the priest, that constituted the material substance of divine worship. Worship was not prepared for Israelite workers in advance; workers prepared the substance of the worship service themselves.[13] In many instances the priest was not even responsible for scheduling the worship. It was the worker, or more accurately, the work itself, that scheduled the worship. Worship began when the harvest dictated (Deut. 16:9). If the harvest was late, the worship was late. As C. E. Armerding notes, "Israel's covenant life was fundamentally tied to the agricultural cycle."[14] Israel's liturgical calendar was in regular conversation with its economic calendar.

The priest's role in these more work-oriented worship services often appears to be somewhat secondary.[15] The priest appears to be a helpmate to

---

13. As Jacob Milgrom notes,

> The rules governing the burnt offering carve out a large area of control for the ordinary Israelite who was offering an animal for sacrifice. All the preliminary rites with the sacrificial animal are performed by the offerer: hand-leaning, slaughtering, flaying, quartering, and washing. The priest takes over at the altar and continues the sacrificial ritual in silence. The rule of thumb for all sacrifices is that the altar is the province of the priest; all other rituals are the province of the offerer. This means that the offerer is directly engaged in this interaction with God. (Milgrom, *Leviticus*, 22)

14. Armerding, "Festivals and Feasts," 311.

15. It should also be mentioned that the priests were often the recipients of these harvest offerings. Having little land of their own, they depended on such offerings to survive. What is notable here is that the priests were clearly instructed not to despise or look down on the work of the farmers' hands. They were commanded to receive that labor as a sacred gift to them. The book of Numbers clearly instructs them to take the fruits of their labor and "eat it as something most holy" (Num. 18:10). Note how many times the worker's offerings are labeled "holy":

> Then the LORD said to Aaron, "I myself have put you in charge of the offerings presented to me; all the holy offerings the Israelites give me I give to you and your sons as your portion, your perpetual share. You are to have the part of the most holy offerings that is kept from the fire. From all the gifts they bring me as most holy offerings, whether grain or sin or guilt offerings, that part belongs to you and your sons. Eat it as something most holy; every male shall eat it. You must regard it as holy." (Num. 18:8–10)

the worker, who is in fact the primary offerer.[16] The priest did not go out into the fields to examine the crops or the herds; the priest did not select the best offering. The workers themselves had the honor, or rather, the weighty liturgical responsibility, of selecting the best craftsmanship to offer Yahweh. The worker, not the priest, had the needed expertise. The farmer alone knew how to spot the flawless lamb, the finest grain, the first and freshest fruit.

Think of it this way: if a worker has to stand in the blazing presence of almighty Yahweh with some piece of his labor, he should be the one to select what product he must carry with him. The work itself would need to be of such a quality and such an amount that the worker would feel comfortable carrying that work into worship. Today's common phrase "I stand by my work" would have carried a rather intense meaning for such a worker.[17]

16. Jeremy Kidwell highlights the importance of the worker's role:
This is not priestly action that excludes the worshipper, but a ritual drama that is performed cooperatively by celebrant and officiant and one that emphasizes the relationship between these two persons and the animal involved. This is a socially inclusive act and, rather than merely commodify the animal involved, it emphasizes the relation among all three individuals. [Gordon] Wenham puts this in particularly vivid (if slightly conjectural) terms: "The ancient worshipper did not just listen to the minister and sing a few hymns. He was actively involved in the worship. He had to choose an unblemished animal from his own flock, bring it to the sanctuary, kill it and dismember it with his own hands, then watch it go up in smoke before his very eyes." In addition to the personal participation of the worshipper, the liturgy as described in Leviticus is deliberately told from the perspective of both the worshipper (1:1–17) and the priest (6:8–13). The choreography of the ritual also emphasizes this closeness. This is the case with the instruction in verse 4, "He shall lean his hand (*smk ydecca*) upon the head of the burnt offering." As [Jacob] Milgrom notes, "sāmak implies pressure." Just as the selection process connotes intimate relationship (as the animal is drawn from one's own flock), so too the ritual itself emphasizes the shared space between the worshipper and the sacrificial animal being offered. This intimacy is underlined by the act of prayer that is implied with the laying on of hands. This liturgical practice is preserved in the Psalter, where a number of Psalms set their prayers in relation to the burnt offering. (Kidwell, *The Theology of Craft and the Craft of Work*, 163)

17. Frederick Holmgren explains how the worker's offering would have been displayed before both God and his community:
"The worshiper is to be identified, must step forth as an individual from the congregation to be seen by all. The liturgy in Deuteronomy 26 rejects anonymous gifts to God. When an offering is brought to the sanctuary, it is expected that the giver will stand up and affirm a partnership with God that is expressed in a humane lifestyle and in specific deeds.

Naturally, there were some worshipers who recited this confession by rote. It was a mechanical act, the thing to do; sacred words slipped from lying lips. To such persons, God declares (by means of an oracle spoken by a priest):

"What right have you to recite my statutes,
or take my covenant on your lips?
For you hate discipline,
and you cast my words behind you.

Mark this, then, you who forget God,
lest I rend, and there be none to deliver!

One should notice here that these were not one-size-fits-all worship services. Workers could bring a wide variety of offerings specific to their own unique vocations. At diverse points throughout the year, barley farmers could bring their barley, cattle herders their cows, bakers their loaves, and so on. Provisions were also made to include a diversity of income levels; for example, a poor person could offer a small bird.[18] There were some restrictions, to be sure, and their offering was not always made by their own hands. But, by and large, the people's diverse works could be gathered in and offered up to God in worship.[19]

Israel's rituals reminded workers not only of their spiritual past but of their vocational past as well. In Deuteronomy 26:1–11, the worker stands before the Lord and recites a prayer recalling that his forefather was a "wandering Aramean" (who had no land to work). He recalls that his forefathers in Egypt were subjected to "harsh labor," that they "cried out to the LORD," who "heard our voice and saw our misery" and "brought us out of Egypt." The memorial function of this prayer carries four vocational reminders for the farmer. First, the farmer's land is a gift, not a possession. Without God's economic intervention, they would be landless, wandering, and unemployed like their forefather. Second, if the farmer is ever oppressed or subjected to hard labor, they too can cry out to God. Third, the farmer serves a God who hears, sees, and responds to these vocational cries. Fourth, the farmer's profits ultimately come from neither the fecundity of nature nor the power of their hands alone. There is another actor in the economic equation. The fruits of the farmer's labor ultimately come from the historical action and intervention of God into their world and economy.[20]

Peter Leithart emphasizes the handcrafted nature of Israel's many tribute offerings. Wine, oil, and bread, for example, represented an amalgamation of God's creation and human craftsmanship—a divine and human collaboration. "Grain," he observes, "was not offered in its raw state; it was either ground

---

He who brings thanksgiving as his sacrifice honors me;
to him who orders his way aright
I will show the salvation of God!"
(Holmgren, "The Pharisee and the Tax Collector," 257–58)

18. Jacob Milgrom writes, "Why was the bird pericope added? Its purpose is to provide the poor with the means to sacrifice the burnt offering. . . . Built into the Israelite system of sacrifices is a mechanism to ensure that all Israelites, regardless of wealth, could communicate directly with God and participate in the spiritual life of their people." Milgrom, *Leviticus*, 23.

19. The desire to express one's unique gifts as a part of worship may be an interesting point of connection with modern Western workers. How can worship leaders tap into this desire and provide formful practices of offering to God of the worker's labors? We will explore this question in chap. 11, "Worship That Gathers Workers."

20. See Christensen, "Deuteronomy 26:1–11," 59.

The Eucharist and the Work of Our Hands

Prayers for the offering in the modern West often are abstract, ethereal, disembodied, and detached from economic life. In contrast, offerings in the Old Testament are grounded in creation, embodied, and deeply embedded in the vocational and economic life of the worshiper who participates in them.

The earthy lyrics of "Ofrenda," a Latin American offertory prayer, help laborers connect the tangible fruits of their labor to the fruits of Christ's work on the cross. The prayer begins with the worker carrying "the wheat of my harvest" and "the grapes of my vineyard" before the Lord. The prayer recalls how wheat and grapes eventually become flour, bread, and wine through human effort and come before the Lord in worship. But the prayer does not stop there. It narrates one more work of transformation—a divine work. The prayer attests to how the worker's humble offerings from creation are then transformed by the work of God into the body and blood of Christ. Somehow the worker's harvest will become Christ's body. According to the Ofrenda, the holy body of Christ is connected to their daily work.

The Ofrenda brings Latin American workers into postures of offering and awe. Through its creational language workers witness the ordinariness of their daily work lifted up and transformed into a gift from God back to them. Within this prayer a worker can see the "fruit of my sweat" as a tangible expression of her love and worship. In the offering she will beg God to receive her workplace offerings because they "carry all my love." [a]

a. "Ofrenda," *Mùsica Católica*, http://musicatolica.me/cancionerocatolico/Song/3149/OFRENDA
   .html.

into flour, baked into bread and wafers, or roasted in the fire (see Lev. 2). Oil, not olives, was spread on the wafers or mixed with the flour that was turned into smoke. The libation that accompanied the tribute offering was not an offering of grapes, but of wine." The substance of the worship was not simply the raw fruit of creation; it was the transformed and handcrafted fruit of human culture. In Israel's worship, we discover God's "creation developed, molded, transformed, glorified by human labor."[21] Here in worship the worker is liturgically reminded that creation is good, that human craftsmanship is

21. Leithart, "The Ecology of the Tribute Offering."

good, and that when creation and craftsmanship are combined, the products of that labor are worthy of being offered in divine worship. Through ritual, the farmer was formed not only to approach work as good and valuable but also, more importantly, to offer that work up as an instrument of worship and praise.

Through these worship services, everyday workers are practiced into a new economy of gratitude. They learn that the correct response to an economic harvest is a liturgical offering of gratitude to both God and neighbor. Profits should lead to praise. Hands that reap a windfall need to quickly be raised in prayer. Unfortunately, in times of great wealth and prosperity, gratitude "is one of the first emotions to evaporate; this requirement [of a liturgical offering] made sure the Israelites gave proper thanksgiving and honour to their bountiful King before enjoying his generous provision (cf. Deut. 26:10–11; Prov. 3:9–10)."[22] Offerings habituated workers into patterns and postures of gratitude, dependence, and humility. Worship services for workers provided the people with a set of material and communal rituals through which they could *practice* their hands, their products, their servants, and their land into the alternative economy of Yahweh.[23]

How did these economic worship services impact the farmers and herders? What was going on in their minds as they led their finest cattle toward the altar? What happened to their hearts as they held a prized goat still while the priest cut its throat?[24] How did these rituals impact their posture toward their marketplace? The biblical text does not answer these questions, nor does it spell out in great detail the full economic meaning or purpose of the rituals.[25] That said, the text certainly invites the modern observer to

22. Sklar, *Leviticus*, 282–83.

23. Brueggemann, *Theology of the Old Testament*, 701.

24. Jeremy Kidwell considers the intensity of this experience:

Along with the priest, [worshipers] would have helped to hold and butcher the sacrifice (and in the case of a bull, likely with the help of others given the weight of the carcass), they would have watched the life-blood—God's absolute possession—be drained from the animal and scattered. Then, they would have watched as the offering was incinerated, with choice (and expensive) cuts of meat being burned down to ashes, consumed by no person. In some cases, though definitely not all, this animal would have represented a prolonged investment of time and nurture, and, in the case of the first two categories [a bull and a male sheep or goat], a choice unblemished male animal. This signified a significant expense, publicly offered, for no purpose other than to offer praise and entreaty to YHWH. (Kidwell, *The Theology of Craft and the Craft of Work*, 165)

25. R. E. Averbeck comments on the scarceness of explanation in texts that describe ritual actions:

One of the reasons ritual texts do not often explain the meaning of the various elements of the rituals is because in ritual activity meaning is primarily displayed rather than explained. One needs to engage with the world of the ritual performance not only

wonder what would happen if contemporary Christian workers found their own ways to physically and communally offer up the best of their labors to God in worship? What might this look like? What spiritual and vocational lessons might be learned?

Eat and Enjoy: Celebrating Work in Worship

Eat the tithe of your grain, new wine and oil, and the firstborn of your herds and flocks in the presence of the LORD your God at the place he will choose as a dwelling for his Name, so that you may learn to revere the LORD your God always. But if that place is too distant . . . exchange your tithe for silver, and take the silver with you and go to the place the LORD your God will choose. Use the silver to buy whatever you like: cattle, sheep, wine or other fermented drink, or anything you wish. Then you and your household shall eat there in the presence of the LORD your God and rejoice.

—Deuteronomy 14:23–26

Israelite workers were commanded to throw parties—lots of them. Each year workers were instructed to host a variety of agricultural feasts that were celebratory, worshipful, inclusive, and lavish.[26] These work and worship parties often involved drinking beer and wine, praising God for the harvest, eating precious cuts of lamb and beef, and sitting with family, coworkers, priests, and the poor and marginalized in the community. It is not at all difficult to imagine that there would have been (at least) three meaningful impacts of these feasts on the workers' lives: emotional, ethical, and theological.

At the emotional level, these feasts reminded workers to stop and actually touch, feel, smell, ponder, taste, and *enjoy* the fruits of their labor. They were obligated to cease their striving and rejoice as coworkers with God celebrating the fruits of their labor. Reaping a good harvest, workers were commanded to go out and lavishly "buy whatever you like . . . anything you wish . . . and rejoice" (Deut. 14:26).

---

cognitively but also experientially if there is going to be a true understanding of the ritual and its internal worldview. . . . Ritual procedures, in turn, carry the ritual performers and other participants along through a physically enacted process of engagement with and participation in the ritual world of the performance and its gods or God (in the case of religious ritual), all of which is embedded within the larger surround world and concerns of the people involved. (Averbeck, "Sacrifices and Offerings," 707–8)

26. On the lavish and celebratory nature of feasting, see Altmann, *Festive Meals in Ancient Israel*; Altmann, "Sacred Meals and Feasts in the Old Testament/Hebrew Bible"; Altmann, "Making the Meal Sacred in the Old Testament."

Celebration is not often considered a spiritual discipline in a modern world that is dominated by self-serious productivity and efficiency. But festivity and frivolity as a liturgical practice were absolutely critical in the life of an Israelite worker. Celebrating one's work in joy and freedom was a spiritual discipline that liberated slaves needed to practice at regular intervals. Freed slaves needed to stop and celebrate the life-giving economy of Yahweh. No longer in subjection to Pharaoh, they worked in the liberating presence of the Lord. Harvest feasting and worship would teach them this theological and economic truth. The festive commands are clear: "Be joyful at your festival. . . . For the LORD your God will bless you in all your harvest and in all the work of your hands, and your joy will be complete" (Deut. 16:14–15).

According to Deuteronomy 14, a farmer who was too distant to carry his offering of crops and cattle to God's dwelling place could convert them

A Chinese Harvest Thanksgiving Hymn

Drawing on the biblical texts of Matthew 6 and Deuteronomy 8, the Chinese hymn "Praise Our God Above" places the farmer under the watchful and generous care of God's provisions. The farmer's work is utterly dependent upon God's larger work with the weather patterns, soil, and rains.

"Praise Our God Above"

Praise our God above who shows boundless love:
spring wind, summer rain, then the harvest grain,
pearly rice and corn, fragrant autumn morn;
though our work is hard, God gives us reward.
God's care like a cloak wraps us country folk;
God makes green things grow, ripens what we sow.
Through him we are strong; sing our harvest song.
Praise God, field and flower, praise God's mighty power.[a]

This song of the workers is intended to inspire and facilitate nature's praise of God as well. Like the psalmists, the singers call out for flowers, grass, plants to praise God for the tangible ways in which God demonstrates his power and care.

a. "Praise Our God Above," *Sound the Bamboo, Christian Conference of Asia Hymnal* (Taiwan: GIA Publications, 2000), 165. Lyrics by Tzu-chen Chao, trans. Frank W. Price, in Christian Conference of Asia. Copyright © 1977 by the Chinese Christian Literature Council Ltd. Used with permission of the Chinese Christian Literature Council.

into silver. How very modern of him! But let the modern reader pause to consider: silver was permitted only as a temporary tool for the ultimate goal of a festive celebration. Silver could serve the feast in three ways. First, silver could allow distant workers to gather, arrange, and enjoy a festive meal over great distances. Second, silver could allow workers who only grow grain, for example, to add the diverse ingredients they really love to their festivities—like their favorite meat or beer. Third, silver could allow more urban workers (merchants and artisans) to convert the trades into a festive meal. Once again, notice that the silver is only a temporary medium. The currency must be immediately converted back into a material feast so that the people's vocations can be held, tasted, and enjoyed. Currency can be selfishly hoarded or responsibly invested. But when you have a massive pile of fresh food, you must enjoy it immediately and you must enjoy it in community. Don't hoard your work for yourself. Don't invest it. *Enjoy it* in the presence of your God and your neighbors. Worker, you must "rejoice in everything you have put your hand to" (Deut. 12:7).

The first benefit of the harvest feasts, therefore, is an emotional one. It trains a community of workers to enjoy the goodness of God and taste the flavor of good work well done. It reminds freed slaves that their new master truly desires that they delight in their work. This is the difference between Egypt's taskmaster and Israel's liberator. Yahweh delights in work that is both free and festive.

The second benefit of harvest feasts is an ethical one. The Feast of Tabernacles, for example, focuses our attention not simply on the fruits that sit on top of the table but on the coworkers and neighbors who sit around the table. The command reads, "Be joyful at your festival—you, your sons and daughters, your male and female servants, and the Levites, the foreigners, the fatherless and the widows who live in your towns. For seven days celebrate the festival to the LORD your God at the place the LORD will choose. For the LORD your God will bless you in all your harvest and in all the work of your hands, and your joy will be complete" (Deut. 16:14–15).

Here at the table the workers are, once again, trained out of the old economy of Pharaoh and into the new economy of Yahweh. As workers look around the table at their neighbors feasting together, they begin to see that the ultimate purpose of their profits, the final end of their work, is not their own personal enrichment and security. No. The ultimate purpose of their work is the flourishing of the whole community.[27] The "work of your hands" will be

---

27. Old Testament scholar Timothy Willis explains that it was expected that harvest ritual "spills over into the everyday lives of the worshippers." It must impact the way they treat their

blessed and "your joy will be complete" if your profits are connected to the flourishing of the community and, most specifically, the flourishing of the vulnerable and the marginalized. Workers are being ethically trained through the liturgy of the feast to see the foreigner, the widow, and the orphan within the economy of God.

Notice, once again, that the presiding priest over the festival is not functioning as a professor of economic ethics. He does not stand up at the table and deliver an hour-long lecture developing abstract theories of social ethics and redistribution. Workers do not sit at the table and read textbooks about theological ethics. Instead, they see it, taste it, smell it, pass it, and watch it take on flesh all around them. They watch it as the master of the farm sits alongside his servants, sons, and daughters. They watch it as he passes precious wine to the widow and the foreigner. They watch as the profits of the farm are transformed into a communal blessing. They do not hear a didactic lecture on theories of social justice; they taste justice themselves.

Getting up from that table, they are better prepared to engage in another year of planting and harvest while keeping the poor, the foreigner, and the widow in mind. As Anastasia Boniface-Malle says, this liturgical feast helps diverse members of Israel's economy reach "beyond the borders of race, ethnicity, class, and gender."[28]

The third benefit of the harvest feasts is a theological one. Yahweh, not the worker, is the host of the harvest feast. Yahweh, not the worker, is the economic origin, essence, and end of the community's work. Yahweh, not a pagan fertility god, is recognized as worthy of harvest praise.

Israelite workers entering into the land of Canaan wrestled with two major theological temptations when it came to the fruits of their labor: first, the suspicion that the harvest was the result of their hard work alone; and second, the suspicion that they had received the harvest from some spiritual source other than Yahweh.[29] Regular feasting "in the presence of the Lord" could

---

own laborers. For "they should 'celebrate' their blessings by imitating the way Yahweh provides for them in the way they provide for those who depend on them." What this means is that you, your workers, and the vulnerable in your community all praise God together for the harvest. After this period of harvest praise, you must go out and provide generously for your workers and the vulnerable—just as God has provided for you. The liturgical rhythms and patterns of gratitude, provision, and praise must be extended and echoed in your public and working life. Therefore the "'bridge' linking worship and general obedience together as celebrative response is founded on the inclusion of those dependent groups in the prescribed worship gatherings." Willis, "Eat and Rejoice before the Lord," 292.

28. Boniface-Malle, "Numbers," 201.

29. This point is underscored by Richard Christensen:

Notice that the offering of first fruits from the land involves the recognition of the living God as the true source of life. Some of Israel's neighbors participated in fertility cults

theologically redirect the workers' hearts and hands toward Yahweh. Fighting the temptation to look back to Pharaoh's economy, they found in feasts the help they needed to direct their eyes forward to God's economy. If feasting ceased, workers would begin to believe that they worked either for themselves or for some other god. Commenting on these feasts, Walter Brueggemann notes, "The festivals, by their very performance, served to generate and sustain a community with a quite distinct ethos. . . . It is no wonder that not showing up for the festival is taken as tantamount to ceasing to be Israel!"[30] Without feasts, workers would forget their true master.

When the Feasts Are Gone

The pervasive presence of work and workers in Israel's "worship feasts" reveals a variety of insights into our own contemporary challenges of faith, work, and worship. It reveals why a twenty-first-century accountant might struggle to connect her digital tithing to her electronic spreadsheets. When she is blessed with a year-end bonus or an unexpected promotion, she may well have no idea how to mark or celebrate that occasion in the presence of her community, the vulnerable, or the Lord. Receiving her promotion, she may keep this delightful vocational news to herself, and the profits might be used to further shore up her savings or send her on a trip. The culmination of her many years of schooling, hard work, and determination may go unshared, unnoticed, and uncelebrated. There will be no one to celebrate with. No one to share with. No one to bless. No one to help her praise God's name for these vocational victories. This lack of space for vocational celebration is a major problem in Western Christianity.[31] As ancient Israel would warn us, it leads to vocational forgetfulness.

The dearth of work-oriented celebrations is having serious emotional, ethical, and theological consequences in contemporary Christian workers.

---

and thus saw their source of life in the energies and vitalities of nature. But Israel is to recognize immediately upon receiving the benefit from the land that the energies and powers that matter are not inherent in nature but have their source in God. The fertility cult is opposed by a faith that is concretely historical. Life and meaning derive not from the power and fecundity of nature but from history and historical remembrance of the acts of God. For readers of Deuteronomy, identity is not tied up primarily in our own inherent natural characteristics but in the One who has called us and redeemed us. (Christensen, "Deuteronomy 26:1–11," 59)

30. Brueggemann, *Worship in Ancient Israel*, 16–17.

31. As Timothy Willis notes, it "is relatively easy to see a connection between eating in a worship setting and a recognition of Yahweh as a provider of agricultural prosperity. It is more difficult to see a connection between traditional worship and God as provider of prosperity based on technology." Willis, "Eat and Rejoice before the Lord," 293.

Emotionally, many Christians simply do not know how to stop, celebrate, and enjoy the goodness of God in their careers. We lack the words, the habits, and the categories to celebrate good work well done. Bonuses, promotions, retirements, and new jobs are not sufficiently celebrated in worshipful festivity and frivolity.

Ethically, neither worship nor feasting plays a meaningful role in the formation of Christian workers today. We don't think about how gathered worship and celebration should train us to relate to our land, profits, coworkers, or the poor. Beyond digital transfers, we do not know how to joyfully respond to our bonuses and promotions in festive ways that bless our community and create delight. This contemporary disconnection between our profits and our worship, our feasting and our community has ethical consequences for our economic and spiritual lives.

Theologically, we lack the celebratory practices that we need in order to meaningfully connect our profits to God's provision and presence. Predictably, in the absence of the feast, we vocationally forget. We imagine that our bonuses and promotions are the result of our own diligence, hard work, brilliance, or good fortune. We make our own harvest. We decide where it goes. And we do this all alone. Or, of course, we begin to attribute our newfound fortunes to some other invisible hand.

The Felicitous Confusion of Worship and Work

> It is my contention that the most morally robust appreciation of the holiness of things and the work that produces them is enabled not . . . by an unmediated personal contemplation of beauty or the goodness of "ideas in things" . . . but rather by their entanglement in a very concrete act of worship.
>
> —Jeremy Kidwell, *The Theology of Craft and the Craft of Work*

Israel's worship was intended to directly engage and confront a person's working life. The modern categories of private and public, sacred and secular, all run up on the rocks when confronted by Israel's strange world of worship.

Consider one final example, the ancient practice of Jubilee. A great ceremonial horn was fashioned to call workers to the universal forgiveness of economic debts, the ritual release of slaves and debtors, and the sacred resting and return of farmland to original tribal ownership. Was Jubilee a time of economic redistribution or spiritual devotion? Was it part of Israel's liturgical calendar or was it the end of the fiscal year? The Jubilee represents a conceptual nightmare for the modern mind to catalog and categorize. Was it religious or secular? Was it worship or work? The answer, clearly, is yes![32]

Hard modern boundaries between the sanctuary and the marketplace come to a conceptual dead end in the sacrifices of Leviticus and the feasts of Deuteronomy. Concluding our examination of the Pentateuch, we see that it would not have occurred to Israelite workers to draw clear, hard, or systematic lines of causation between their working and worshiping lives. Their work and their worship would have regularly trespassed the cognitive boundaries that modern Westerners have erected.

Finally, we find little evidence in the Pentateuch of a systematic, abstract, or theoretical "theology of work." There is a simple explanation for this perceived oversight: *the Pentateuch's theology of work was already deeply embedded, enacted, and embodied in its practices of worship.* Hence there was no felt need for an explicitly delineated theology of work. Walter Brueggemann helpfully explains that for liturgically formed communities like Israel, worship tends to take on "an internal logic of its own in the community of practice, an internal logic not accessible to outsiders and about which the community does not trouble to speak very clearly or precisely."[33] As the worlds of worship and work become increasingly porous and conversant with one another, the individual worker increasingly experiences an acute difficulty separating the two activities. The Pentateuch, as we can see, did not consider this to be a problem.

32. See Brueggemann, *Worship in Ancient Israel*, 18.
33. Brueggemann, *Theology of the Old Testament*, 653.

6

The Psalms

Singing God's Work into Ours

Let your work be manifest to your servants,
  and your glorious power to their children.
Let the favor of the Lord our God be upon us,
  and prosper for us the work of our hands—
  O prosper the work of our hands!
—Psalm 90:16–17 NRSV

When it comes to work and worship, we might not expect too much from the book of Psalms. The Psalter's primary focus is clearly on God, not workers. Moreover, these ancient songs, poems, and prayers were collected largely to serve worshipers in the sanctuary, not workers in the fields. We don't expect the psalms, which are focused on God and composed for the sanctuary, to intersect with the raw reality of everyday work in the fields and the marketplaces. And yet, that is exactly what the psalms do.

The lyrics of the psalmists are shot through with workplace images, questions, and issues. Israelite merchants, shepherds, and farmers were regularly exposed to a multiplicity of labor-oriented metaphors and imagery strewn throughout their songbook.[1] A rudimentary word search quickly reveals the repetitive appearance of workplace terms and images:

1. Scripture regularly uses agricultural metaphors and terms to help workers understand and connect with God. Oded Barowski writes, "Israel's closeness to the soil and her dependence on it are evident in the use of agriculturally related terminology as metaphors throughout her

grapes—1	ox—5	fields—11
plow—2	skill—5	fruit—11
reap(er)—2	labor—6	wealth—11
toil—2	shepherd—6	gold—12
weary—2	grow faint—7	sheep—12
bribe—3	vine—7	free—17
crops—3	bulls—8	poor—21
harvest—3	grains—8	oppress—24
sow—3	insects—8	work—30
goats—4	foundations—9	servant—59
build—5	plant(ed)—10	hands—121[2]
cattle—5	rain—10	

The psalms sing of rains and harvests (Pss. 67:6; 85:12; 147:8). They pray about being weary and worn out (Pss. 6:1–6; 31:10; 102 inscription). They shout about carrying work to God in thanksgiving (Pss. 51:19; 66:15; 107:22). They protest about evil people prospering in the marketplace (Ps. 73:3–12). They lament about being cheated and falsely accused (Pss. 55:11; 62:4; 69:4; 109:4). This, quite simply, is a songbook for workers.

The psalms are not a spiritual escape from Israel's markets and fields. Their lyrics emerge out of, and directly engage, the lives and labors of the people.[3] John Goldingay explains that when the people cry out, "Prosper for us the work of our hands—O prosper the work of our hands!" they mean what they say.[4] "Hey God," they shout, "just grant that all the hard work we do in sowing and plowing, in building and planting, pays off rather than being a waste of time. Please, for your name's sake, don't let all of this hard work slip away. Establish it."

The psalms have a unique ability to directly engage the vocational long-ings of workers—both ancient and contemporary. Their lyrics are capable

---

literature. Proverbs and allegories, blessings, prophetic speeches, and psalms use agricultural symbolism extensively. Gideon (Judg. 8:2), Jotham (Judg. 9:8–15), Samson (Judg. 14:8), and Nathan (2 Sam. 12:1–4) use agricultural allegories when trying to clarify a problem. Israel was likened by the prophets to a vineyard (Isa. 5:1–8), a grapevine (Jer. 2:21; Ezek. 17:6–10; Hos. 10:1)." Barowski, *Agriculture in Iron Age Israel*, 11–12.

2. The word search is based on the New International Version.

3. Those interested in exploring the topic of work in the psalms further might benefit from exploring the commentary on the psalms recently completed by the Theology of Work Project at www.theologyofwork.org.

4. Goldingay, *Psalms*, 3:34.

of accomplishing two functions at once. They're specific enough to connect with the raw day-to-day experience of an ancient farm laborer in the fields, yet they're broad enough to resonate with the vocational experiences and emotions of a twenty-first-century financier in a New York City high-rise.[5]

Worshiping Workers into God's Work

> I meditate on all your works
> > and consider what your hands have done. . . .
> Show me the way I should go,
> > for to you I entrust my life.
>
> —Psalm 143:5, 8

Examining the workplace images and metaphors strewn throughout the psalms, we make one discovery that is both immediate and instructive. Within their lyrics the "works of God's hands" are primary, while those of human hands are nearly always secondary. Whenever the psalmists mention a specific workplace issue, that discussion is almost always surrounded with voluminous accounts of God's work and God's actions.[6] Through the psalms, Israel's workers are continually instructed to ponder and sing about the work of God's mighty arms, hands, and fingers (Pss. 8:3; 77:15; 136:12).

In the psalms, the works of God's hands provide an interpretive lens for the work of our hands—not the reverse. The Psalter here is functioning under a simple but powerful assumption: a worker can't understand the place or purpose of their work in the world until they learn to sing, pray, and meditate on God's work in the world. Singing about God's work with force, conviction, and regularity is the critical hermeneutical lens through which a worker can more clearly understand and begin their own labors in the world. God, accordingly, has a lot of diverse "jobs" in the psalms.

protector (7:9)	provider (16:5)
maker of the stars (8:3)	midwife (22:9)
manager (8:5–6)	teacher (25:12)
judge (9:16)	planter (44:2)

5. Our usual disclaimer applies here. Those who want a full and exhaustive historical examination of the psalms need to look elsewhere. Our goal here is to briefly excavate and examine a few select intersections between worship and work in the psalms. We're primarily interested in contemporary appropriations of the psalms for modern workers.

6. There are many examples of this. The best might be Psalm 104.

scheduler (74:17)	seamstress (139:13)
tender of grapes (80:8–9)	craftsman (139:14)
liberator of those who toil (81:6)	physician (146:8)
irrigator (104:13)	foster parent (146:9)
public defender and advocate for the poor (113:7)	border guard (147:13)
	cook (147:14)

God is also repeatedly depicted as an engineer carefully laying sturdy foundations for cities and for the very earth itself (Pss. 24:2; 87:1; 89:11; 102:25; 104:5).[7]

Psalm 23 famously depicts the almighty God working as a humble shepherd. John Goldingay notes that herding sheep in the ancient world was "a despised occupation."[8] It was dangerous work—smelly, dirty, and difficult. Our modern visions of a quiet and peaceful hillside filled with fluffy white sheep grazing wistfully on wavy green grass should be replaced with fearful encounters with wild beasts, bandits, and robbers followed by images of muddy, cold, and sleepless nights next to filthy animals. Yet the psalmist displays no discomfort describing God's work in the world using the humble vocation of the shepherd.

The primary purpose of Psalm 23 is obviously to illustrate something about the work of God—not the work of shepherds. However, imagine a group of shepherds singing this psalm together night after night. Those from higher socioeconomic classes might look down on their humble vocation, but in this psalm the shepherds are invited to sing about a deity whose work is somehow comparable to theirs. Shepherds image God when they protect those under their care, skillfully locate fresh water for their flocks, ward off danger, and provide a sense of rest and security. *Singing Psalm 23, a group of shepherds can gather to praise a deity who is not at all embarrassed to be compared to them.*

In the second half of Psalm 23 God suddenly takes on a whole new job: a party host. Like a waiter, Yahweh patiently sets a table, prepares a meal, and fills drinks (a little too full). The psalmist makes it clear that the faithful

7. John Goldingay remarks, "'Founding' is thus equivalent to 'building,' 'making,' or 'creating,' which have the same implication. But the verb 'found' is especially familiar in connection with the founding of the temple and other buildings, especially after exile. Naturally, that is regularly portrayed as human work, which it literally was (Ezra 3:6–12; Hag. 2:18; Zech. 4:9; 8:9). The founding of Zion was the work of the Jebusites, taken on by David and subsequent kings. The psalm begins by claiming the founding of Zion was actually Yhwh's work." Goldingay, *Psalms*, 2:633.

8. Goldingay, *Psalms*, 1:348.

African Liturgy around the Work of God

The intimate proximity of God to humble work and workers described in the Bible is not off-putting to every community. Speaking out of his own cultural experience of Cameroon, Jean-Marc Éla argues that the liturgies of the African church must do three things. First, they must remind the people that God is a worker like them. Second, they must continually emphasize the immanent presence of God in their fields and huts. Third, their liturgical seasons must be responsive to the agricultural seasons of the workers. He writes,

> Each stage of the planting cycle can open a window to contemplate the God of the peasants—God the potter, God the worker, and God the shepherd of the people. Similarly [the people] must become aware of God's presence in the hut of the mother whose granary is empty. They must recognize God in the shade of the faidherbia trees where the thirsty peasant stops to recover his strength. We search for God through the voice of a people pleading for rain in a time of drought. Then Jesus Christ appears as God with a peasant's black face and hands toughened by labor under the burning sun. Humanity is thus linked to the God of Revelation through its quest for food, and nothing can come between work and prayer.[a]

Pastors and worship leaders need to help workers practice the presence of God in their daily labors. One way this can be done is through the songs and prayers used in corporate worship on a weekly basis. Incorporating psalms and songs that speak of God's presence in an array of workplaces will form workers to be alert to encountering him there. Placing the liturgical calendar in direct conversation with the economic seasons and cycles in your community brings work and worship together.

a. Éla, *My Faith as an African*, 8.

work of God will encircle, follow, and nourish him "all the days" of his life. The psalmist's daily work—however mundane—will be protected, guided, and nourished by the overflowing work of God.

In Psalm 65 the Israelites sing of "God the farmer," who, according to Goldingay, is busy "driving home with his cart so full of rich grain that it

is overflowing from the cart and thus from its tracks."[9] He translates verses
9–10 in this way:

> You have attended to the earth and watered it;
>   you greatly enrich it.
> God's stream is full of water;
>   you prepare their grain because thus you prepare it,
> Saturating its furrows, smoothing its grooves,
>   you soften it with rains, you bless its growth.
> You have crowned the year of your goodness;
>   your cart tracks flow with richness.[10]

Here the laboring deity "attends" to the soil "like a farmer caringly watering his animals. God thus enriches the land and makes it abundant. God
constructs a fine irrigation system, with a stream or channel delivering water in
a controlled way from God's storehouses."[11] Farmers gather in the sanctuary
to sing of God as the digger of channels, the director of waters, the blesser
of seeds, and the harvester of grains.

Comparing the almighty God of the universe to a lowly sheep herder or
farmer may have been disruptive and perhaps even a little embarrassing to
the ancient ear. The song does not quite have the same effect on the modern
ear. The terms "shepherd" and "farmer" are too remote for most of us, too
arcane. It might be a helpful exercise for contemporary worshipers to imagine
singing an adapted version of Psalm 23 in which God is depicted as our ICU
nurse, our security guard, our waiter, or our HR representative. These careers
are uncomfortably close to our own—awkwardly adjacent. Singing songs that
compare the extraordinary works of almighty God to our quotidian labors
fills us with a sense of discomfort that is both appropriate and revealing. That
discomfort should be interrogated.

The truth is Western Christians don't always like the idea of almighty God
working intimately at their side. For a variety of reasons, we much prefer the
distant god of the deists. We prefer a god who commanded us to work in
Genesis 1 and then politely left us alone.

While many Western Christians might be uncomfortable singing a congregational song about "God the farmer" or "God the ICU nurse," Nicaraguan
campesinos have no such qualms. In a song by Carlos Mejía Godoy, "Vos Sos
el Dios de los Pobres" ("You Are the God of the Poor"), from a special Mass

9. Goldingay, *Psalms*, 2:282.
10. Goldingay, *Psalms*, 2:273.
11. Goldingay, *Psalms*, 2:281.

composed for Nicaraguan peasants, worshipers sing, "You are . . . the God who sweats in the factory" and "Christ is a laborer too."[12] A second verse by Heidi Michelsen says of God:

> I've seen you sweeping floors
>> And cleaning toilets and
>> Bussing some tables at the mall.
> I've seen you selling chiclets on the corner
>> Without any shame in this role at all.
> You change diapers, cook, and iron,
>> You sew a new eye on Maria's doll.
> You say to Juana, "I'll watch the children"
>> So she can go out and have a ball.[13]

Both the Nicaraguan Mass and the psalms can push workers to seek intimacy with God *in and through the more mundane aspects of life in the marketplace*. Their daily sweat, their stress, their late nights in the office, and their early mornings in the libraries are all spiritually "thin spaces" in which workers can be renewed through the intimate presence of God.

The psalms depict God faithfully at work in the world alongside the worker. Sometimes Yahweh's works are grand and cosmic, such as laying the foundations of the earth and handcrafting the stars (Pss. 19:1; 24:2; 102:25). Sometimes they are small and humble, such as shepherding lambs, gently watering seeds, attending to the soil, and carefully knitting together infants in their mothers' wombs (Pss. 23:2; 65:9; 139:13). Whether great or small, cosmic or quotidian, God's complex works surround our own. Singing together in the sanctuary, we are reminded of this simple but life-changing truth: *God's work gives meaning to ours.*

The Sailor's Song

In Psalm 107 we encounter a group of sailors working hard at sea. Out on the open water, the sailors witness the mighty works of God in the wind and the waves. When they return to the quiet harbor, the sailors feel compelled to go to the sanctuary. They need to talk about God's "works with joy," for they

> went out on the sea in ships;
>> they were merchants on the mighty waters.

12. Godoy, "Vos Sos El Dios De Los Pobres."
13. This verse, by Heidi Michelsen, is used with permission.

An Entrepreneur Reads Psalm 107

Uli Chi is an award-winning technological entrepreneur and founder and chair of Computer Human Interaction, a 3-D virtual reality software company. As a Christian and an entrepreneur, he is committed to pursuing his work guided by a commitment to Scripture, honoring the image of God in each person.[a] Appropriately, he reads Psalm 107 as an entrepreneur; he can do no other. In his notes on the passage below, we see how his vocation in business shapes his reading. Being an entrepreneur involves risk, uncertainty, lament, teamwork, and vision amid chaos. While reading his notes, notice how Dr. Chi's liturgical reflections on the sailor's psalm connect with his entrepreneurial vocation.

1. *Context:* "Doing business on mighty waters" (NRSV), "they were merchants on mighty waters" (TNIV), and "Some of you set sail in big ships; you put to sea to do business in far away ports" (The Message). Notice in the NRSV the reference to "the deep" (v. 24) and "the depths" (v. 26) which echo Genesis 1:2. Entrepreneurial work takes place in the context of things that are "formlessness and void." Business creation requires both new "form" and "content" to be created. Bringing order out of chaos is one of the qualities I look for in hiring folks to work in entrepreneurial settings.

They saw the works of the LORD,
   his wonderful deeds in the deep.
For he spoke and stirred up a tempest
   that lifted high the waves.
They mounted up to the heavens and went down
     to the depths;
   in their peril their courage melted away.
They reeled and staggered like drunkards;
   they were at their wits' end.
Then they cried out to the LORD in their trouble,
   and he brought them out of their distress.
He stilled the storm to a whisper;
   the waves of the sea were hushed.

2. *Goal:* Most entrepreneurs have a sense of their ultimate destination ("their desired haven," v. 30), even when they don't know how to get from point A to point B. This provides orientation and stability amidst uncertainty.

3. *Journey:* I love the description in vv. 26–28. It describes for me the unexpected joys and difficulties of entrepreneurial work. Extraordinary highs ("they mounted up to heaven") and lows of fear and anxiety ("down in the depths")—places from which we cry "to the Lord in [our] trouble" (v. 28).

4. *Labor and Liturgy:* Verses 32–33 connect the business experience with congregational worship. Work is not just a personal experience but should also have a public expression.

5. *Risk:* Entrepreneurs risk their own livelihoods as well as the livelihoods of those who work with them on the same "ship." I realize how much is at stake for everyone involved in my work. There is a "fellowship" of those who engage in work together.

6. *God's Sovereignty and Mystery:* "For he commanded" (v. 25) reminds me of what C. S. Lewis says about Aslan being good, but not tame, in *The Lion, the Witch and the Wardrobe*. Work is intended to be a good adventure but it often takes us out of our comfort zones and takes us out into the untamed world. Vocational risk requires trust.

a. You can read more about Uli Chi's biography and work at https://depree.org/profile/uli-chi, and watch his discussion of how his faith and work intersect on Seattle Pacific University's YouTube channel: "God's Call to Create and Serve through Business," https://www.youtube.com/watch?v=7W5E343OgGo.

> They were glad when it grew calm,
>   and he guided them to their desired haven.
> Let them give thanks to the Lord for his unfailing love
>   and his wonderful deeds for mankind.
> Let them exalt him in the assembly of the people
>   and praise him in the council of the elders. (Ps. 107:23–32)

Having intimately experienced God's work in their workplace, the sailors' response is revealing. They rush to give their vocational testimony in the assembly. *Workplace praises, stories, and theological insights are offered up in the sanctuary.* The sailors' offering of vocational praise in worship is not abstract or spiritual; it comes directly from the lived encounter with God's presence and power in their working lives at sea.

Songs That Shape Workers

> Come, let us go up to the mountain of the LORD,
>   to the temple of the God of Jacob.
> He will teach us his ways,
>   so that we may walk in his paths.
>
>   —Isaiah 2:3

Why should workers "consider," "ponder," and "meditate on" the works of God (Pss. 77:12; 111:2; 143:5)? Why should they gather to "proclaim the works of God" (Ps. 64:9) or "tell of his works with songs of joy" (Ps. 107:22)? Why should workers vow that they will "meditate on all your works and consider all your mighty deeds" (Ps. 77:12)?

One answer can be found in the *responsive* relationship between God and workers in Israel. According to Christopher Wright, the ethical imagination of Israel is marked by its responsive character. In short, God works and the people respond to that work with works that echo his. Responsive work *begins* with a time of meditating on, singing of, and shouting about the many works of God in the sanctuary. Only then can workers respond to God's works with faithful works of their own in the world. An Israelite's finite works in the fields and markets are expected to echo and attest to God's infinite works throughout the world. Human work must be *responsive* to God's work, and that is why worshipers must continually rehearse God's works in song.[14]

By singing about God's patterns of holy work, workers can begin (ever so slowly) to conform their patterns of work to God's. Pondering God's works of beauty and justice, workers must respond with works of their own that reflect those divine patterns. The people were commanded, "Be holy because I, the LORD your God, am holy" (Lev. 19:2). Wright asserts that this holiness command is not theoretical but rather "thoroughly practical."[15] This earthy, gritty holiness of God "includes generosity to the poor at harvest time, justice for workers, integrity in judicial processes, considerate behaviour to other people (especially the disabled), equality before the law for immigrants, honest

---

14. See C. Wright, *Old Testament Ethics*, 25; Jensen, *Responsive Labor*.

15. See C. Wright, *Old Testament Ethics*, 39. While it is common to discuss the *imago Dei* as a foundational concept for theologies of work, here we are exploring another possible foundation: the *imitatio Dei*. Tim Keller makes much of the "God the worker theme," as does the Talmud. Interestingly, the Talmud uses the *imago Dei* to develop an ethical vision centered on the *imitatio Dei*. God's command "Be holy as I am holy" is an invitation to imitate God. The *imago Dei* is the foundation for *imitatio Dei*. The command shows us how to bear God's image by imitating his actions. See Keller, *Every Good Endeavor*, 19–30; Cohen, *Everyman's Talmud*, 210–12; cf. Goldingay, *Israel's Life*, 585–606.

trading. . . . A favourite metaphor used in the Old Testament to describe this feature of Israel's ethics is that of *walking in the way of the* LORD."[16]

Singing in the sanctuary enables workers to rehearse God's patterns of work so that they can begin to "walk in the ways of the Lord" in and through their daily work.[17] Through song workers can fill their lungs with the many works of God. As they sing and shout about God the shepherd, the farmer, the artisan, the artist, the advocate, the irrigator, and the engineer, they begin to develop their redemptive imagination for their own work. They can begin to see their own labors in cultivation, commerce, management, and craftsmanship in a new—and divine—light. Through worship, they can see that they were created to reflect the labors of their creator—to cultivate the earth, to care for animals, to provide for the vulnerable, to build and to decorate, just as their God has before them. Their worship provides them with a responsive pattern, a logic for their work to follow.[18]

It is one thing to read a book about justice; it is another thing to sing a song about God's justice standing shoulder to shoulder with a coworker or a business partner. Gordon Wenham describes the formative power of the psalms in this way:

> By singing a hymn or reciting a psalm, a worshiper is taking personal ownership of the words of the text. . . . This public dimension [of gathered worship] creates a strong social pressure to conform to the beliefs or values of the text being recited. . . . If a preacher instructs the listeners to do something, they can just ignore it if they dislike it. . . . But it is quite different with a liturgical text. To pray a psalm is to address both God and fellow worshipers. Thus, either other worshipers will notice the silence of the person who does not pray it aloud, or God will take note of the hypocrisy of the person who prays it aloud but disagrees with it. Liturgy does not simply invite assent; it demands it.[19]

16. C. Wright, *Old Testament Ethics*, 38–39.

17. The Old Testament calls the Israelites to rehearse songs in worship about God's laboring over creation, crafting of its beauty, formation of humanity, resting and delighting in his work, shaping Israel, feeding the animals and humans, and liberating the slaves. Walter Brueggemann notes that God is "portrayed as a potter, who with skill, sensitivity, and delicacy, forms the human person (Gen 2:7–8), forms the animals and birds (Gen 2:19) and the earth (Isa 45:18; Ps 95:5), and forms Israel (Isa 43:1, 7, 21; 44:2, 21, 24; 45:9, 11). . . . The verb *form* (*yṣr*) may signify a certain satisfaction or delight on the part of Yahweh . . . (. . . the delighted exclamation of Gen 1:31, 'It was very good,' is likely an aesthetic judgment)." Brueggemann, *Theology of the Old Testament*, 250–51.

18. For, as Christopher Wright writes, it is in and through worship that an Israelite's "deepest convictions are to be found, not in systematic doctrinal or ethical formulations, but in doxology. . . . Israel's worship shows the same dynamic as Israel's ethics; namely, that it is based on God's prior action." C. Wright, *Old Testament Ethics*, 45.

19. Wenham, *Psalms as Torah*, 204–5.

Reflecting God's Character through Our Work

The Porter's Gate is a sacred-arts collective created to help the church engage in acts of intentional hospitality to those outside the community. In 2017 the collective convened sixty musicians, songwriters, scholars, and pastors to have a conversation focused on work, worship, and vocation. A focal question for the artistic gathering was this: "What would it look like to create music that affirms the work of the people and invites workers to bring their work into worship and to take worship back into their work?"[a] The verses in their song "Day by Day" highlight the ways various vocations reflect God's character and contribute to God's mission in the world. This song habituates workers into aligning their work with God's purposes by offering their work as a sacrifice to him.

"Day by Day"

Verse 1
Server, you remind us of our Savior's bowl and towel.
Teacher, you are raising up a child to be kind.
Lawyer, give us hope that justice one day will surround us.

Refrain
May God's kingdom come,
On earth His will be done.
Lord, be close to us,

Wenham is clear that the formative power of the psalms is not automatic. Worshipers can ignore both a lecture and a song. That said, the psalms point out the porous nature of human bodies and souls when they are engaged in song. When lungs are filled, voices raised, hands outstretched, heads bowed, and knees bent in worship to God, human beings are particularly susceptible to liturgical transformation. *By leading us to actively respond to God's works with our hearts, minds, and hands, the psalms can train workers to "walk in the ways of the Lord."*[20]

20. Joel LeMon claims that "the Psalter presents an ethic of prayer." By this he means that the Psalter understands something critical about the formation of a person's ethical public life. Such a life depends not simply on the intellectual reception of a set of theological or ethical ideas. Instead, the Psalter believes that "right actions rely on constant dialogue with God." Psalms make the case that "prayer is the sole foundation of righteous behavior, informing and shaping every action in the lives of the faithful." LeMon, "Psalms," 98.

Lord, have mercy on us,
Lord, please put Your hand on us day by day.

Verse 2
Farmer, you are working for a table full of bounty.
Painter, with each color you are teaching us to see.
Nurse, yours are the healing hands that touch the poor and broken.

Verse 3
Carpenter, you frame a house for those who need protection.
Laborer, you lift a heavy burden for the weak.
Leaders, build a city that all children may rejoice in.[b]

Not every song on Sunday morning will have such explicit reference to daily work, nor should they. But the present dearth of musical resources that address the weekday realities of workers in many American churches perpetuates an unhealthy divide between corporate worship and daily worship through the laity's work.

a. The Porter's Gate Worship Project, https://www.portersgateworship.com/about.
b. Lyrics and music by Lowana Wallace and Isaac Wardell, featuring Joy Ike, from *Work Songs* (Porter's Gate Publishing, 2017), available at https://theportersgate.bandcamp.com/track/day-by-day-feat-joy-ike. Used with permission of Porter's Gate Publishing.

Giving Workers a Voice

Evening, morning and noon
    I cry out in distress,
    and he hears my voice.
            —Psalm 55:17

Plowmen have plowed my back
    and made their furrows long.
            —Psalm 129:3

I will come to your temple with burnt offerings. . . .
Come and hear, all you who fear God;
    let me tell you what he has done for me.
            —Psalm 66:13, 16

Whenever workers, ancient or modern, enter a sanctuary, they carry with them a wide variety of workplace experiences and emotions. Any given week, diverse workers have a variety of things they need to say to God. Some need to shed tears and some need to shout in praise. Some need to give thanks and some need urgent intervention. The vivid words and images of the psalms enable workers to articulate and offer their working lives to God in profound and transformative ways. Within today's faith and work movement much is made of carrying the biblical lessons of Sunday into Monday. The psalms enable the opposite. They give the worker an opportunity to carry their raw emotions of Monday into Sunday. The psalms not only describe, they demand a two-way dialogue between work and worship, a honest conversation between the street and the sanctuary.

It is not always easy or natural to speak honestly with God about work. It takes practice, even skill. It is something that needs to be learned. As John Goldingay observes, the psalms assume "that we do not know instinctively how to talk with God but rather need some help knowing how to do so."[21] The psalms offer workers a vocabulary for use in honest dialogues with God. Here the worker has access to 150 psalms of both lament and praise, confession and thanksgiving, heartfelt petitions and promises. All of these lyrics have the potential to make their way to the lips of a worker on any given Sunday.[22] As Bernhard Anderson writes, "Most of scripture speaks *to* us while the Psalms speak *for* us."[23]

The psalms not only permit workers to express a wide variety of emotions, they enable an impressive depth of emotion as well. Nearly every worker comes to a low point in their career, a point at which they can relate to the psalmist's cry about having fallen into "a pit."[24] Likewise, nearly every worker experiences moments in which they, in a fit of rage, want to ask God to hurl their coworkers, clients, or overseers into "a pit."[25] Whether they admit it or not, many workers can identify with the psalms of rage—even the violent ones. Walking through a toxic workplace, workers have little difficultly relating to the psalmist's cry that they are "surrounded"[26] by "enemies."[27] At the close of a particularly stressful season, who among us cannot relate to the psalmist's cry, "My strength is dried up" (Ps. 22:15)? Hopeless workers should give thanks that the word "pit" shows up as frequently as it does!

The psalms will not romanticize work in a fallen world. They will not instruct anyone to "whistle while you work." These songs will tell the raw truth—sometimes in an all-out rage—that work is not what it is supposed

---

21. Goldingay, *Psalms*, 1:22.
22. Goldingay, *Psalms*, 1:23.
23. Anderson, *Out of the Depths*, ix.
24. Pss. 7:15; 28:1; 30:3; 30:9; 35:7; 40:2; 57:6; 69:15; 88:4; 88:6; 103:4; 119:85; 143:7.
25. Pss. 9:15; 35:8; 55:23; 94:13; 140:10.
26. Pss. 17:9, 11; 22:12, 16; 27:6; 40:12; 49:5; 88:17; 109:3; 118:10, 11; 140:9.
27. "Enemy/enemies" is mentioned ninety-three times in Psalms.

to be. Commenting on Psalm 137, Rodney Sadler describes how early African American communities were bound closely to the psalms through their experiences of toil and hardship on plantations. He writes,

> The Psalms have been a significant religious resource to the African American community . . . who have suffered the grave indignity of oppression, enslavement, segregation, and second-class citizenry. . . . The visceral nature of the Psalter—a book that grew out of the experiences of a people who themselves were familiar with lamentation and praise amid oppression, dislocation, and community crisis—became a source language for formerly enslaved Africans and African Americans, providing them a means of expressing their angst and anguish in intimate fellowship with their God.[28]

Powerful and privileged workers often struggle to understand and identify with the rage of these lament psalms. Those on the underside of a rapacious economy do not. Sadler suggests that if the privileged would like to understand the rage psalms, they should start by listening to the stories of harassed workers who know a thing or two about workplace injustice. He writes, "Because the sufferings and joys experienced by African Americans and the laments and praises voiced by the ancient psalmists cohere so readily, African American narratives may provide critical insight into the origins of certain psalms, particularly those that emerge from contexts of oppression and exile."[29]

Here the psalmists' laments need to be in conversation with the slaves' cry from Exodus. Oppressed and suffering workers laboring in the fields of Egypt scream out in prayer, and Yahweh responds. The birth of Israel as a nation is located in the cry of a worker's lament and the response of a liberating God. Learning to lament about work is the beginning of a new life for Israel. It can mark the beginning of a new life for a modern worker as well.

If Exodus assures workers that they can scream out to God about work, Psalms provides workers with the words they are allowed to scream. Therein workers can find a whole battery of vivid language to express their workplace rage—a rage they might not even realize is there. Through these songs a broken-down worker is equipped to cry out, "I have done what is righteous and just; do not leave me to my oppressors" (Ps. 119:121). If they must, workers may even find themselves demanding retribution: "Silence my enemies; destroy all my foes" (Ps. 143:12); "Send forth lightning and scatter the enemy; shoot your arrows and rout them" (Ps. 144:6). In Psalm 109 a merchant is

28. Sadler, "Singing a Subversive Song," 447.
29. Sadler, "Singing a Subversive Song," 448.

Learning Fervent Prayer from the Korean Practice of *Tong-sung Ki-do*

Depending on one's context, it can be uncomfortable for workers to express their vocational stresses and laments in communal worship. The Korean practice of *tong-sung ki-do* stands out in stark contrast.

Those familiar with twentieth-century Korean history will know about the intense suffering Koreans endured under Japanese colonization, the Korean War, and military dictatorship. *Han* is the word used to describe this experience of deep suffering.[a] The term carries with it experiences that Andrew Park describes as "frustrated hope," "the collapsed feeling of pain," "being forced to let go of something valued," "resentful bitterness," and "a wounded heart."[b] *Tong-sung ki-do* is a distinctly Korean form of prayer that grows out of this prolonged experience of *han*.[c]

The literal translation of *tong-sung ki-do* is "praying together out loud." It is an expression of Spirit-filled prayer often heard in early morning prayer gatherings of Koreans, although it is also used in individual prayer. *Tong-sung ki-do* is fervent, persistent, emotionally loaded prayer. It vocalizes to God the deep sufferings and joys of the community as a form of both lament and surrender. It is described by some as having its roots in biblical characters struggling with God in prayer (Gen. 32:22–32; Exod. 2:23–25; Jer. 31:15; Luke 22:44). Major Young Sung Kim describes the form *tong-sung ki-do* takes in Korean Salvation Army congregations:

> During worship, usually at the time of special prayer request, the minister or the worship leader will call the congregation to pray in unison. The whole congregation joins together to pray aloud indi-

falsely accused in the marketplace. Here the worker asks God for economic retribution:

> My God, whom I praise,
>   do not remain silent,
> for people who are wicked and deceitful
>   have opened their mouths against me. . . .
> May a creditor seize all he has;
>   may strangers plunder the fruits of his labor. (Ps. 109:1, 11)

vidually but spontaneously at the same time in unison. Some time, in the beginning of prayer the congregation may shout, "Lord! Lord! Lord!" in unison as a corporative sign of engaging the prayer warfare. Usually the congregation is given a specific time period, with a common theme of petition or supplication.[d]

Tong-sung ki-do holds together the individual and communal dimensions of prayer by creating space for each Christian to bring their pain, lament, and longings before God as a collective expression of prayer. Each pray-er participates "in the larger picture of God's work in the community as a whole."[e] Through such practices the anguished longings and hurts of each person find an audience with God and solidarity in community.

One wonders how *tong-sung ki-do* might inspire communities of workers to express a wider range of emotions in prayer, especially in non-Korean churches. What if more churches were places in which workers expected to find solidarity with others who themselves are collectively expressing deep vocational anguish?

a. Pak et al., *Singing the Lord's Song in a New Land*, 39–40.
b. Park, *The Wounded Heart of God*, 15–20.
c. Pak et al. explain that the Japanese curfew was lifted at 4:00 a.m. every day. It was then the church bells would ring, followed by prayers at the church at 4:30 a.m. This was a form of embodied protest against being exiled in their homeland. They write, "In this context of being silenced and oppressed [under Japanese occupation], *tong-sung ki-do* was an act of resistance, a breaking of the imposed silence. . . . [It] became a psychological catharsis in which the people could freely express their agony before God, and it provided a way of being released from the burden of their oppression. It also served them as a way to gather up new strength to go on living with new hopes." Pak et al., *Singing the Lord's Song in a New Land*, 40.
d. Kim, "Tongsung Kido."
e. Yu, "Tongsung Kido."

When a worker, ancient or modern, has been unjustly treated in the marketplace, these are the sorts of words they want to say—and often do. The songs of the Psalter do not suppress the worker's rage. Instead, their candid lyrics put words to workers' anger and train workers not to shout into the abyss but to carry their vocational rage directly to God.

No doubt, such words of vocational rage can make polite and submissive Christian workers feel awkward. But the psalmists prod them onward and declare that sometimes words of rage need to be voiced. As John Goldingay says, "The Psalms make it possible to say things that are otherwise unsayable."[30] Worship must not be a time of pretend. If rage needs to be expressed, it needs to be expressed. God already knows the rage is there. Moreover, as J. Clinton McCann insists, "In the face of monstrous evil, the

30. Goldingay, *Psalms*, 1:22.

Spirituals and Work Laments

African American spirituals grew out of the centuries-long communal experience of slavery and forced labor. African slaves were kid-
napped, bred, raised, and sold like chattel to satisfy the rapacious
economic lusts of white Americans. Their songs of lament are psalm-
like prayers that express primal cries for life, dignity, and liberation.
Yolanda Smith explains that many African American spirituals "origi-
nated in the work context."[a] She mentions one particular work song
that specifically discusses the relationship between oppressed workers, their work, and their overseers.

> Captain, O captain, you must be cross,
> It's six o'clock an' you won't 'knock off!'
> Captain, O captain, you must be blin',
> You keep hollerin' "hurry" an' I'm darn nigh flyin'.

There's nothing simple or flat about the relationship between the
spirituals and the daily work of the slave. Some spirituals sought to
undermine the oppressor; some sought to give the slaves hope; some
rhythms made the working day pass more easily; some expressed
deep and gnawing sorrow. No matter the vocational purpose, the
chants, dances, and lyrics were in deep conversation with the lived
experience and raw cry of the worker.

The composer R. Nathaniel Dett makes an interesting comment
about the enduring vitality of spirituals and folk songs in the African
American community: "With other races, the making of the folk song
was incidental to life; with the creators of the spiritual, it was life itself. On the plantation, the makers of these songs were slaves, hire-
lings, chattel, with minds and bodies subject to the wills and whims

worst possible response is to feel nothing. What *must* be felt—by the victims
and on behalf of the victims—are grief, rage, and outrage. In the absence
of these feelings, evil becomes an acceptable commonplace. In other words,
to forget is to submit to evil, to wither and die; to remember is to resist, to
be faithful, and to live again."[31] Vocational lament is here a profound act
of faith.

31. McCann, *Introduction to the Book of Psalms*, 119.

of their masters. . . . This gave to the spiritual an intensity of projection comparable to no other folk expression in the world."[b]

It is their capacity for bringing to speech the seemingly unspeakable experience of godforsakenness, oppression, and violence that make the spirituals unique. It also accounts in part for why the psalms were so popular among African slaves.[c]

Neither the mourning slave nor the lamenting psalmist would surrender their voice to the extinguishing forces of evil from their masters and enemies. Holding fast to the God of the oppressed gave them a counterinterpretation of their true identity, value, and dignity. The slave was a "brother," and his enslavement stood in direct opposition to God's purposes for creation.

Both the spirituals and the psalms function as condensed forms of spiritual vitality and resilience that are desperately needed among oppressed workers today. The emotional residue of the original workers who sang these songs lives on in their words today. Contemporary workers in oppressive circumstances looking for raw language need look no further than the psalms and the spirituals.

a. Y. Smith, *Reclaiming the Spirituals*, 71.
b. Darden, *People Get Ready!*, 69.
c. See Sadler, "Singing a Subversive Song," 447.

Praying against the Boss

John Goldingay assigns a rather uncomfortable title to his reflections on Psalms 9–10: "How to Pray against the Powerful." These two prayers call on God to visit justice and vengeance on marketplace leaders who are taking advantage of the weak and vulnerable. While the powerful imagine that they are a law unto themselves, these songs declare a firm *no*; they exist under and are subject to the law of God.

Imagine a CEO reciting prayers like these in worship. Correctly framed, haunting questions may soon emerge for him: "When my employees go home from a day spent in my company, when they pray to God, when they gather for worship, what do they say to God about me? What do they ask God to do to me? Are my workers asking God to visit justice and even vengeance on me?" Psalms 9–10, according to Goldingay, may prompt overseers to recognize themselves as "the people who are being prayed against."[32]

32. Goldingay, *Psalms*, 1:184.

Liturgical Hospitality for the Worker

Contemporary forms of worship can sometimes feel like a one-way conversation. Workers sit in the pews and are the passive recipients of sermonic monologues directed *at them*. The sanctuary speaks, the worker listens.

The psalms, however, initiate a dynamic conversation, a vocational dialogue between the sanctuary and the streets. In their lyrics we find agricultural issues, economic challenges, and marketplace questions all carried directly into the sanctuary. Great harvests along with horrific drought and injustice are all being brought forward. Commenting on David's psalms in particular, Derek Kidner argues that the prayers come "straight from life: from the battlefield or 'the cave,' not from the sanctuary." Composed on the street, only later were the psalms adapted for use in the sanctuary. This "is the opposite direction of flow" that we might expect.[33] We would expect Jerusalem's sanctuary to speak to its streets; we would not expect the streets to talk back.

The Psalter, Kidner argues, is not an inert "liturgical library, storing up standard literature for worship." Instead, the songbook is like a "hospitable house," a home that has welcomed a disorganized collection of real people's praises and petitions. The hospitable house is "well lived in, where most things can be found and borrowed after some searching, and whose first occupants have left on it everywhere the imprint of their experiences and the stamp of their characters."[34]

With a spirit of liturgical hospitality, the psalms invite workers to enter God's hospitable house. The psalms welcome their workplace experiences—praises and pains alike. Once inside, workers are encouraged to decorate God's hospitable house with their workplace thanksgivings, confessions, and laments. Is this how we treat our places of worship today?

Raising Dirty Hands in Worship

> Who may ascend the mountain of the LORD?
>   Who may stand in his holy place?
>   —Psalm 24:3

> You have set our iniquities before you,
>   our secret sins in the light of your presence.
>   —Psalm 90:8

33. Kidner, *Psalms 1–72*, 30.
34. Kidner, *Psalms 1–72*, 32.

An Israelite worshiper needed to examine their daily work *before* they entered the house of worship. Consider your marketplace behavior this week. Are your hands clean? Look at the basket of produce you are about to bring before the Lord. Were these fruits earned honestly? Does that calf represent your best and most holy effort?

If your workplace behavior disqualifies you from worship, all is not lost. The Scriptures prescribe two actions. First, leave the sanctuary immediately and return to the marketplace. Make immediate restitution with those you have wronged (Lev. 6:1–6). Second, return to the sanctuary and reckon with your sin in the presence of your God (Lev. 6:7). A horizontal reconciliation with economic neighbors in the marketplace needs to accompany a vertical reconciliation with God in the sanctuary.[35] Psalm 15 reflects this integrated sentiment:

> LORD, who may dwell in your sacred tent? . . .
> The one whose walk is blameless . . .
> who keeps an oath even when it hurts,
>   and does not change their mind;
> who lends money to the poor without interest;
>   who does not accept a bribe against the innocent. (vv. 1, 2, 4–5)

Lyrics like these remind the worker to stop and reflect on their marketplace behavior before they enter the sanctuary. Do you intend to raise dirty hands in worship today? Considering the week you've had, are you worthy of approaching the sacred tent? To climb God's holy mountain, enter the gates, and dwell in the Lord's house of worship is a profound blessing, for "it is good to be near God" (Ps. 73:28). The ancient Psalter pushes contemporary Christians to reckon with their workplace behavior both before and within worship. To glibly reply, "Well, Jesus paid it all, so I'm good now," is to fail to wrestle with, and ultimately release, the real guilt that haunts (or should haunt) a worker on a Sunday morning.

Seeing Work through Worship

"Your work *is* worship." This well-meaning and increasingly popular phrase is vulnerable to a dangerous misinterpretation. The mistake runs something

---

35. Christopher Wright elaborates on this theme: "Israel's worship was to be marked by a deepened commitment to ethical response at the horizontal level. . . . Even coming into the presence of the LORD at all in worship was subject to ethical criteria. . . . [Worship in the sanctuary] is acceptable only from those who, in the everyday conduct of their lives, mirror the ethical standards of the God they presume to worship—those, in short, with clean hands and a pure heart." C. Wright, *Old Testament Ethics*, 45–46.

like this: if my daily work is worship, then why do I need to participate in the gathered worship of the church? There is a multiplicity of theological rejoinders to this line of thinking. The psalms offer one interesting reply.

The psalmists appear to believe that worship in the sanctuary can enable a worker to more clearly interpret their work—and the marketplace as a whole—in the light of God. Psalm 73 offers a fine example of this. Here we find an Israelite merchant troubled by a marketplace that appears to have no justice. He sees bad businesses flourishing everywhere with seemingly no negative consequences.

But then he confesses, "I entered the sanctuary of God," and a larger perspective on the market is revealed.

> But as for me, my feet had almost slipped;
>   I had nearly lost my foothold.
> For I envied the arrogant
>   when I saw the prosperity of the wicked. . . .
> This is what the wicked are like—
>   always free of care, they go on amassing wealth. . . .
> When I tried to understand all this,
>   it troubled me deeply
> till I entered the sanctuary of God;
>   then I understood their final destiny. (Ps. 73:2–3, 12, 16–17)

In the sanctuary, workers are able to peer through the cluttered economy of the world to see the deeper—and truer—economy of God. From Zion's heights, they are able to see that the economy of the world is short-lived. Worship in the sanctuary enables workers to see the final destiny of the oppressor and the true nature of economic flourishing.

The psalm closes with a revealing comment about the critical importance of liturgical space and proximity.

> Those who are far from you will perish. . . .
> But as for me, it is good to be near God.
>   I have made the Sovereign LORD my refuge;
>   I will tell of all your deeds. (Ps. 73:27–28)

Place, space, and proximity matter. Simply put, contemporary workers need to regularly *and physically* withdraw their bodies from the economy of the world. Worship needs to physically gather the bodies of workers into a worship space so that they may stop and examine the economy of the world in the light of the deeper economy of God.

When Israelite workers climbed Zion's hilltop and participated in Yahweh's world of worship, they stood at a critical vantage point from which they could begin to see their own world of work more clearly.[36] From Yahweh's "world of worship" they could see their fields anew as spaces of divine provision, beauty, and value. They could begin to recognize the ways in which their fields stood in rebellion to the justice, rest, and generosity of God.[37] As Walter Brueggemann says, "Worship models and enacts an alternative world of sanity that prevents Israel from succumbing to the seductive insanities of a world raging against the holiness of Yahweh."[38]

Worship Puts Work in Its Place

Two women arrive for worship: a coffee laborer in Guatemala and a coffee executive in Seattle. The executive has spent her week developing a global corporate strategy, restructuring departments, moving processing plants, and shifting massive workforces from one country to the next. Her week has been one of (seeming) power, control, and dominion. The coffee laborer, on the other hand, has had a very different week. One of her friends was laid off, and the other was injured during the coffee harvest. Her upper-class sister made fun of her job over the phone. On Friday she learned that, in an effort to increase profits, her farm's American buyers are shifting their production to Indonesia.

Now it is Sunday. These two very different workers (and two very different weeks) are both being gathered into worship. As we have seen, the psalms are able to directly engage both the manager and the managed. The psalms neither

36. How can a sanctuary enable workers to better see their world of work? Walter Brueggemann argues that when Israelites gathered for worship, they were collectively engaged in a creative act of "world-making." Cooperating with God, worshipers create a "world of worship." This world reflects divine order, beauty, justice, abundance, and grace. The world of worship surrounds the worker with the works of God in song and story, poem and praise. Through gathered "public worship Israel is engaged in constructing a world in which Israel can viably and joyously live." Brueggemann, *Israel's Praise*, 6. This alternative "world of worship" critiques the dominant patterns of the "world of work." Moreover, it reminds Israelite workers what is truly lasting and valuable—and what is not. It reminds workers of the true patterns of the economy of God and helps them to walk in the ways of the Lord. See Brueggemann, *Israel's Praise*, 158; Brueggemann, *Theology of the Old Testament*, 665.

37. Notice, for example, how one's marketplace vision can be transformed by a sanctuary song: "Do not be afraid when some become rich, when the wealth of their houses increases. For when they die they will carry nothing away; their wealth will not go down after them" (Ps. 49:16–17 NRSV).

38. Brueggemann, *Theology of the Old Testament*, 665.

romanticize nor demonize their participation in the marketplace. Instead, the psalms put their work and the economy as a whole "in its place" within the larger work and economy of God.

Psalm 104 offers a particularly illuminating example of this.[39] Within its lyrics, Israelite workers would have seen their labors as one thread within the "magnificent quilt" that is the complex creational economy of God.[40] They would have begun to see that "every thread contributes to a whole, woven by a supremely skilled craftworker."[41]

For the coffee executive, Psalm 104 can humble her pretensions to power and omnipotence. She is reminded that she is not a coffee demigod. Her labors are dependent on a much larger ecosystem of divine and human labor. Through Psalm 104, the executive sings not of her work but God's:

> All creatures look to you
>   to give them their food at the proper time.
> When you give it to them,
>   they gather it up;
> when you open your hand,
>   they are satisfied with good things.
> When you hide your face,
>   they are terrified;
> when you take away their breath,
>   they die and return to the dust. (vv. 27–29)

39. This psalm deftly situates the finite work of humans within the seemingly infinite works of God, the land, and all its creatures. The psalm discusses at great length the complexity and significance of God's labors in and through the rivers and the rain, the trees and the soil, the birds and the cattle, while, in contrast, the humans labor receives little attention at all. As we will see, this particular worship song carries with it the potential to impact the coffee executive and the coffee laborer in two very different ways.

40. Psalm 104 reveals one more interesting counterpoint to popular theologies of work that are built primarily off of Genesis 1 and 2. John Goldingay notes that in this particular worship song people are invited to sing about a God who is constantly, busily, and almost obsessively at work throughout every nook and cranny of creation. "Whereas Genesis portrays creation as effortless, the psalm portrays it as requiring expenditure of divine energy in constraining and harnessing other dynamic forces." Goldingay, *Psalms*, 3:197. Here workers are not gathering to sing about a distant clockmaker who has completed his work and is now on a permanent sabbatical. No, in this song, workers shout that "God is a gardener sprinkling rain from the heavens. God is a farmer growing crops. God feeds the lions. . . . God is not on a Sabbath but continues to work. When God gives, these beings eat, to their full; when God does not, they are terrified." Goldingay, *Psalms*, 3:198. This psalm reminds workers that they do not labor within an autonomous created order or some sealed-off and self-sufficient globe. Our labors and our lives are constantly and completely dependent on the continuing labors of God.

41. Goldingay, *Psalms*, 3:191.

The executive's corporate success is deeply dependent on the rains of the Pacific, the soil of Guatemala, the pollination of the bees, and the skilled hands of the laborer. She is not autonomous. She is not "self-made." She is a small contributor to the much larger and much more complex economy of God. The soil and workers of Guatemala are not hers to rule. Her company relies on the sovereign hand of the divine farmer. The lyrics of Psalm 104 not only humble her, they invite her to return to her work with a liturgical vision of her redemptive calling within this larger chain of production.

While psalms like this might humble the manager, they can have the opposite effect on the managed. As the laborer fills her chest with this song, her humble head is lifted, her back is straightened, and her eyes reflect a reaffirmed purpose. She is no longer "just" a laborer on a dusty patch of forgotten land. She is now an important contributor to the economy of God. She has not been forgotten; she has not been abandoned. She is beloved and valued. She is part of God's work in the world. She sings to God:

> From your lofty abode you water the mountains;
>> the earth is satisfied with the fruit of your work.
> You cause the grass to grow for the cattle,
>> and plants for people to use,
> to bring forth food from the earth,
>> and wine to gladden the human heart,
> oil to make the face shine,
>> and bread to strengthen the human heart. (Ps. 104:13–15 NRSV)

Those who would marginalize or dehumanize her should be warned: this laborer has an immortal advocate who both hears and responds to her cry. She has a direct line to the one who waters the mountains and brings forth the fruit.

But perhaps we're being too simplistic in our treatment of these two workers. Perhaps our coffee executive is not self-centered or domineering at all. Perhaps she is truly anxious about a global coffee market that she cannot control. Perhaps she is overwhelmed by her responsibilities for thousands of workers. Once again, this worship song offers some insight into her work. The worker's finite role in Psalm 104 can be welcome news to workers who have convinced themselves that the "weight of the world" rests on their shoulders. Immersed in the world of this psalm, the anxious executive is reminded that she is not carrying the world—God is. Her finite role in the grand economy of God is not to be mourned. Her vocational finitude is a liberating liturgical discovery, something that the stressed-out executive can positively revel in.

This is the poetic and prophetic power of the psalms. As a complex work of liturgical art, the psalms can accomplish something that a didactic sermon cannot. The exact same lyrics can impact diverse workers in diverse ways. They can humble powerful workers and lift up downtrodden workers. They can invigorate the lazy and offer rest to the exhausted. This is the poetic power of the psalms. They can put work in its proper place within the larger economy of God.

Psalm 104 invites workers to sing themselves into the deeper truth that *it is the Lord* who created the land, plants, animals, and their work. *It is the Lord* who sovereignly waters, feeds, and sustains them. For twenty-two long verses Israelite farmers must sing about the economic contributions of God, the land, and the animals, before their agricultural contribution is even mentioned—in only one verse (v. 23)! The land and its animals are not mere "tools" or "resources," they are sacred participants in a divine economy. Psalm 104 liturgically places workers—both powerful and humble—within this larger economy of God.

Conclusion: A Sanctuary That Offers Rest

The modern world of work has a way of training workers to believe that everything depends on them. Christian workers in particular can convince themselves that God desperately *needs* their work. Their work is holy; therefore it is urgent. Psalm 50 offers a firm (and freeing) rebuttal. Yahweh declares:

> I have no need of a bull from your stall
>> or of goats from your pens,
> for every animal of the forest is mine,
>> and the cattle on a thousand hills.
> I know every bird in the mountains,
>> and the insects in the fields are mine.
> If I were hungry I would not tell you,
>> for the world is mine, and all that is in it. (vv. 9–12)

The message of Psalm 50 on this point is simple: while God might delight in your workplace offerings, God does not *need* any of it. Both God and the world will survive just fine without you. For the weary worker, this is profoundly good news. You may rest.

Psalm 127 offers a similar message of relief. It speaks specifically to the worker "who needs to make sure that everything gets done."[42] This particular

---

42. Goldingay, *Psalms*, 3:502.

prayer, Goldingay explains, "confronts us in our pretensions about our work being indispensable and bids us relax."[43] Self-important and exhausted workers must "be vigilant against" what Goldingay calls "a blasphemous anxiety to do God's work for him."[44] Gathered in communal song, faithful workers are reminded "not to get overwhelmed" by their work but rather to rest in the work of God.[45]

> Unless the LORD builds the house,
>   the builders labor in vain. . . .
> In vain you rise early
>   and stay up late,
> toiling for food to eat—
>   for he grants sleep to those he loves. (Ps. 127:1–2)

The psalm invites workers into a liturgy of rest, to ponder their vocational finitude, contingency, and ultimate dependence on the mighty work of God. The song reminds workers that their efforts are "not the only factor in making things happen."[46] And, in this liturgical discovery, workers can begin to rest in the assurance that God "grants sleep to those he loves." Gathered together in song, workers remind one another through its lyrics to rest, not in their work but in God's.[47] For the Lord says,

> I removed the burden from their shoulders;
>   their hands were set free from the basket.
> In your distress you called and I rescued you. (Ps. 81:6–7)

43. Goldingay, *Psalms*, 3:502.
44. Goldingay, *Psalms*, 3:506.
45. Goldingay, *Psalms*, 3:502.
46. Goldingay, *Psalms*, 3:502.
47. Goldingay, *Psalms*, 3:503.

7

The Prophets

Decrying the Destruction
of Work and Worship

By your many sins and dishonest trade you have desecrated your sanctuaries.

—Ezekiel 28:18

The prophet does not mind someone going into the temple—he is only bothered if a person does not take the temple with him when he comes back out!

—David Fagerberg, *Consecrating the World*

While this book is primarily concerned with how worship and work can
begin to cohere and flourish, this chapter examines how worship and work
can begin to separate and die. Here our two guiding questions are as follows:
How might unfaithful worship impact the integrity of our work? And how
might unfaithful work impact the integrity of our worship?

The prophets offer two straightforward warnings. First, if workers regularly
engage in unfaithful worship practices, the integrity of their work will suffer
in a variety of ways. Second, if workers regularly engage in unfaithful work
practices, the integrity of their worship will suffer as well. The perversion of
gathered worship in the sanctuary leads to the perversion of Israel's scattered
work in the marketplace and vice versa.

According to the prophets, the temple and the marketplace are profoundly
interdependent. On the positive side, when the ways of the Lord are honored

in both worship and work, flourishing will flow freely back and forth between the temple and the fields. On the negative side, when the ways of the Lord are dishonored, idolatry and injustice will flow freely. If there is any form of disorder in the marketplace, there is most likely some form of idolatry going on in the temple. If God is not responding to the people's worship, there is most likely some form of injustice going on in their work.

What follows is a brief and selective reading of the prophets. We are peering through one small facet of the complex jewel that is Israel's prophetic witness. We are focused solely on what the prophets have to say about the (dis)integration of work and worship.

Because the prophetic voice here is largely that of critique and deconstruction, our time will be spent exploring the prophets' *negative* evaluations of worship and work. Do not misunderstand their rhetorical broadsides. Prophets are not against "the market" or "the temple." Instead, they are against the perversion of *God's* market and *God's* temple. The prophets' negative screeds against priests and merchants are fueled by a positive, but fierce, desire for holy work and holy worship. These prophetic critiques haunted their original audience, and they should haunt us as well. Instead of sanding down their rough edges, we invite readers to feel the intended discomfort and allow the prophets' cries to illuminate the ways in which our own work and worship diverge from God's holy design.

Empathizing with Idolaters

> Their land is full of idols;
>   they bow down to the work of their hands,
>   to what their fingers have made.
>
> —Isaiah 2:8

> Shameful gods have consumed the fruits of our ancestors' labor.
>
> —Jeremiah 3:24

To the contemporary ear, the ancient practice of idolatry sounds reprehensible and unimaginable. How could Israelite farmers and merchants engage in such a horrible practice? In this section it is our (counterintuitive) task to help the reader understand and *even empathize* with the common practice of idolatry among ancient workers.

Imagine for a moment that you're an ancient farmer plowing a dry and dusty hillside that has not seen rain in months. If the rains do not come next week, you may well lose your crops, your land, and your livelihood. Your family will be enslaved to a wealthy landowner or to the king, one of whom will take your land. You're desperate. Your family farm, your very life hangs in the balance, so you will listen to anyone, you will try anything.

Within the fragile agricultural economy of ancient Israel, the idolatrous worship of rain gods like Baal made sense. Baalism was profoundly logical, rational, and practical. After all, throughout Canaan it was widely accepted that "Baal was the god of wind and weather, who dispensed dew, rain and snow and the attendant fertility of the soil."[1] Canaanite workers developed liturgies to feed Baal and convince him to provide the rain and fertility that they so desperately needed.[2] In Canaan's economy, Baal worship "had an obvious and immediate *relevance to daily life*. The Israelites were a rural farming people. They heard the claim that it was Baal who was responsible for the grain, the wine, the wool, and the flax which provided their food and clothing (Hosea 2:8–9)."[3] Baal was not a transcendent god; he was embedded in the people's deepest vocational longings and fears. These vulnerable farmers thought they could cover their economic bases and worship both Baal and Yahweh. "They must have thought it possible to combine the best of Yahwism with the best of this other fascinating religion which had its focus in the yearly rhythm of planting and harvesting so close to the lives of these people."[4]

These vulnerable farmers, whom we label "idolaters," were not monsters. They were neither stupid nor superstitious. They were making rational decisions based on the dominant economic thinking of the time. Their idolatry was driven by a vocational desire for deeply good things—food, family, security, and fruitful work. Their sense of vocational fragility and contingency drove them to seek economic security in fertility gods like Baal and Asherah.

If we define idolatry as *an inordinate trust in the work of human hands*, then the ancient practice of idolatry no longer seems quite so arcane and remote to modern life. Contemporary workers tossed by the economic waves of the global marketplace regularly feel fragile and vulnerable. They fear for their own careers, security, and success. They're willing to put their trust in just about any work of human hands that promises to secure their future. They regularly put inordinate trust in technology, fashion, titles, and wealth. It is harsh to say, but modern workers will regularly sacrifice even their own children by depriving them of their time and attention in order to secure their financial future. Moreover, through pious prayers and fervent songs, modern

---

1. Möller, "Prophets and Prophecy," 827.
2. See Milgrom, *Leviticus*, 21.
3. Limburg, *Hosea–Micah*, 24
4. Limburg, *Hosea–Micah*, 24.

worshipers regularly try to cajole God into giving them economic blessings. Idolatry is not a thing of the past. It is a present and pervasive power in contemporary work and worship.

It is important for us to empathize with these ancient idolaters. It is important to draw close to them and relate to their vocational fears, their contingency, their yearning for economic security. Lacking empathy, modern readers will not be able to recognize idolatry's power and presence in their own work and worship.

Keeping this firmly in mind, we begin our selective examination of three prophets: Amos, Hosea, and Isaiah. Each of these prophets reveals a unique way in which worship and work can go terribly wrong. Amos and Isaiah blame corrupt workers, markets, and fields, while Hosea blames corrupt worship leaders, sacrifices, and songs. While their context is remote, their economic and liturgical insight is uncomfortably close to home.

Idolatry and a Corrupt Economy

> Woe to you who add house to house
>   and join field to field
>   till no space is left. . . .
> They have no regard for the deeds of the LORD,
>   no respect for the work of his hands.
>   —Isaiah 5:8, 12

During the prophetic age of Amos and Hosea, economic indicators were soaring for the wealthy few—and dropping for the poor majority. Small farmers increasingly lost their ancestral lands to the rapacious grasping of wealthy landowners and oppressive kings. Israel's patchwork quilt of family farms was gradually being acquired and centralized under the aristocratic ownership of the palace and the wealthy few. Newly homeless, these farmers were quickly transformed into migrant workers.

The powerful continued to expand their land and estates through a variety of legitimate and illegitimate means.[5] Some local farmers were falsely accused in the courts. Upon conviction they were imprisoned, killed, or turned into indentured servants. Their ancestral lands were then free for the taking. Other farmers lost their land through overwhelming debts. During periods of drought farmers were offered high-interest loans to see them through;

5. Mays, *Amos*, 143.

ancestral lands were put up as collateral. When workers could not pay, lands were confiscated.[6] Some farmers lost their land through simple violence or fraud, others from high taxes, and still others from their own irresponsibility.

Though the causes were complex, the end was simple. Israel's agricultural economy was rapidly becoming centralized—and unequal.[7] Rural farmers were marginalized, while elite landowners and urban merchants were quickly growing in power.[8] As Ellen Davis notes, these "formerly free peasants became serfs, doubtless on land their own families had long held."[9] Without land of their own, migrant laborers were increasingly vulnerable to the swings of the market and the rapacious taxes of the state.

Yahweh's original desire for freed slaves, working their own crops, offering them up in holy work and worship was being despoiled. The holy and gracious economy of Yahweh was being replaced by Baal's economy of grasping and greed. African scholar Yoilah Yilpet here recognizes that Israel's economic poverty had a liturgical consequence: the poor laborer's "lack of grain, wine and oil, used to represent all agricultural products, affects the worship services in the temple ([Joel] 1:9–10). The very ability to worship God is compromised by the inability to provide the offerings commanded. . . . African readers can identify with their despair."[10]

In Israel there were no divisions between church, state, and market. Israel's elites—be they political, religious, or economic—were all cooperating with one another in their collective marginalization of poor workers. Israel's priesthood, for example, was regularly engaged in the collection of palace taxes, the settling of trade disputes, the praise of the crown, and the processing of various grains and meat.[11] Sanctuary, market, and palace were united as one.

6. Davis, *Scripture, Culture, and Agriculture*, 123.

7. Davis, *Scripture, Culture, and Agriculture*, 121.

8. Ellen Davis comments:

   [Israel's markets became a] centralized system of commodity agriculture controlled by the crown. The old subsistence economy, as it had been practiced in semiautonomous villages cooperating within regional networks, was supplanted by intensified and specialized agriculture. The new system was designed to maximize production of the three most important commodities: grain to feed the cities (the state's administrative and trade centers), and wine and olive oil, the more expensive products, to provide export revenue and to satisfy (directly or indirectly) the taste for luxury now cultivated among the few who were rich. (Davis, *Scripture, Culture, and Agriculture*, 122–23)

9. Davis, *Scripture, Culture, and Agriculture*, 124.

10. Yilpet, "Joel," 1054.

11. According to Ellen Davis, "There was a clear connection between Israel's food economy and the priesthood. . . . [Priests] issued loans to farmers to pay for animals and seed. They calculated and collected taxes in the form of agricultural products; these might be stored, redistributed to forced labor gangs and soldiers, or exported. . . . Sanctuaries [were] places for *food processing*, along with storage and redistribution: 'At sanctuaries throughout Israel,

A Boy's Song of Lament

This congregational song from the Philippines speaks of a child who is heartbroken by seeing his father beaten down by his incessant labors and his mother by hunger and sadness. Out of the mouth of babes comes wisdom. In this song, based on one of the darkest lament psalms (Ps. 88:1–2), we follow the lead of a child resisting the dehumanization of exploitation by breaking his silence and crying out to God for help and deliverance.

"A Boy's Prayer"

While I am asleep,
may you never leave my side.
And may your loving care,
include my parents also.

My father is tired,
for he works all day and night.
And yet the pay he gets
has never been sufficient.

My mother's in tears,
every day we face our meals.
For she has never seen
enough food on our table.

And there's one more thing
that I have to ask of you,
Don't let me go astray
when I awake tomorrow.

Though I'm not out of school,
may I learn to put to use
the little that I know,
so I can earn a living.[a]

a. I-to Loh, *Hymnal Companion to "Sound the Bamboo": Asian Hymns in Their Cultural and Liturgical Contexts* (Chicago: GIA Publications, 2011), 257. Lyrics by Rody Vera, trans. Roland S. Tinio; music TOTOY; Jonas Baes. Copyright © 1990, Christian Conference of Asia, GIA publications, Inc. Used with permission.

---

priests slaughtered and butchered livestock, decanted wine and olive oil, and parched grain.'" Davis, *Scripture, Culture, and Agriculture*, 133, quoting Matthews and Benjamin, *Social World of Ancient Israel*, 192.

The priests supported the palace, the palace supported the nobles, the nobles supported the priests. No one supported the worker.

This corrupt unity of temple, palace, and market meant that the priesthood and its worship services were deeply implicated in a corrupt economic system. The wealth produced by this dishonest economy was regularly brought into the sanctuaries. Worship leaders accepted these contaminated offerings and raised them up to Yahweh in a perverted act of praise.

This is the economic and liturgical context into which Amos and Hosea step. Their prophetic critiques were directed against a marketplace, a sanctuary, and a palace that were, together, perpetuating the corruption of holy worship and holy work. This context should help us understand why the prophets cry out against the corruption of economics, politics, and liturgy. It explains why, in one breath, a prophet will criticize sacrifices *and* taxes, songs *and* wages, vineyards *and* temples.

Moving forward, Hosea's critique will primarily focus on the corrupting influences of unholy sanctuaries, while Amos's will focus on the corrupting influences of unholy markets. Hosea will blame the worship leaders. Amos will blame the workers. And both, sadly, will be right. Both markets and temples, worship leaders and workers, are capable of poisoning God's holy designs for worship and work.

Amos: Blaming Merchants and Markets

Israel's merchants worried that their worship was no longer "working." They worried that God was not responding to their liturgies the way they had hoped. Amos confirmed their fears. The Lord declared through Amos,

> I hate, I despise your religious festivals;
>   your assemblies are a stench to me.
> Even though you bring me burnt offerings and grain offerings,
>   I will not accept them.
> Though you bring choice fellowship offerings,
>   I will have no regard for them.
> Away with the noise of your songs!
>   I will not listen to the music of your harps. (Amos 5:21–23)

The merchant's songs are no longer music to God's ears; they are noise. The fruits of their labor are no longer pleasing to God's nostrils; they are a stench. In the past their work was worship; now it is an abomination. What has gone wrong? Who is to blame?

The answers can be found in the twenty-four verses that surround this passage. They point the finger of blame toward cheating in the markets, corruption in the courts, and crushing taxes from the state.[12] In short, Amos declares, the sins in the streets are destroying the songs in the sanctuary.

Note that the Israelites are still actively "worshiping" Yahweh in this passage. They're still singing songs and praying prayers. They're still offering up their work to God through festivals and sacrifices. For all we know, they are "doing worship" correctly. And yet their worship is not only disgusting to God but is also having no discernable impact on their working lives. The sanctuary, which was supposed to train workers to walk in the ways of the Lord, is failing. Faith, work, and worship are falling apart.

Amos 8 adds another element. Here the prophet addresses a group of merchants who are eager and impatient for a worship service to end. The merchants can't wait to leave the sanctuary so they can rush back to the marketplace to make more money. They're itching to escape the liturgy so they can cheat their customers, game the market, gouge the poor, and squeeze every last cent out of their shoddy products. Once again, these workers are still participating in "orthodox" Yahweh worship. They're singing the right songs, they're praying the right prayers. And yet, once again, their worship has no discernable impact on their work. It is here that Amos speaks:

> Hear this, you who trample the needy
>   and do away with the poor of the land, saying,
> "When will the New Moon be over
>   that we may sell grain,
> and the Sabbath be ended
>   that we may market wheat?"—
> skimping on the measure,
>   boosting the price
>   and cheating with dishonest scales,
> buying the poor with silver
>   and the needy for a pair of sandals,
>   selling even the sweepings with the wheat. . . .
> "In that day," declares the Sovereign Lord, . . .
> "I will turn your religious festivals into mourning
>   and all your singing into weeping. . . .
> I will send a famine through the land—
> not a famine of food or a thirst for water,
>   but a famine of hearing the words of the LORD.

12. Mays, *Amos*, 142.

> People will stagger from sea to sea
>   and wander from north to east,
> searching for the word of the LORD,
>   but they will not find it." (Amos 8:4–6, 9–12)

In a sinful world, we expect some merchants to lie, cheat, and steal. We also expect prophets to rise up and condemn them. What we do not expect is this: Amos predicts that the corruption of their work will lead to the corruption of their worship. Note how the marketplace evil discussed above is immediately surrounded both above and below by discussions of worship. The merchants disregard worship on the front end, and their worship falls apart on the back end.

According to Amos, unfaithful labor will destroy liturgy in two principal ways. First, when these workers raise filthy hands and fruits up to God in worship, God will respond by turning their songs into "mourning" and "weeping." Their harvest feasts will no longer be festive. The joy in their worship will dissipate. The second consequence is that worship will no longer nourish the workers. The prophet predicts that workers will leave worship feeling famished and thirsty. They will wander about craving spiritual intimacy with God, longing for some word of divine direction. Merchants "will stagger from sea to sea" in their spiritual quest for divine connection, and "they will not find it." When marketplaces are filled with greed, merchants will hear nothing from God in the sanctuary. If wealthy merchants refuse to hear the cries of workers in the marketplace, Yahweh will refuse to hear their cries in the sanctuary. Work without integrity leads to worship without integrity.[13]

Going through the motions in the sanctuary will not transform our working lives. In all of Scripture, Amos 8 is perhaps the best example of this truth. The passage is a cold shower for those suffering from what we might call "liturgical fundamentalism." By this moniker we mean to indicate the romantic belief that a good worship service can fix just about any problem with the

---

13. James Limburg expands on this disconnect between work and worship:
  The businessmen Amos addressed have divided their lives into watertight compartments, one marked religion, the other business. They are scrupulous in closing down for the holy days. No doubt they are to be found among those thronging to the sanctuaries on the sabbath! During the rest of the week their religion is not involved, though, and the customers who enter their places of business are doubly cheated, when they buy and when they sell. Religion, after all, is religion and as for the rest—well, business is business! . . . This prophetic word rejects that dichotomy between faith and life. Religion, it says, has to do with the whole of life, holy day and holy place, but also every day and every place. It also compels its hearers to examine their attitude toward possessions and wealth, with a reminder that in the ancient church one of the seven deadly sins was greed. (Limburg, *Hosea–Micah*, 122)

human condition. Liturgical fundamentalism believes that good worship—on its own—can transform a worker's marketplace behavior. Amos 8 destroys this myth.

Here is the fundamental mistake of the liturgical fundamentalists: while they can see the formative liturgical power of the sanctuary, they can't see the formative liturgical power of the marketplace, nor can they recognize the ways in which marketplace liturgies undermine the formative power of the sanctuary. Consider Amos's merchants as an example. All week long they practiced and habituated the marketplace patterns of cheating, stealing, taxing, lying, grasping, and greed. These economic patterns were (de)forming their hearts in powerful and profound ways, habituating them into the economy of the world. These potent marketplace liturgies easily overpower the liturgies of the sanctuary. One Sabbath day of gracious rest can't compete with six greedy days of grasping acquisition. Formed by a perverse marketplace, Israel's merchants entered the sanctuary with impenetrable hearts closed shut.

It is not difficult to spot the contemporary relevance. Participation in inhumane businesses is not only economically destructive; it is spiritually and liturgically destructive as well. Amos shatters any illusion that liturgical formation in the sanctuary can "do it all" or "go it alone." Which liturgy is more formative: one hour in the sanctuary or fifty hours in the marketplace? The inability of sanctuary liturgies to compete with marketplace liturgies underscores a critical point: workers need to participate in faithful liturgies more than once a week. If workers hope to remain faithful in corrupt economies, they will need to develop and practice their own "counterliturgies" on a daily basis in the workplace.

Amos clearly demonstrates that workers do not enter the sanctuary as blank slates. They already have the patterns of the world's economy written on their hearts. Workers don't sit passively in the pews waiting for worship songs and prayers to write the patterns of God's economy on their hearts. Amos's merchants are immune to holy worship. Their ears are closed, their hearts are hard, and their minds are fixed on the profits that could be had once "worship" is over. They are raising greedy hands that only know how to grasp, cheat, and consume. A single worship service can't change work or workers on its own.

Amos's critiques are devastating. But the prophet is not without hope. While the sanctuary has proven ineffective and impotent, God's sovereign power to transform and save is not. Amos closes his book with a promise that, after a period of devastating exile, Yahweh will restore Israel to holy worship and holy work. Yahweh declares,

Worship Arising from the Lips of Field Workers

Faced with overwhelming corruption and oppression, some workers can (quite understandably) seek a liturgical escape from the world (and their work). The Peruvian hymn "Que se alegren" ("Let Them Be Joyful") avoids this temptation to spiritual escapism. Instead it utilizes the imagery of the Beatitudes to inspire a more earthy hope in the midst of injustice. Rather than seeking to transport workers to some heavenly abode, this song roots the hope of Peruvian workers in God's faithfulness to their land and their vocations. The song calls for farmers, the poor, and the persecuted to be joyful because "within them are the burning flames of hope" that promise "one day" they will receive "new and fertile lands" belonging to them.

Christ comes not to rescue them from their land and labor but to liberate them to work the new creation in joy and freedom. Christ, God with us, comes alongside marginalized workers to labor and struggle at their side.

> They will rebuild the ruined cities and live in them.
> They will plant vineyards and drink their wine;
> they will make gardens and eat their fruit.
> I will plant Israel in their own land. (Amos 9:14–15)

By the work of the Lord, workers will be restored to their land, their labors, and their liturgies once again. As both Isaiah and Micah promise, these workers "will beat their swords into plowshares and their spears into pruning hooks" (Isa. 2:4; Mic. 4:3). Saved by Yahweh—not the power of human worship—these farmers will be free, once again, to work and worship before the face of God. When work and worship disintegrate, you could (like Amos) blame the workers. On the other hand, you could (like Hosea) consider blaming worship leaders.

Hosea: Blaming Worship Leaders and Sanctuaries

> The more priests there were, the more they sinned against me.
>
> —Hosea 4:7

Bad liturgy eventually leads to bad ethics. You begin by singing some sappy sentimental hymn, then you pray some pointless prayer, and the next thing you know you have murdered your best friend.

—Stanley Hauerwas and William Willimon, *The Truth about God*

In ancient Israel and in contemporary America, gathered worship can easily be twisted and manipulated to cover up a wide variety of marketplace sins. Human beings are well practiced at using worship to distract workers from economic depravity and devastation. We can use worship to pacify oppressed workers who should be speaking up. We can use it to assuage the guilt of the economically powerful who have a responsibility to change things. There are all sorts of ways in which corporate worship can either ignore, excuse, or empower marketplace evil.

Postmodern forms of spirituality are not immune from marketplace manipulation. Eastern and alternative forms of spiritual practice have become increasingly popular in the twenty-first-century marketplace. Global corporations regularly create intentional spaces for yoga classes, practices of meditation and mindfulness, spiritual-empowerment retreats, and more. Some research has found that these worship practices make corporate workers more productive, efficient, and happy. But Jeremy Carrette and Richard King are troubled by the way these spiritual practices fail to challenge some of the more destructive effects of global capitalism. They write, "In a sense, the most troubling aspect of many modern spiritualities is precisely that they are not troubling enough. They promote accommodation to the social, economic and political mores of the day and provide little in terms of a challenge to the status quo or to a lifestyle of self-interest and ubiquitous consumption."[14]

As we will see in our discussion of Hosea, all forms of corporate worship and spiritual practice can be twisted to cover up economic evil and pain. Worship leaders—be they ancient or contemporary, Western or Eastern—can play a role in destroying the moral integrity of the marketplace and the work that happens therein.

---

14. Carrette and King, *Selling Spirituality*, 5. They go on to write, "We wish to challenge the way in which the concept of spirituality is being utilised to 'smooth out' resistance to the growing power of corporate capitalism and consumerism as the defining ideology of our time. We do this not out of some misguided belief that traditional religious institutions and systems have been free from authoritarian and oppressive structures of their own, but rather out of a concern that cultural diversity is being eroded by the incessant march of a single worldview—an economically driven globalization—driven by a triumphalist and corporate-oriented form of capitalism" (17).

Groaning and Hope in Our Labors

"Not in vain" is the repeated refrain of the song below. These words fall fresh on workers in every industry and social status. The labor that God intended to be good and life-giving to humankind has been impacted by sin. All workers know this experientially at some level. Pastors and worship leaders serve workers well when they combine the prophetic critique of sin and injustice with the hope of a God-redeemed creation, people, and work.

"Your Labor Is Not in Vain"

Verse 1
Your labor is not in vain
though the ground underneath you is cursed and stained.
Your planting and reaping are never the same,
but your labor is not in vain.

Refrain
For I am with you, I am with you.
I am with you, I am with you
For I have called you,
called you by name.
Your labor is not in vain.

Verse 2
Your labor is not unknown
though the rocks they cry out and the sea it may groan.
The place of your toil may not seem like a home,
but your labor is not unknown.

Verse 3
The vineyards you plant will bear fruit;
the fields will sing out and rejoice with the truth,
for all that is old will at last be made new:
the vineyards you plant will bear fruit.

Verse 4
The houses you labored to build
will finally with laughter and joy be filled.
The serpent that hurts and destroys shall be killed,
and all that is broken be healed.[a]

a. Lyrics and music by Wendell Kimbrough, Paul Zach, and Isaac Wardell, featuring Paul Zach and Madison Cunningham, from *Work Songs* (Porter's Gate Publishing, 2017), available at https://theportersgate.bandcamp.com/track/your-labor-is-not-in-vain-feat-paul-zach-and-madison-cunningham. Used with permission of Porter's Gate Publishing.

Hosea's prophetic witness poses a number of sharp and incisive questions to contemporary pastors and worship leaders: This Sunday, will you accept offerings that emerge from perverted marketplace structures and practices? Will the worship *that you lead* challenge the economic idols and injustice active within your city? If your worship is silent on these economic issues, doesn't that lend them legitimacy? What responsibility do you have, as a worship leader, to challenge unfaithful work and workers who enter the sanctuary?

Throughout his prophetic speeches Hosea constantly uses the vivid and sometimes disturbing sexual metaphors of adultery and prostitution to illustrate Israel's economic and liturgical infidelity. The nation has been unfaithful to her lover. She has been unfaithful in both the markets and the fields, on her throne and on her altars. In every facet of her life Israel has become, quite simply, a prostitute.

Ellen Davis explains that Hosea used the evocative metaphors of "disordered sexuality" to characterize the nation's unfaithful "participation in an exploitative religious, political, and economic system."[15] Israel was Yahweh's unfaithful lover, and its adultery was manifest on the throne, in the market, and at the altar. Notice how Hosea intermingles the metaphors of spirituality, sexuality, and agriculture in the following passage.

> Let her remove the adulterous look from her face
> and the unfaithfulness from between her breasts. . . .
> She has not acknowledged that I was the one
> who gave her the grain, the new wine and oil,
> who lavished on her the silver and gold—
> which they used for Baal.
> Therefore I will take away my grain when it ripens,
> and my new wine when it is ready.
> I will take back my wool and my linen,
> intended to cover her naked body.
> So now I will expose her lewdness
> before the eyes of her lovers;
> no one will take her out of my hands.
> I will stop all her celebrations:
> her yearly festivals, her New Moons,
> her Sabbath days—all her appointed festivals.
> I will ruin her vines and her fig trees,
> which she said were her pay from her lovers;

15. Davis, *Scripture, Culture, and Agriculture*, 132.

> I will make them a thicket,
> > and wild animals will devour them.
> I will punish her for the days
> > she burned incense to the Baals. (Hosea 2:2, 8–13)

Notice that the Israelites are still bringing their work into worship. The critical difference here is that the worship leaders are allowing the workers to offer their grain, wine, and oil *to both Yahweh and Baal*. The consequences of this bifurcated worship are simple: God will put a stop to their worship and their work ("I will stop all her celebrations . . . I will ruin her vines and her fig trees").

The tragedy is not simply that Israel's workers have taken two economic lovers (Yahweh and Baal) but that *their worship leaders have actively blessed the affair through corporate worship*. Through unfaithful teaching and perverted worship, Israel's priests are leading workers away from Yahweh's economy of justice and grace. Through Hosea, God speaks now to the priests:

> There is no faithfulness, no love,
> > no acknowledgment of God in the land. . . .
> My people are destroyed from lack of knowledge.
> Because you have rejected knowledge,
> > I also reject you as my priests. . . .
> The more priests there were,
> > the more they sinned against me. (Hosea 4:1, 6–7)

Israel's worship contributed to unfaithful work and worship in a variety of ways. They were accepting and blessing offerings in the sanctuary from corrupt economic practices. They were allowing the merger of unfaithful work and worship to go on unchallenged.[16] Worst of all, the priests were perpetuating a market system of economic oppression and liturgical idolatry that was actively destroying Israel—and its workers.[17]

The corruption of Israel was flowing freely from the sanctuary out into the marketplace and back again, and worship leaders were facilitating the unholy intercourse. Being limited to "the sanctuary" did not let the priests off the hook. According to Hosea, these worship leaders were actively contributing to the adulterous prostitution of the marketplace, the fields, and the very

16. Davis, *Scripture, Culture, and Agriculture*, 131.
17. Hosea explicitly connects the priests to the corruption of the royal house (5:1) and equates them with bands of robbers (6:9).

land itself (1:2).[18] Israel's priests were unfaithful lovers. Through corporate worship they welcomed another lover (Baal and perverted wealth) into the marriage bed.

These worship leaders needed to be distinct, set apart from the world's unholy ways of worship and work. To Hosea's great dismay, Israel's priests were not set apart; they lacked holy strangeness. They had been assimilated into the worship and work of the nations (Hosea 4:6–9). Adulterous fruits from adulterous markets were being accepted, honored, and blessed in adulterous worship. Israel's worship and work looked like everyone else's. It was normal, no longer strange. Without Israel's holy strangeness, these worship leaders could no longer lead workers into God's alternative economy.

In his prophetic critique, Hosea promises that *creation itself* will put a stop to the priests' prostitution of worship and work. "Thorns and thistles," he predicts, "will grow up and cover their altars. Then they will say to the mountains, 'Cover us!' and to the hills, 'Fall on us!'" (Hosea 10:8). According to Ellen Davis, the "transport of goods from farm to sanctuary will cease for the Lord declares, 'I am about to block up her way with thorns and I shall erect a fence about her. . . . I will cause all of her celebrations to cease.'"[19] Israel's adulterous worship and work must cease. If it does not, the land itself will rise up to stop its own desecration.

As we noted, Hosea's was an age of constant worship. At that time Israel had "a thriving religious life."[20] Every day new priests, altars, and sanctuaries were springing up all over Israel. And yet *the proliferation of worship in the sanctuary was destroying its work in the marketplace*. God declares, "The more priests there were, the more they sinned against me" (Hosea 4:7). Hosea says the same about the proliferation of altars (10:1–3).[21] The increase of communal worship was actually stoking Israel's economic and liturgical lust.

Jutta Krispenz notes that part of the problem was that these priests were catering to the liturgical desires of the workers. Rather than leading holy worship, the priests sought to give the workers an experience they would find "pleasant" (Hosea 4:13).[22] Such worship leaders would seek to serve the existing "ritualistic tendencies within people." This worship would not, in any way, challenge or "contradict the people's desire."[23] So, while workers

18. For Hosea, there was "no clear separation between politics and religion, between [worship] and the personal conduct of life." Krispenz, "Idolatry, Apostasy, Prostitution," 10.

19. Davis, *Scripture, Culture, and Agriculture*, 133.

20. Krispenz, "Idolatry, Apostasy, Prostitution," 27.

21. Although this proliferation of altars "should promote the proximity of God, they only excite God's wrath." Krispenz, "Idolatry, Apostasy, Prostitution," 25.

22. Krispenz, "Idolatry, Apostasy, Prostitution," 16.

23. Krispenz, "Idolatry, Apostasy, Prostitution," 28.

were often engaged in worship, their liturgies were often self-centered and hedonistic (4:7–8, 13; 8:13). Thus, though they cried out loudly and often in worship, "Our God, we acknowledge you!" (8:2), God grieves, "They do not cry out to me from their hearts" (7:14).[24]

Finally, as Ellen Davis notes, in Hosea 9 we encounter "a seamless blending of the themes of sexuality and eating, of offspring and harvest, of love and worship, and economics and international politics."[25] We see that, for Hosea, these are all "inseparable aspects of Israel's life."[26] The farmers are about to celebrate their harvest festival. The workers are ready to rejoice in worship for another fruitful year. Hosea, once again, ruins the party.

> Do not rejoice, Israel. . . .
> For you have been unfaithful to your God;
>> you love the wages of a prostitute
>> at every threshing floor.
> Threshing floors and wine presses will not feed the people;
>> the new wine will fail them. . . .
> They will not remain in the LORD's land;
>> Ephraim will return to Egypt. . . .
> They will not pour out wine offerings to the LORD,
>> nor will their sacrifices please him. . . .
> Their treasures of silver will be taken over by briers,
>> and thorns will overrun their tents. . . .
> They consecrated themselves to that shameful idol
>> and became as vile as the thing they loved.
> Ephraim's glory will fly away like a bird—
>> no birth, no pregnancy, no conception. . . .
> Give them wombs that miscarry
>> and breasts that are dry. (Hosea 9:1–4, 6, 10–11, 14)

Fields created for fertility—like wombs and breasts—will go dry and miscarry. Israel did not acknowledge the work of Yahweh, in either its sanctuaries or its

24. Krispenz, "Idolatry, Apostasy, Prostitution," 27.

25. Davis, *Scripture, Culture, and Agriculture*, 135. Davis carefully charts the ways in which the worship and work of Israel's farmers fell apart. She argues that Hosea uses the metaphors of fornication and adultery to refer "to the whole religio-political system of controlled agriculture . . . endorsed by priests and prophets at the central shrines" (131). Hosea sees Israel's flourishing and faithfulness as deeply interconnected. Healthy nations need faithful worship, faithful work, and faithful sexuality; a virus in one realm quickly spreads to the others. Davis points out that this intimate connection between unfaithful sexuality, liturgy, and economics is found in Ezekiel's prophetic vision as well (Ezek. 18:11–13) (135).

26. Davis, *Scripture, Culture, and Agriculture*, 135.

markets. Because of this, free farmers will become slaves; they "will return to Egypt" (Hosea 9:3) and be exiled from both worship and work.

Although Israel's future is grim, Hosea closes with words of hope. On the day of the Lord the people will once again be reconciled to a holy marriage of fruitful work and worship. God promises,

> "There I will give her back her vineyards,
>   and will make the Valley of Achor a door of hope. . . ."
> "In that day," declares the LORD,
>   "you will call me 'my husband';
>   you will no longer call me 'my master.'
> I will remove the names of the Baals from her lips;
>   no longer will their names be invoked. . . ."
> "I will betroth you to me forever;
>   I will betroth you in righteousness and justice,
>   in love and compassion. . . ."
> "I will respond to the skies,
>   and they will respond to the earth;
> and the earth will respond to the grain,
>   the new wine and the olive oil,
>   and they will respond to Jezreel.
> I will plant her for myself in the land." (Hosea 2:15–17, 19, 21–23)

Isaiah: Disappointed in Worship? Reexamine Your Work

> For day after day they seek me out;
>   they seem eager to know my ways. . . .
> "Why have we fasted," they say,
>   "and you have not seen it?
> Why have we humbled ourselves,
>   and you have not noticed?"
>   —Isaiah 58:2–3

In chapter 58 the prophet Isaiah is addressing a group of frustrated workers gathered in a sanctuary. They are complaining to God because he is not responding to their worship. They have been saying all the right prayers, singing all the right songs, and offering all the right sacrifices. They are crying out to God in worship and getting nothing but silence in return. Are their liturgical practices broken? Why isn't their worship "working"? God finally gives the workers an answer:

> On the day of your fasting, you do as you please
>   and exploit all your workers. . . .
> You cannot fast as you do today
>   and expect your voice to be heard on high.
> Is this the kind of fast I have chosen,
>   only a day for people to humble themselves?
> Is it only for bowing one's head like a reed
>   and for lying in sackcloth and ashes?
> Is that what you call a fast,
>   a day acceptable to the Lord?
> Is not this the kind of fasting I have chosen:
> to loose the chains of injustice
>   and untie the cords of the yoke,
> to set the oppressed free
>   and break every yoke? . . .
> Then your light will break forth like the dawn,
>   and your healing will quickly appear. . . .
> Then you will call, and the Lord will answer;
>   you will cry for help, and he will say: Here am I.
> If you do away with the yoke of oppression, . . .
> You will be like a well-watered garden,
>   like a spring whose waters never fail. . . .
> If you keep your feet from breaking the Sabbath . . .
> and if you honor it by not going your own way . . .
> then you will find your joy in the Lord. (Isa. 58:3–6, 8–9, 11, 13–14)

According to Isaiah, the integrity of a person's work directly impacts the integrity of their worship. The best way to "honor" God's Sabbath is by "not going your own way" in your everyday life and work.[27] In this passage *economic* acts of self-centered dominance are set in direct opposition to *liturgical* acts of fasting (fasting, after all, is an action that embodies self-denying submission).[28]

Why was worship not "working"? Why was it incapable of (trans)forming the lives of Israel's workers? John Goldingay argues that their liturgies had become self-centered and self-serving. Entering the sanctuary, worshipers did "what pleased them—what worked for them, what resonated with their own experience. They were eager to know Yahweh's ways (v. 2) but they also wanted to walk in their own ways (v. 13)."[29]

---

27. "Therefore, while the people act as if they are devoted to God, this passage indicates that they live their lives as if they actually have no interest in God." Barram, "Between Text and Sermon," 460.

28. Goldingay, *Isaiah*, 326.

29. Goldingay, *Isaiah*, 327.

The ghost of Egypt's rapacious economy haunts every verse of this passage. Israel's elites were mimicking Pharaoh. Israel's markets were mimicking Egyptian slave fields. What must be done? Isaiah instructs worshipers to immediately leave the sanctuary and loose the economic chains, untie the cords, and break every yoke. These, after all, were the exact actions Yahweh took when he released the Israelites from their hard labor in Egypt.[30] But Isaiah goes further than the other prophets before him. He declares that *the fair treatment of workers is actually a form of holy worship.* Promoting justice in the workplace is a holy sacrifice, an act of worship that produces a pleasing aroma.

Finally, Isaiah predicts that acts of economic justice will liberate more than employees; these acts will liberate employers as well. The economic patterns of grinding and grasping are a great burden to carry. Both the employee and the employer have to bear their weight. By offering justice to their employees, Isaiah argues, employers can experience a profound liberation that is both spiritual and economic. We already know that Israel's employers have long cried out to God in the sanctuaries and have received no answer. We know that they are weary of shouting into the darkness and receiving no response. *Isaiah offers hope for the renewal of worship amongst the wealthy through the just treatment of their workers.*[31] Through marketplace justice, God will once again respond to their sanctuary prayers.

> Then you will call, and the LORD will answer;
>   you will cry for help, and he will say: Here am I. . . .
> You will be like a well-watered garden,
>   like a spring whose waters never fail. (Isa. 58:9, 11)

The restoration of the marketplace to Yahweh's holy design is a critical first step in the restoration of the sanctuary. The prayers of employers are no longer desperate monologues, liturgical cries into the abyss. The vocational conversation can begin again when Yahweh returns to the sanctuary and says, "Here am I."

---

30. Westermann, *Isaiah 40–66*, 337.
31. Allen, "Between Text and Sermon," 192.

8

The Early Church

Worship and Work in Ancient Christianity

Baking, pouring, washing.
Gifts of God for the people of God.

—Jill Crainshaw,
When I in Awesome Wonder

Before we explore the intersections of worship and work within ancient Christianity, imagine the following scenario. It's Sunday morning of Labor Day weekend. You and two worship leaders are in Chicago for a conference on worship. The three of you decide to attend an unfamiliar church in the neighborhood of your hotel.

Arriving late to worship, the three of you find a seat near the back. A congregational song allows you to slip in unnoticed. As you look around the sanctuary, you notice something rather strange. Every member is holding an object in their hands. At the invitation of the leader, the people begin to move toward the front. One by one the worshipers begin to pile their objects on the floor immediately surrounding the Lord's Table. You spot a teenager carrying some textbooks, an old man carrying a hammer, a woman with a briefcase, a young man with a laptop, another with a set of keys. You spot a woman with a baby bottle. Is that man carrying a muffler? A group of children lay down some crayons and a soccer ball. As the pile grows, so does your confusion and curiosity. You and your two friends watch as worshipers lay down phones and shovels, a basket of fresh croissants, wrenches and uniforms, stethoscopes and neckties. The Communion table is now completely surrounded, but the people keep coming. Here comes a circular saw and a day planner, a case of wine and a plate of muffins, a set of blueprints and a coffee pot. Finally, bringing up the rear, an old man carefully lays down a small wooden ship that has been skillfully placed inside a small bottle. The people return to their seats and the song comes to an end.

Thoroughly confused, you and your two friends watch as the pastor walks around the table. With a smile on his face, he inspects the items. Moving in front of the table, he raises his hands and announces, "Let's stand and pray together!"

Lord of all creation,
You have given us this work,
You have planted us in this city.
We serve in hospitals, businesses, homes, and schools,
Places to care and create, places to serve and to bless.
We come to you today grateful for all these vocations,
Grateful for the opportunity to join you and your work in this city.

And so today we present our humble and imperfect works to you.
We ask that, through the redeeming power of your Son,
You would take our fallen and finite tasks
And turn them into worship,
Works of praise, pleasing to you.

In the power of your Spirit
Take our meager and imperfect crafts,
Use them to feed, and serve, and bless this city.
Through the power of your Spirit
May these fruits produce an aroma,
An aroma that is sweet to you
And all who are blessed by them.

Lord, some of these callings frustrate us.
Many of these callings cause us pain.
From injustice and discrimination at work, we pray for deliverance.
From pain, we pray for your healing.
For those straining to receive a new calling,
We pray that your voice would be heard strong and clear.

God, we confess that we do not always offer our best at your table.
We confess that sometimes we do not offer our all.
We hold back.
We try to control these callings.
We think they belong to us.
We think they exist to bless us alone.

Forgive us, Lord.
These labors we offer today are imperfect,
Sometimes they are outright rebellious.
Forgive us for our unfaithfulness at work.
Clean our soiled hands and hearts.
Renew our minds.

By your grace and through the power of your Spirit
Take these callings and make them yours.
Break these callings open and feed your people.
Pour these callings out and quench their thirst.

May the work of our hands,
The offerings of our whole lives
Give you pleasure
And bring you praise.
In the name of the Father, Son, and Holy Spirit.
Amen.

Taking it all in, you and your friends watch as the pastor reaches into the pile of offerings and takes a single croissant and a bottle of wine. He lifts them high in the air and gives thanks to God for the creation of grain and the crafting of the baker, for the creation of grapes and the crafting of the vintner. Finally, saying the words of institution, the pastor gives thanks to Christ for his work of salvation, a work that gives the people's work meaning and purpose.

Elders approach the table, and they open the case of wine and begin to pop the corks. They pour the wine and steal a quick smell of its rich aroma. The elders tear open the crispy croissants. The people file forward toward the table again. This time they have nothing to bring, nothing to offer. They bring empty hands that can only receive. You and your two friends come before the elder. He offers you the baker's croissant and the vintner's wine and says, "The work of Christ, completed for you."

The congregation sings another song, and then it's time for the benediction. Everyone stands. The pastor briefly reminds them to attend the Labor Day

prayer walk through Chicago's financial district. Finally, he asks the congregation to physically turn around and face the back door. You and your two friends
share quizzical looks, but you decide to obey. You have, after all, gone along this
far. With your backs to the preacher and your faces to the street outside, the
following words of blessing are spoken over your shoulder and out into the city.

Now go, church.
Leave here.
Go in the name and in the power
Of the Father, the Son, and the Holy Spirit.

Go and extend your worship into your work.
Go and extend Christ's service into your service.
Take the grace that you've received at this table
And extend it to all for whom you care.
Remember the hospitality you've found here.
Offer it to others tomorrow.

Go and work.
Honor the One who is working on you.
Do so by making beautiful things,
By serving in beautiful ways,
By speaking up for the weak whose beauty is being maligned,
By filling this city with the aroma of good and beautiful work.

Reflect the beautiful work of your heavenly Father,
Nourished now by the grace and mercy of Christ,
In the power of the Holy Spirit.

God has already accomplished the great work.
God goes before you and behind you.
God works at your side.

You depart in silence. A little stunned, the three of you decide to share a walk
through the neighborhood so that you can reflect on what just happened.

As they begin to talk, you quickly discover that your two friends, both
worship leaders themselves, had very different assessments of the Sunday
service. Your first friend loved it. She uses words like "groundbreaking" and
"innovative," "creative" and "new." She believes that the service represents
something terrifically original and imaginative. Your second friend, however,
shares a different reaction. He viewed the service as messy, disorganized,

Celebrating the Fruit of the Workers' Labors

The Korean hymn below draws on Jesus's description of his Father as a "worker" in John 5:17. The lyrics teach us that work, and therefore workers, are to be respected and dignified for their role in stewarding creation and its development. By putting talents, gifts, and energies to good use, the worker will reap a community of hope and a fertile land.

"Jesus Christ, Workers' Lord"

Jesus Christ, workers' Lord, we are servants to you.
This wondrous world, all of the earth, all creation is yours.
We would work, helping to grow lovely flowers so rare.
Labor and toil, joined with your gifts, bring fresh fruits of love.

Workers we, giving our lives in full service to you.
With freedom blessed, under your rule, citizens all are we.
On the fields sowing the grain, harvest soon we'll reap:
in factories, making the tools, tools to meet our need.

Royal are we, working to serve Jesus, Savior and King.
One family living in peace partners sharing the earth.
Tools in hand we have reaped rich harvest of grain.
By grace of God, we will receive gifts enough for all.

This lost world, in God's name, we would reclaim in love.
New life is brought, marvelous gift, all inherit the earth.
Now may we from the dust fertile land restore,
That there shall come God's paradise,
Life from death shall arise![a]

a. I-to Loh, *Hymnal Companion to "Sound the Bamboo": Asian Hymns in Their Cultural and Liturgical Contexts* (Chicago: GIA Publications, 2011), 118. Lyrics by Byung Soo Oh, trans. T. Tom Lee, para. Elise Shoemaker, music: KEUN-LOH; Jim Kim Kook. Copyright © 1990, Christian Conference of Asia, GIA publications, Inc. Used with permission.

and possibly sacrilegious. Putting the worldly items of daily work around a sacred altar was disrespectful, he says. Croissants should not be used in Communion. What is a dirty muffler doing so close to the holy table? This is just another example of a church throwing out holy tradition in order to be new, revolutionary, and relevant. While the worship service struck her as delightfully revolutionary, it struck him as horrifically revolutionary.

The next two chapters exploring work and worship in the early church will attempt to undermine *both* of these reactions. They will demonstrate that this Labor Day worship service is not, in fact, terribly new or revolutionary at all. Within the earliest worship practices of ancient Christianity one can find a variety of rituals that point us in exactly this sort of direction.

Notes on Historical Method

As with our discussion of the Old Testament, we need to share a couple of notes about our historical reading and appropriation of early Christian worship. First, like the ancient Israelites, early Christians were not perfect or omniscient; they did not "solve" the issue of worship and work. Our purpose here is not to romanticize or resurrect a flawless or imagined Christian past. Not only is this a bad idea, it's impossible. Recent historical scholarship has revealed that we actually know precious little about the first three centuries of Christian worship.[1] We simply do not have enough historical information to accurately reconstruct a cohesive definition of what constituted "ancient Christian worship." What we do know is that early worship services throughout the Roman Empire were both diverse and dynamic in their historical development. Recent academic debates about the historical development of the Lord's Supper in the early church are an excellent case in point. They're a complex, scholarly hornet's nest—something we want no part of.[2] This is not a history book. This chapter and the next will not seek to resolve these complex debates about what constituted "early Christian worship." That is far beyond the scope of our study.

Instead, we will explore a variety of illuminating ways in which early Christian worship directly engaged the daily work of early Christians. These ancient moments of intersection will inform our contemporary reflections on the reconciliation of work and worship in the modern world. The vast cultural distance between the early Christian world and our own obviously limits this endeavor. But the rewards outweigh the challenges. The worship of the early church has something important to offer those of us wrestling with the modern divide between faith, work, and worship.

Throughout these two chapters we will investigate how early worship practices directly engaged people's callings and careers, their material products, their industries, cities, streets, and surrounding fields. We will explore how early Christians carried the fruits of their labor before their worshiping

---

1. See Bradshaw, *The Search for the Origins of Christian Worship*; Bradshaw, "Difficulties in Doing Liturgical Theology," 184–86.
2. See Bradshaw, *Eucharistic Origins*.

communities, how their work was shared to bless pastors, the poor, and the surrounding city. We will witness how some early worship leaders carefully examined the ethical character of workers and the work products they offered before admitting them into the worship. We will even witness how early worship services broke out of designated "worship spaces" and extended into the streets, markets, and fields.

Like the ancient Israelites before them, early Christians did not produce a systematic "theology of work." These ancient workers did, however, gather together for regular worship that directly engaged their work. And it was *through worship* that these workers slowly learned, week after week, to gather, prepare, and offer their work for the upbuilding of their community and the glory of God. Their worship trained them to offer God more than a symbolic portion of their work; it demanded that they offer their whole selves—their lives and their very bodies—as a living sacrifice, holy and pleasing to their God (Rom. 12:1).

The Worldly Worship of the Early Christians

> The pattern of the Christian Year has its origin in the agricultural rhythm of the Mediterranean region.
>
> —Andrew Pearson, *Making Creation Visible*

> By using the natural elements (water and oil) and human products (bread and wine) in the liturgy, the church shows reverence for God's creation while deepening its relationship with God.
>
> —Mebratu Kiros Gebru, "Liturgical Cosmology"

It is the second century. In Corinth, Antioch, Alexandria, and Rome, early Christians are gathering for worship. Diverse craftspeople, farmers, cooks, and weavers make their way through their city streets. They carry in their hands a wide variety of foods and other goods from their fields, kilns, shops, and kitchens. Assembling in one another's homes for the communal meal, they bring their unique offerings to worship.[3] They carry the elements of worship in their hands. Women carry the body of Christ, kneaded on their rough-hewn kitchen tables and baked in their wood-fired ovens.[4] Men carry

---

3. Note, for instance, the many households where believers met that are mentioned in the New Testament: Acts 2:46; 12:12; 16:40; 20:18; Rom. 16:3–5; 1 Cor. 16:19; Col. 4:15; Philem. 2.

4. Marcelle Del Verme explains, "That is a loaf made from the first kneading of dough, ἀπαρχή being the equivalent of ראשית alluding to Num 15:20–21 (cf. also Neh 10:38). In all

the blood of Christ, grown in their fields, crushed in their presses, and stored in their cellars. Sailors carry their fish in from the harbor, their scales glistening in the sun. If the community is having a fortunate year, the worship meal might include homemade cheese, sweet honey and savory meat, fresh olives and a robust collection of flavorful herbs.

With their work in hand, they gather for worship. In one corner of the room a pile of extra clothing, coins, tools, food, and other household items has grown to a significant size. After worship, the deacons will distribute the extra items, food, and crafts to the local poor.[5] The aroma fills the senses of the carpenter, the tentmaker, and the sailor as they gather for the meal and wait for the songs, prayers, and teaching to begin.

Early Christian worship was earthy, aromatic, and a bit messy. Everyone contributed. It was not highly intellectual or theoretical. Worship did not spiritually transport workers out of their city or the material concreteness of their lives and labors. Instead, like Israel's earthy and smoky worship, early Christian liturgies directly engaged the mundane materials of urban life and labor. *Early Christian worship was permeated with a holy form of worldliness.*[6]

While we know precious little about the precise content and structure of early Christian worship services, we do know that they often took place around handmade tables, with handmade food, in handmade homes. We

---

probability the Didachist is referring to the biblical and Jewish offering known as חלה, the portion which every housewife set aside for the priests when she was kneading dough in the bread-trough. This precept taken up by the Didachist . . . was still in force and generally observed during the period of the Second Temple and even after." Del Verme, *Didache and Judaism,* 171n21. See also Milavec, "When, Why, and for Whom Was the Didache Created?," 69n16; Bradshaw, *Early Christian Worship,* 64.

5. As stated earlier, historians have now thoroughly demonstrated that we know surprisingly little about the earliest practices of the Eucharist in the ancient church. What historians do appear to agree on is that early Christian practices of eating and drinking in community and in thanksgiving to Christ were deeply diverse throughout the Roman Empire. Our purpose here is not to jump into these dense historical discussions but rather to highlight one small—but very important—aspect of the ancient meal that appears to pop up again and again throughout the diverse historical records: the practice of the laity offering their gifts in conjunction with a meal.

In its earliest stages, the Lord's Supper was a meal that someone had to prepare. The supper did not fall out of the sky into the laps of the early Christians. Someone had to plow and pick, nurture and tend, harvest and slaughter, cook and serve these meals. The body and blood of Christ at the table of early Christians would have been made by—you guessed it—early Christians. The work of their hands was brought into worship, where it was lifted up to God as an offering, and then blessed, broken, and shared. The meal could happen only if the people worked and the people offered. Here members of the early church heeded the Israelites' belief that one should not appear before the Lord empty-handed.

6. See Mouw, *Called to Holy Worldliness.*

A Rural Hymn of Harvest Praise

Scripture is filled with a rich and robust set of images of the land and its fruits. This earthy imagery shaped the spiritual vision of Christians, both ancient and modern. The following hymn begins with the harvest practices familiar to an agrarian community. The gathering in of the crops into God's temple provides a summons for a celebration of the final eschatological ingathering of the glory of the nations into God's holy city.

"Come, Ye Thankful People, Come"

Come, ye thankful people, come,
raise the song of harvest home;
all is safely gathered in,
ere the winter storms begin.
God our Maker doth provide
for our wants to be supplied;
come to God's own temple, come,
raise the song of harvest home.

All the world is God's own field,
fruit as praise to God we yield;
wheat and tares together sown
are to joy or sorrow grown;
first the blade and then the ear,
then the full corn shall appear;
Lord of harvest, grant that we
wholesome grain and pure may be.[a]

a. Lyrics by Henry Alford (1844), melody by George J. Elvey (1858), Hymnary.org, https://hymnary.org/media/fetch/139853.

know that the elements of worship were not prepackaged on behalf of workers. The meals were prepared by workers and for workers—by hands well worn from a life of labor in the city. The apostle Paul himself was a bivocational worship leader. As a tentmaker he was no stranger to the Mediterranean market. In the days before worship, Paul was in the streets hawking his tents with the rest of the merchants. Workers constituted the leadership and work products the substance of worldly worship in the ancient church. Celsus, a pagan antagonist of early Christianity, specifically criticized the church for attracting a motley crew of uneducated workers. These early communities, he writes, were full of "wool-workers, cobblers, laundry-workers, and the most illiterate and bucolic yokels."[7]

Scholars are increasingly pointing out this earthy character inherent to the earliest forms of Christian worship. Nathan Mitchell remarks, "Christian worship is inherently worldly. Its primary symbols are drawn from the messiest activities of human life: giving birth and dying, washing and smearing bodies with oil, eating and drinking, unburdening one's heart in the presence of another. All of this is the septic stuff of the world's drama—and the stuff of Christian liturgy as well."[8] Matthew Whelan adds,

> It may be obvious—but I think it bears repetition—that the church roots its worship in everyday life and its activities. Baptism builds upon bathing, the Eucharist upon eating, anointing the act of salving one's skin, and so on. Manifold aspects of the liturgy appeal to the senses—sight, sound, smell, taste, and touch. The fact that the liturgy involves elements of the creation displays reverence for them as the church gathers to worship the incarnate God revealed within them. Indeed, the liturgy gives voice to the praise of God within the created order (Ps. 148). Moreover, the liturgy not only roots the church within that order but returns her to it.[9]

Whelan's final phrase is critical for our purposes. Early Christian worship *did not* facilitate a worker's escape from creation or daily work. Instead, the worldliness of worship rooted workers in the earth, in their work, and in their city. Bread and wine, hands and feet, water and oil—all of these material and vocational creations were made holy and consecrated to the Lord in worship. "For everything God created is good, and nothing is to be rejected if it is received with thanksgiving, because it is consecrated by the word of God and prayer" (1 Tim. 4:4–5). "So whether you eat or drink or whatever you do, do it all for the glory of God" (1 Cor. 10:31).

It was only natural, therefore, that if a worker wanted to offer some home-grown olives or homemade cheese, early worship leaders soon devised a liturgy to include the fruits of this labor in their communal worship. For, "If anyone should offer cheese and olives, let him say thus: 'Sanctify this milk that has been coagulated, coagulating us also to our love. Make also this fruit of the olive not depart from your sweetness, which is a symbol of your richness that you have poured from the tree for life for those who hope in you.'"[10]

---

7. Origen, *Against Celsus* 3.55, quoted in Stevenson, *A New Eusebius*, 151.

8. Mitchell, "The Spirituality of Christian Worship."

9. Whelan, "Prefiguring the Salvation of the World," 194.

10. "Blessing of Cheese and Olives," quoted in Bradshaw, Johnson, and Phillips, *The Apostolic Tradition*, 52.

Modern Longing for Holy Worldliness and Liturgical Materialism

Three contemporary writers, Kathleen Norris, Jill Crainshaw, and Tish Harrison Warren, have done much to revive what we might call the holy worldliness of Christian worship. Norris claims that good Christian worship "grounds me again in the real world of God's creation, dislodging me from whatever world I have imagined for myself."[11] Crainshaw adds, "To wonder at the stuff of worship Sunday after Sunday is to embrace life."[12] For her, the worldly elements of worship enable people to see the quotidian things of this earth through the lens of divine glory. The *spiritual* power of Christian worship is here connected to its *materiality*.

Warren explains that the worldly character and mundane materiality of Christian worship make sense when we consider that God made human beings to live and labor in the materiality of his creation. She writes, "God made us to spend our days in rest, work, and play, taking care of our bodies, our families, our neighborhoods, our homes. . . . What if days passed in ways that feel small and insignificant to us are weighty with meaning and part of the abundant life that God has for us?"[13]

Each of these three women living amidst the abstraction of modernity reflect in their own unique ways a longing for an ancient Christian materialism—a holy worldliness. Their liturgical reflections on life and labor call us to see God's creation, to gaze on its materiality, in much the same way the poet Elizabeth Barrett Browning would have us do.

> Earth's crammed with heaven,
> And every common bush afire with God;
> But only he who sees, takes off his shoes,
> The rest sit round it and pluck blackberries.[14]

The fact that it is women who have played such a leading role in helping the modern Western church to reflect on the connection between mundane material labor and holy liturgy is worthy of further discussion.

The materiality of early Christian meals, offerings, and liturgies must have played a critical pedagogical role in helping workers forge cognitive connections between spirit and matter, worship and work, theology and life. As we

---

11. Norris, *The Quotidian Mysteries*, 26.
12. Crainshaw, *When I in Awesome Wonder*, 9.
13. T. Warren, *Liturgy of the Ordinary*, 22.
14. Browning, *Aurora Leigh*, 246.

Earthy Vocational Worship with Apples

In Ukraine, the church's Feast of the Transfiguration is also known as the Savior of the Apple Feast Day. This festival ushers the material and vocational lives of Ukrainian farmers into worship. The festival coincides with the onset of autumn and the beginning of the apple harvest season in August. As the apples ripen and the season begins to change (i.e., transfigure), workers are invited to reflect on Christ's transfiguration and the transformation that is needed in those who labor in his fields.

Throughout Ukraine, communities of workers carry baskets of apples, grapes, and pears to be blessed in a special worship service. After the service the community celebrates by eating the fruit together. The labor festival has its roots in pre-Christian society. Rather than destroying the pagan harvest festival, the people of the church reimagined it and incorporated it into their own Christ-centered liturgical calendar. The annual worship service serves to cultivate gratitude to God in the fields and dependence on his provisions for the harvest that lies ahead.[a]

a. "Apple Spas Is the Most Important of Three Savior Days."

discuss later, modern churches would be wise to follow their lead in rediscovering the benefits of more material and tactile forms of worship. Worship that engages our senses and bodies, our tongues and stomachs, and the physical work of our hands can go a long way in helping workers ground their worship and work in the earth—as opposed to the clouds.

Protecting the Holiness of Worship and Work

Let each one leave the church to take up his daily tasks, one hastening to work with his hands, another hurrying to his military post, and still another to his post in the government. However, let each one approach his daily task with fear and anguish, and spend his working hours in the knowledge that at evening he should return here to church, render an account to the Master of his whole day, and beg forgiveness for his falls.

—John Chrysostom, "The Eighth Instruction," in *Baptismal Instructions*

Early Christian worship welcomed the smell of sweat and the mundane materiality of human agriculture, industry, and commerce. It was impressively hospitable to work and workers who had been consecrated with oil to the holy service of God in the world. However, the presence of *unholy* work and *unholy* workers in worship was another story entirely. Dishonest fruits, ill-gotten gains, and crooked crafters attempting to enter into worship often encountered a cold reception. In fact, the first reported crooked offering brought into Christian worship ended in an immediate death sentence (see the story of Ananias and Sapphira in Acts 5:1–11).

If the preceding section painted a generous and hospitable picture of work's inclusion in early Christian worship, this section presents the rougher edge of the early church. The moral purity and holiness of both worship and work were things that early Christians sought to protect—sometimes with firm communal discipline.

Baptism was a critical rite of initiation within their worshiping life (John 1:31–33; 3:5; Acts 10:48; 16:31–33; 1 Cor. 12:13; Col. 2:11–12). The ritual signaled the beginning of a new life in Christ and a new calling within the city. Baptism represented a worker's holy ordination to the priesthood of all believers.[15]

In the early church, candidates for holy baptism were required to have their professional lives, crafts, and career choices carefully examined by the church before they could participate in the baptismal liturgy.[16] One of the earliest Christian documents on corporate worship includes an entire chapter titled "Concerning the Crafts and Professions." The ancient worship instructions direct worship leaders to "inquire about the crafts and work of those who will be brought in to be catechized."[17] This document outlines a long list of prohibited careers associated with dishonesty, idolatry, sex trafficking, imperial violence, magic, immodest theatrical performances, gladiatorial games, and schools of pagan philosophy. Unrepentant participation in these industries disqualified a worker from baptismal worship service. Full communion with Christ in the sanctuary demanded full communion with Christ in the marketplace (cf. Luke 19:1–9).

The early church, knowing that its list of prohibited careers was not exhaustive, went on to remark, "If we have left out any other thing, the things themselves will inform you, for we all have the Spirit of God."[18] In other words,

---

15. Eastwood, *The Royal Priesthood of the Faithful*.

16. See Bradshaw, Johnson, and Phillips, *The Apostolic Tradition*, 87–95.

17. See the Sahidic version of §16.1 in Bradshaw, Johnson, and Phillips, *The Apostolic Tradition*, 88.

18. See the Sahidic version of §16.17 in Bradshaw, Johnson, and Phillips, *The Apostolic Tradition*, 92.

examine the fruits of the applicant's labor; the quality and impact of their work will demonstrate their spiritual readiness to participate in the liturgy of baptism. How many modern books on baptism call for an inquiry into the professional lives of the participants? We have yet to find one.

If an ancient worker from a prohibited industry sought admittance to worship and the rite of baptism, priests were given strict instructions on how to respond. Leaders were told, in no uncertain terms, "Do not catechize them and baptize them, until they have renounced all occupations of this sort, and three witnesses have testified for them that they really have renounced all these vices."[19] Some professionals with "unclean hands" needed to separate themselves from their problematic industries for three years before their hands could touch the Lord's Supper.[20] Ancient liturgical documents advise that these workers be excluded from worship "until they are purified first from these impure occupations."[21] Once these workers repented, the church was to have them thoroughly "examined for a time, for the evil is hard to wash out."[22]

Suppose that a worker renounces his morally suspect craft or career. Suppose he is fully examined and then ultimately baptized. Suppose further that he regresses back into his sordid profession. Ancient worship leaders had a clear process in place for this vocational backsliding. Liturgical documents state that if workers "are found after baptism in vices of this sort, they are to be excluded from the church until they repent with tears, fasting, and alms."[23] Notice the twofold role of worship in this vocational crisis. First, the worker's participation in morally suspect work excludes him from worship. Second, the worker's road to redemption runs primarily through liturgical practices— not theological education. Through the liturgical practices of tears, fasting, and alms, the worker is ultimately restored to the worshiping community.

The worker can't be allowed to live two lives. Perverted work and holy worship cannot coexist. Life, labor, and liturgy need to be faithfully interwoven. Mending together holy lives of integrity was a difficult process that sometimes required the community to say "No."

Admitting sinful workers into holy worship was not the only challenge the early church would wrestle with. The church also reflected on the liturgical

---

19. *Canons of Hippolytus* §15, in Bradshaw, Johnson, and Phillips, *The Apostolic Tradition*, 91.

20. Bradshaw, Johnson, and Phillips, *The Apostolic Tradition*, 97.

21. *Canons of Hippolytus* §11, in Bradshaw, Johnson, and Phillips, *The Apostolic Tradition*, 89.

22. *Apostolic Constitutions* §8.32.7–13, in Bradshaw, Johnson, and Phillips, *The Apostolic Tradition*, 89.

23. *Canons of Hippolytus* §15, in Bradshaw, Johnson, and Phillips, *The Apostolic Tradition*, 91.

A Puritan Prayer Guide for Marketplace Protection

The marketplace is not inherently evil, but, as we argued earlier, neither is it neutral. Workers must be savvy about the ways in which the liturgies of the workplace can lead them astray. The Puritan Lewis Bayly guides workers in the practice of daily prayer and names the marketplace pitfalls that can inhibit faithfulness.

> Think not any business or haste, though never so great, a sufficient cause to omit prayer in the morning: But meditate— . . .
> That in going abroad into the world, thou goest into a forest full
> of unknown dangers, where thou shalt meet many briers to tear
> thy good name, many snares to trap thy life, and many hunters to
> devour thy soul; it is a field of pleasant grass, but full of poisonous
> serpents: adventure not, therefore, to go naked amongst these
> briers, till thou hast prayed Christ to clothe thee with his righteousness; nor to pass through these snares and ambushments,
> till thou hast prayed for God's providence to be thy guide; nor to
> walk barefoot through this snaky field.[a]

a. Bayly, *The Practice of Piety*, 151.

admittance into worship of the products and profits of sinful work. Early workers and worship leaders alike were instructed to carefully examine and consider the ethical quality of the fruits being offered in worship. The *Didache*, which contains one of the earliest records of ancient Christian worship, was particularly concerned that worshipers offer only "pure" sacrifices to God. It advises Christian workers to "break bread and give thanks, confessing your faults beforehand, so that your sacrifice may be pure."[24] The *Didascalia*, another early church text, instructs worship leaders not to accept impure or dishonest offerings. Leaders are told to "be constant . . . with all care and with all diligence . . . to search out concerning the things that are given."[25] Worship leaders were specifically prohibited from accepting offerings from "hypocritical lawyers," "dishonest tax-gatherers," "those who alter weights or measure deceitfully," or "inn-keepers who mingle water (with their wine)."[26] Nor could priests accept offerings "from rich persons who keep men shut

24. *Didache* 14.1, in Niederwimmer, *The Didache*, 194.
25. *Didascalia* XVIII, in Connolly, *Didascalia Apostolorum*, 156.
26. *Didascalia* XVIII, in Connolly, *Didascalia Apostolorum*, 158.

up in prison, or ill-treat their slaves, or behave with cruelty in their cities, or oppress the poor."[27]

Notice that the liturgical warning is not simply for the workers who offer defiled products but is also for the worship leaders who accept them. No matter the amount offered, no matter how desperately the money or food is needed, priests should never "nourish widows from these" sources, and if they do, they "shall be found guilty in judgement on the day of the Lord."[28] Not letting up its moral intensity, the *Didascalia* declares that worship leaders "have no pretext to say, 'We do not know,'" regarding the moral integrity of the fruits being offered.[29] The document ups the ante and declares that it is better for the church and its impoverished dependents "to be wasted with famine than to receive from evil persons."[30] In addition, "If a widow be nourished with bread only from the labour of righteousness, it shall even be abundant for her; but if much be given her from (the proceeds) of iniquity, it shall be insufficient for her. But again, if she be nourished from (the proceeds) of iniquity, she cannot offer her ministry and her intercession with purity before God."[31]

This last sentence from the *Didascalia* is both critical and crushing. We see here that polluted profits and fruits offered in holy worship will corrupt more than the individual worship of the rebellious worker. *Their polluted offerings will corrupt the worship of the widow who receives it and offers it to God in thanksgiving.* The virus of this evil work spreads throughout the community's worship.

The integrity of holy worship had to be protected from morally compromised professionals, their industries, and their profits. The materiality of the community's worship was intimately connected to its life and labor in the world. Rebellious commerce could not be allowed to poison the bread and wine of the table, the oil of anointing, the coins of the offering, the waters of baptism, or the alms distributed to the widows. Church historian Maxwell Johnson notes that, for an early church father like Irenaeus, the community's "offering cannot be separated from the lives of those who offer it."[32] Or, as Augustine would later write, "To bless God in the churches, brethren, means so to live that each one's life may give glory to God. To bless God in word and curse Him in deed is by no means to bless Him in the churches.

27. *Didascalia* XVIII, in Connolly, *Didascalia Apostolorum*, 158.
28. *Didascalia* XVIII, in Connolly, *Didascalia Apostolorum*, 158.
29. *Didascalia* XVIII, in Connolly, *Didascalia Apostolorum*, 159.
30. *Didascalia* XVIII, in Connolly, *Didascalia Apostolorum*, 159.
31. *Didascalia* XVIII, in Connolly, *Didascalia Apostolorum*, 158–59.
32. Johnson, *Praying and Believing in Early Christianity*, 122. See Irenaeus, §17.5 in *Against Heresies* IV, in Coxe, Roberts, and Donaldson, *Ante-Nicene Fathers*, 1:484.

Almost all bless Him with their tongues, but not all by their works. But those whose conduct is inconsistent with their profession [of faith] cause God to be blasphemed."[33]

Augustine's concern for an intimate and integral connection between word and deed, worship and work, resonates with what we saw earlier in the Old Testament. Johnson deftly points out the Jewish-Christian continuity here:

> From the Hebrew prophets through Augustine of Hippo we have repeatedly seen this kind of concern for the verification of worship in the very lives of the communities who offer it. Whether the prophetic critique of Amos, the words of ritual critique and reform addressed to early Christian meal fellowships by the gospel and other New Testament writers, catechumenal formation, liturgical homilies, or development in the concept of the Eucharist as the sacrifice of Christ and the church, the concern that Christians live according to how they worship and believe is, indeed, a consistent concern through the ages.[34]

Early Christian prohibitions around work and worship ring rather harsh and negative in our modern ears, but readers should remember that these negative warnings emerge from a view of work and worship that is fundamentally positive. These prohibitions emerge from an early Christian belief that good work can be holy, can serve and bless one's neighbor and community, can participate in the mission and worship of God. Therefore, if what workers do with their hands, minds, and bodies in the marketplace truly matters to God, it should matter in the sanctuary as well. Work cannot be an afterthought in worship, an ancillary issue, a necessary evil. Work and how workers worship matter deeply to God. As Clement of Alexandria argued in the second century,

> Practise husbandry, we say, if you are a husbandman;
> but while you till your fields, know God.
> Sail the sea, you who are devoted to navigation,
> yet call the whilst on the heavenly Pilot.
> Has knowledge taken hold of you while engaged in military service?
> Listen to the commander, who orders what is right.[35]

Sexuality, race, violence, and politics were flash points in the early church, and the modern Western church (appropriately) continues to debate these

---

33. Augustine, *On the Psalms*, 1:255–56, quoted in Phillips, "Liturgy and Ethics," 86.

34. Johnson, *Praying and Believing in Early Christianity*, 126.

35. Clement of Alexandria, *Exhortation to the Heathen* 10, in Coxe, Roberts, and Donaldson, *Ante-Nicene Fathers*, 2:200.

issues today. Serious differences on these issues can, and often do, rip modern churches apart. The wrong opinion or the wrong action can get a worship leader fired, end a pastor's ordination, or excommunicate a member.

Although the early church and the modern church share a common intensity on these issues of sexuality, race, politics, and violence, they are surprisingly divergent on the issue of work. Modern Western churches simply do not discuss the presence and participation of rebellious workers, industries, and profits in corporate worship. These churches are willing to go to great (and often uncomfortable) lengths to protect the purity of their worship from perceived sexual and political corruption, but the vocational and economic corruption of corporate worship does not seem to bother them at all.

What do the early church's concerns about professionals and the profits they offer reveal about them? What does our lack of concern about these things reveal about us? A tangible example might help illustrate the point. It is common for modern churches to show a great deal of concern that their young people be well prepared to make holy sexual choices as they emerge into adulthood (i.e., preserve their sexual purity). Do these churches demonstrate the same level of concern that their young people be well prepared to make holy vocational choices? Are parents asking youth leaders to adequately prepare their children to use their vocations to serve their neighbor, improve their city, and glorify their God?

Our purpose here is not to resurrect the ancient practice of barring pagan sorcerers and gladiators from corporate worship. Nor is our hope that pastors will start examining the quarterly reports of accountants and controllers who worship in their sanctuaries. No, the purpose is to reveal a significant blind spot within our modern approach to worship and discipleship. Western churches still have "hypocritical lawyers." They still have the modern equivalents of "inn-keepers who mingle water (with their wine)," "those who alter weights," and powerful leaders "who keep men shut up in prison . . . [and] behave with cruelty in their cities."[36] Our purpose, rather, is to pose the following questions: *What would it look like for contemporary pastors, elders, and small-group leaders to actually know the workers they disciple and the industries they engage?* How might fellowship groups "be constant . . . with all care and with all diligence . . . to search out concerning the things that are given"?[37] How might the community take seriously the ancient call to gather work into worship that is holy, just, and praiseworthy?

36. *Didascalia* XVIII, in Connolly, *Didascalia Apostolorum*, 158.
37. *Didascalia* XVIII, in Connolly, *Didascalia Apostolorum*, 156.

Street Worship

> The structure of the Church is designed to run in a straight line from the sanctuary, through the nave, and out the narthex: a linear structure that directs the force of the liturgical explosion onto the street.
>
> —David Fagerberg, *Consecrating the World*

Modern churches often think of worship as an activity that is carefully bounded within a specific worship space. The sanctuary is a "sacred space," while the marketplace is a "secular space." Worship is appropriate in the former but not the latter. It should be no surprise that our premodern sisters and brothers did not recognize or respect these spatial separations in quite the same way.

During the fourth century, after the age of Christian persecution had come to a close, the underground liturgies of the early church started to go public. The songs and prayers of early Christian worship started bursting out of their designated worship spaces and spilling into the streets.

Early "stational liturgies" are an excellent case in point. These liturgies functioned like an urban worship parade snaking its way through city streets and markets. Entire congregations marched, sang, and prayed their way through city squares and even around the city walls. Worshiping in the streets, Christian workers were publicly and liturgically declaring the lordship of Jesus Christ over the whole life of the city. John Baldovin, an expert on these street-based liturgies, remarks that, for marching Christians, religious buildings "were not the only loci of Christian worship. Since the *civitas* itself was holy, the public places and streets of the city were fit places to worship as well." These processions "were a means of expressing the public and cultural nature of Christianity and an expression of that faith as pilgrimage and process."[38] Worshipers not only verbally proclaimed but also physically enacted a *public* gospel that would eventually transform the political, economic, and cultural character of the Mediterranean markets they were marching through. Like the Christian practices that engaged the economy (*oikonomia*) of the Christian home (Eph. 5:21–6:9; Col. 3:18–4:1; 1 Pet. 2:18–3:7), new Christian practices had to be developed to engage the economy of the city.

These street processions not only proclaimed the publicness of the Christian gospel, they also contested the publicness of the pagan gospel. Greek and Roman forms of pagan spirituality were deeply public and pervasive at this time. Urban markets in Rome, Corinth, and Athens were shot through

---

38. Baldovin, *The Urban Character of Worship*, 266.

Riding Kenya's Prayer Train to Work

In Western contexts haunted by the ghosts of Christendom, going public with Christian faith, let alone Christian worship, seems absurd and unthinkable. Attempts to repristinate ancient stational liturgies could appear foolish, impractical, and even offensive. But must we completely forfeit the public character of Christian faith and worship in our pluralistic cities? Might there be something within these ancient street liturgies that could inform our contemporary engagement with modern thoroughfares and marketplaces?

On a southbound train to Nairobi, Kenya, you can find Pastor Helen Wangui Tiphy and her husband, Bishop Joseph Tiphy Gachuhi. Amidst a crowded coach of commuters, these two pastors preach and lead communal prayers and songs. Their unique train-based liturgy began in 1998 when "a group of Christians traveling to work together on the train decided to start a group and received permission to use the carriage to worship, pray, and sing." Since then, the train's "Fellowship Coach" is used every morning and evening for this worship gathering.[a]

The reason for the growth of this commuter worship service, says Pastor Wangui Tiphy, is that it meets the needs of people trying to cope with the stresses of life, unemployment, overwork, and despair. And this touch point for commuters between work, pain, and prayer is the inroad for a public worship service during the daily commute.

Perhaps this example from our Kenyan brothers and sisters will fall on deaf ears in the United States. Perhaps it seems too audacious and "churchy" for our culture today. But is the proper response to carry on with our privatized approach to prayer and discipleship? Should we sit on our hands and muffle our ears to the deep pains and hardships of workers moving through our cities? Wouldn't a better approach be to cultivate public spaces and practices through

with pagan crafts, products, rituals, and economic practices. The values of paganism were embedded in the economic sinews and industrial structures of the Roman markets. Early Christian processions were directly contesting the economic principalities and powers of the city.

For centuries prior, paganism had conducted its own public processionals through imperial cities, fields, and marketplaces. "These popular processions

which workers can carry their vocational pains, petitions, and praises to God in worship?

Take, for example, the New York churches surrounding Wall Street following the financial crisis of 2007. Many worshipers in these congregations worked for the financial firms that either contributed to or were impacted by the subprime mortgage debacle. These workers, no doubt, were processing a wide variety of emotions, from guilt and shame, to sadness and anger, to fear and confusion. Imagine that a collective prayer walk had been organized to snake its way through the city's financial district. Imagine that prayers of confession and lament had been offered—prayers for the families affected by the crisis; prayers for repentance, economic transformation, and protection; prayers for the pensions, jobs, and homes that had been lost. How might this have impacted the workers who participated in this public practice? How might it have impacted the workers who witnessed the procession from the sidewalk?

Consider another example. In Grand Rapids, Michigan, a growing number of people are biking to work during the warmer months. There have been a number of hit-and-run accidents and biker deaths caused by vehicles in recent years. The city has tried to respond by putting in bike lanes and instituting a mandatory five-foot buffer zone around bicyclists.[b] Could there be an openness in the city to a public blessing of the bikes for divine protection? Could these blessings draw on the old blessing of the ships still practiced today in some maritime communities?[c] If God blessed our coming and going then, could he do the same today?

While these examples should not be copied woodenly, the *publicness* of these ancient (and contemporary) street liturgies should inform the *prayerful* ways in which we move through our streets and markets.

a. "Kenya's Prayer Train."
b. "Grand Rapids Drivers Must Give Bikes More Room under New 'Safe-Passing' Law."
c. Theology of Work Project, "The Blessing of a Ship," comp. and ed. David Welbourn.

encircled the cities, forming a magical ring of protection."[39] In essence, the early Christians needed a liturgical procession of their own to contest the economic and cultural values, practices, and processions of Roman paganism.

But more than mere cultural contestation, early Christians needed a way to liturgically communicate and cultivate their own spiritual and civic relationship

39. Baldovin, *The Urban Character of Worship*, 235.

with the city. Emerging from the catacombs, Christians needed to ensconce their own ways of engaging the spiritual, economic, and political life of the city. These early worship processions may very well have helped early disciples understand Christ's imminent presence and power in the streets and markets of their city.

Early Christian shop owners, artisans, farmers, political officials, and business leaders walked and worshiped with their priests through the markets. Small house churches and worshiping communities spread thinly throughout a Roman city could now liturgically connect with one another as they processed from church to church. In so doing, workers reminded each other that they were not alone in the city, that they were united, and that their gospel was a public one with implications for the life of the entire city.

These processions had the added bonus of reminding the pagan powers that their patterns of civic life were contestable. One scholar even labels these early Christian processions a "liturgical conquest of space."[40] Whereas modern worshipers will (quite understandably) be uncomfortable with the militant metaphor, the early church was not. The city and its marketplace represented a public clash of oppressive principalities and powers—both spiritual and economic. What we have here is a parade of workers asking Christ to bring renewal to the city's markets, shops, and fields. They're declaring that civic life and labor exist under the reign of Christ, not Caesar.

Ancient Christians worshiping their way through the streets believed that the communal liturgies had public consequences for the economic life, protection, and flourishing of the city. *To pray, sing, and process through the city was a public service, a civic duty.* These processions emerged from "the conviction that the city was sanctified through the existence in it of the worshiping community."[41] According to this early liturgical imagination, Baldovin explains, the city was defended as much by worship "processions as it was by walls and military and political power. Thus, the city as a holy civilization was a concept that was expressed above all liturgically."[42] In other words, one of the best things that Christian workers could do for the health of their city was to walk, pray, and sing their way through it.

The Field Parade: Rogationtide

Soon enough the worship of the early church would break out of the walls of the sanctuary and the city entirely. During the Middle Ages, priests pro-

40. Wannenwetsch, *Political Worship*, 262.
41. Wannenwetsch, *Political Worship*, 262.
42. Baldovin, *The Urban Character of Worship*, 257.

cessed with worshipers out through the city gates and into the surrounding fields. During these "rogation liturgies," workers, children, and priests walked, prayed, and chanted together around their village's crops. They walked and worshiped in an act of embodied penance, praise, and spiritual solidarity with local farms and farmers.

These field-based worship services directly interceded on behalf of local farms and farmers before the face of God. The workers' prayers and songs asked God for protection from agricultural disease, disasters, and demons.[43] Rogation worship services were often observed during the most tenuous agricultural moments—moments when fragile plants were budding in the spring and particularly susceptible to a late frost. Farmers prayed collectively for divine blessing and provision for the work of their hands. Their physical movements liturgically marked the boundaries of human cultivation around the local village. Their prayers petitioned God's providential work to be made manifest in their agricultural labor. Farmers prayed for forgiveness for the sins of the past year and asked (Latin *rogare*, "to ask") for God's merciful protection over the work that lay ahead.

Rogation liturgies took on a variety of forms in different times and places throughout Europe. In one iteration, prayer "altars decorated with flowers and greenery were set up at every stop [around the village fields], where the priest would bless the fields and the beasts as the faithful sang the litanies."[44] In Venice, a seafaring community, the rogation liturgy needed to be reimagined for nautical life. Here the "maritime ceremony assembled the entire community in a flotilla of boats" so that they might bless "the rich fishing ground and harbor that nurtured the city."[45] "As was the case with most liturgical rites, Rogation Days could be adapted to a wide variety of local conditions, which meant that its significance was highly pliable. In many respects, the rituals were merely containers into which people poured the meanings that were vital to them."[46]

While these rogation liturgies have ancient origins, they have been continually revived and reimagined throughout the history of the church. A contemporary rogation prayer reads as follows:

Let us ask God to have mercy on our tired land,
and to prosper the work of our soiled hands.

43. See Stilgoe, "Jack-o-Lanterns to Surveyors."
44. Roy, *Traditional Festivals*, 1:393.
45. Muir, *Ritual in Early Modern Europe*, 76.
46. Muir, *Ritual in Early Modern Europe*, 76.

Let us ask God to forgive our delusion of self-sufficiency
so that we may praise him for his provision and goodness.[47]

Additional rural liturgies were developed throughout church history to bless, support, and encourage those who worked in the fields. Specific blessings for plows, seeds, and animals were later developed. With the "Loaf Mass," medieval farm workers in England celebrated the Lord's Supper with a special loaf of bread made from the first grain harvested from the local fields.

Rural churches throughout history and around the world have continued this ancient tradition of developing liturgies for farmers. These vocationally conversant liturgies enable farmers either to request or to render gratitude for another year of gracious protection and provision for their labor in the fields. As John Stilgoe notes, farmers "might pray for a good harvest across the entire kingdom, but undoubtedly their thoughts centered on the fields beneath their feet."[48]

Conclusion

Reenacting ancient liturgies on modern streets in the original Latin would not be a great idea. But might contemporary churches reimagine work-oriented street liturgies for their own cities? What profit might be gained from organizing a prayer walk around a new factory or through a city's struggling commercial district?

Various prayer walks could conceivably accomplish at least four things. First, in times of economic blessing and flourishing, these walks could direct workers' thanksgiving *to God* for the good, productive, and fruitful work that takes place within local businesses. Second, in times of economic injustice, corruption, or disaster, these walks could provide workers with a physical way to tell God about their economic heartbreak and frustration. Worshipers could reflect on and confess their own complicity in distorted and dysfunctional markets as they walked. Or, if they are not complicit, workers could cry out to God for rescue. Third, walkers could ask the Holy Spirit to transform their local marketplace for the flourishing of all citizens. Fourth, these walks could have a spiritually formative impact on the diverse workers and pastors who participate in them. By including a variety of workers, denominations, in-

---

47. Ambrose, *Together for a Season*, 45.
48. Stilgoe, "Jack-o-Lanterns to Surveyors," 16.

dustries, ethnic groups, and socioeconomic classes, these processions could express the unity and solidarity of the church at work in the city.

Modern pastors and professionals alike have largely accepted a highly privatized understanding of their faith and their worship. Public processions and public expressions of prayer in commercial spaces would most likely be uncomfortable for pastors and professionals alike. This discomfort reveals something important, something that should be interrogated.

Every single day modern workers move through powerful corporations, factories, marketplaces, and even digital spaces. These public spaces attempt to form and shape workers' hearts and desires in a multiplicity of ways. Readers may remember the work of Jeremy Carrette and Richard King from an earlier chapter. They complain that marketplace rituals and liturgies are simply too powerful and too formative. What we need, they argue, are new spiritual practices capable of contesting the broken values, habits, and systems of the global marketplace. For, they insist,

> Since the earliest stages of human history, of course, there have been bazaars, rialtos and trading posts—all markets. But The Market was never God, because there were other centers of value and meaning, other "gods." The Market operated within a plethora of other institutions that restrained it. As Karl Polanyi has demonstrated in his classic work *The Great Transformation*, only in the past two centuries has The Market risen above these demigods and chthonic spirits to become today's First Cause.[49]

In reviewing the worship processions of the early church, contemporary Christian workers discover that they don't need to invent a *new* marketplace spirituality to resist the gods of the market. They already have an ancient liturgy waiting to be rediscovered and reimagined. In the stational liturgies, contemporary Christians have the beginnings of a spiritual practice from their own history ready and waiting to contest the idols of the modern marketplace.

49. Carrette and King, *Selling Spirituality*, 173.

9

The Early Church Offering

Work Becomes Worship in Christ

Whoever has the firstfruits of the earth is to bring them to the church, the first of their floors and the first of their presses, oil, honey, milk, wool, and the first produce of the work of their hands.

—*Canons of Hippolytus* §36

The Church . . . herself is offered in the offering she makes to God.

—Augustine, *City of God*

This chapter is a continuation of the preceding one. Here we dig into the most important intersection of worship and work in the early church: the offering. Over its first few centuries, the church developed a remarkably rich theology and practice of vocational offering. As we will see, the modern church has much to learn from the unique (and sometimes surprising) ways in which ancient Christians offered their work in worship.

The fact that the early church developed vocationally conversant practices of offering should not surprise us. There is a simple explanation as to why: many early Christians were Jews. Ancient Jewish practices of agricultural sacrifice, offering, and feasting played a pivotal role in shaping the liturgical imagination of the early church.[1] There were, of course, important differences between ancient Jewish and Christian practices. However, as we will see, it is the *continuity* that is particularly striking. The New Testament texts often were used by early church leaders to demonstrate how Israel's agricultural offerings and sacrifices were not abolished, but rather *transformed*, by the death and resurrection of Christ. Like their Jewish brothers and sisters before them, early Christians *continued* to offer the first fruits of their labor in worship. They did so, however, in and through the grace of Jesus Christ, their high priest. The Christocentric nature of work in worship in Christianity is, therefore, where this chapter must find its conclusion.

Offering Your Work in Early Christianity

Historical reports of early offerings in the church vary greatly, but this much is true: many early Christians carried a wide variety of work products with them as they gathered for worship.[2] Sometimes these products were given to deacons or priests at the door.[3] Sometimes their humble works were carried all the way into the worship space.[4] These diverse offering rituals were constantly evolving over the first few centuries. Depending on the context, workers presented products with differing levels of liturgical ceremony, pomp, and circumstance. Like the ancient Israelite farmers before them, early Christians offered fruits from their fields, including grapes, figs, pomegranates, olives, apples, prunes, quinces, cherries, almonds, and more.[5]

While agricultural offerings like these were common, early Christianity was, by and large, a city-based and therefore industrial and commercial

1. See Skarsaune, *In the Shadow of the Temple.*

2. Sources that discuss the early church bringing offerings up to the altar include Jungmann, *The Sacrifice of the Church*; Jungmann, *The Mass of the Roman Rite*; Wannenwetsch, "Eucharist and the Ethics of Sacrifice and Self-Giving."

3. Robert Taft notes that in the East "the faithful offered bread and wine to be consecrated at the eucharist . . . the faithful gave their gifts to the deacons in the sacristy as they arrived for the liturgy; the deacons selected as much bread and wine as was needed and brought it to the altar. . . . This is the nub of the problem. As [Dom Gregory] Dix says, we know that the laymen offered *prosphorai* [gifts], and that the deacons presented these gifts at the altar, but 'what we do not know, as regards the pre-Nicene church generally, is when and how the deacons received them from the laity.'" Taft, *The Great Entrance*, 17–18.

4. According to the *Didascalia* (third-century Syria), "Offerings were handed over to the deacon before mass. . . . It would seem that the people, one by one, left their gifts with the first deacon as they arrived in church at the beginning of the liturgy." Taft, *The Great Entrance*, 18. For a thorough discussion of the historical origins of the offertory and "great entrance" in the Eastern tradition, see Taft, *The Great Entrance*, 3–52.

5. See Bradshaw, Johnson, and Phillips, *The Apostolic Tradition*, 170.

religious movement. Therefore, the agricultural rituals of ancient Judaism had to develop to serve this more urban faith. Church historian Aaron Milavec, reflecting on this commercial and industrial shift in the offering ritual, reminds us that urban professionals like "craftspeople and merchants had as much cause to thank God for their prosperity as did the farmer."[6]

Historical records tell us that urban Christians offered a wide variety of handcrafted products from their kitchens, kilns, and workshops.[7] Early commercial and industrial offerings included, but were not limited to, articles of clothing, bread, currency, cheese, oil, wine, and a variety of crafts.[8] From these accounts we see that early Christianity demonstrated a remarkable degree of liturgical hospitality and flexibility when it came to welcoming workers and their diverse crafts into worship.

A Threefold Liturgical Theology of Work

Following the workers' presentations, deacons or priests would designate the workplace offerings for one of three distinct purposes: some were distributed to the poor, some were given to the ministries of the church, and some were directly included in the celebration of corporate worship (communal meals; oil for anointing; sacred offerings of milk, honey, and fish; and the Eucharist). Thus, early Christian farmers and merchants who carried their work into worship could expect their work to serve one of three functions in the global work of Christ: poverty relief, ministry support, and worshipful communion.

All three of these functions were considered a part of the church's "liturgy" in the city. In ancient Greek society, a *leitourgia* was any generous work done

6. Milavec, *The Didache*, 80.
7. Milavec, *The Didache*, 80.
8. According to Aaron Milavec,

> It appears that the category of first fruits has a Jewish foundation that has been artfully adapted for gentiles making their living as craftspeople and merchants. . . . The extension of first fruits when "opening a jar of wine or oil" (*Did*. 13:6) or when receiving an augmentation "of silver and of clothing and of every possession" (*Did*. 13:7) finds no counterpart in ancient Judaism and might serve to suggest that craftspeople and merchants had as much cause to thank God for their prosperity as did the farmer and the baker. The novice, it will be remembered, was trained to regard everything he or she possessed as the Father's "free gifts" (*Did*. 1:5) and to "accept the deeds befalling you as good things, knowing that, apart from God, nothing happens" (*Did*. 3:10). In light of this understanding, undoubtedly the first and best products of the kiln, the loom, and the forget were set aside for first fruits and given to the prophets so that they could give thanks to God. (Milavec, *The Didache*, 522)

The Meaning of *Leitourgia*

The word *leitourgia* first emerged in ancient Greek villages as a way to describe a curious new civic behavior. From time to time, a village would encounter a great and costly communal need. The town either required or desired a new civic building, a festival, a school, or some great military expense. The high cost of these communal goods was too great for the town's treasury to bear. The village leaders would go to the wealthiest persons in the community and request—or often command—that they "perform a liturgy for the city." By "liturgy" they meant a costly, generous, and sacrificial act of service for the flourishing of the whole community—*leitourgia, a work of service on behalf of the people.*

Later on, the Greeks also used the word *leitourgia* to describe acts of self-giving service, nurture, and generosity between friends and parents, animals and their young, and slaves serving their masters. This ancient Greek habit lives on today in the practice of contemporary Christians strangely declaring that they are going to attend a worship "service." For twenty-first-century readers who have spent a lifetime dividing up worship and work, spiritual and material, private and public into neat little categories, the choice of *leitourgia* is a curious and even surprising one. And yet, the choice reveals that neither the ancient Greeks nor the ancient Jews would make such a stark division between civic service and spiritual practice. For a wealthy landowner in an ancient Greek village "to perform leitourgia was simultaneously to care for the bodily needs of the community and to reverence the gods."[a] Likewise, for a Jewish priest to offer a sacrifice in the temple was simultaneously to reverence Yahweh and perform a public service on behalf of the entire nation for its civic flourishing. The Jewish priest entered the temple not for a time of private or personal spiritual empowerment but rather as an act of public service,

for the flourishing of the city in honor of the gods—and was considered both spiritual and vocational.

The Greeks honored their gods by caring for their city. Moreover, they cared for their city by honoring the gods. Within the liturgical imagination of the ancient Greeks, these two vertical and horizontal functions were inseparable. The liturgical imagination of ancient Christianity affirmed this instinct, and for what happened in the temple had vast public consequences that were economic, agricultural, political, military, cultural, and even meteorological. Worship, in the Jewish imagination, was an act of public service and sacrifice for the public good—*leitourgia*.

In her book *Missional Worship, Worshipful Mission*, Ruth Meyers comes to a similar conclusion. Contemporary American perspectives vastly underestimate and greatly limit the power and purview of gathered worship in Americans' lives. A true wrestling with the first-century Jewish understanding of the publicness and civic orientation of worship will greatly expand the way in which we understand and practice gathered acts of praise. Meyers concludes that it is time to retire the definition of liturgy as "the work of the people."

> The phrase "the work of the people" emphasizes the people who gather, those who proclaim and respond to the Word and offer intercession, the assembly that celebrates a holy meal. By not also turning our attention beyond ourselves to the need of the world for God's reconciling love, continuing to think of liturgy as "the work of the people" impoverishes our celebrations. . . . When I use the term "liturgy," I have in mind *both* the structured ritual activity that involves texts and actions, using symbols, speech, song, and silence, *and* the assembly's work for the common good, its public service as a gathered community and as the people of God in the world. Liturgy as work for the common good is thus a form of participation in the mission of God.[b]

Attending to the Greek origins of *leitourgia* and, more importantly, the early Jewish understanding of the public nature of worship will pay great dividends for our desire to cultivate worship that is less privatistic and more vocationally conversant.[c]

a. Holman, *The Hungry Are Dying*, 57.
b. Meyers, *Missional Worship, Worshipful Mission*, 29.
c. For a historical and linguistic discussion of *leitourgia*, see Garnett, "Liturgy, Greece and Rome." See also the chapter "Leitourgia and the Poor in the Early Christian World," in Holman, *The Hungry Are Dying*, 31–63; Kittel, *Theological Dictionary of the New Testament*, 216 and 222; Ward, *The Politics of Discipleship*, 182–83.

the Greek term *leitourgia* was adopted by the church. This helps us understand why early Christians would feel comfortable adopting a pagan term like *leitourgia* to describe their own practice. Christian liturgies were theological *and* civic, spiritual *and* material.

Within the threefold offering, the Christian worker was providing for the poor in their city, strengthening the ministry of their church, and honoring their God in worship: all three of these actions constituted their *leitourgia*.

Offering your work to the poor in the name of the Lord was just as much a liturgy as offering your work at the Lord's Table.[9] A Christian merchant's work and worship were united, integrated, and interwoven through this threefold liturgy. *In and through the practice of offering, work and worship became one.*

As seen through the threefold offering, early Christians' everyday work had civic, ecclesial, and devotional purpose. The offering communicated an emerging Christian conviction that human work should further the threefold cause of love, mission, and adoration in the world.

The words "love," "mission," and "adoration" were not abstract theological concepts for early Christian workers. Week after week, farmers, merchants, and artisans watched the hard-earned fruits of their labor being directed toward this threefold purpose. Historical evidence is scant, but it is difficult to imagine that this regular practice did not have an impact on early Christian theologies of work. Indeed, this sorting of work through the threefold offering maps rather nicely onto Arthur Geoghegan's historical description of ancient Christian theologies of work.[10] Early Christianity, it would appear, had a *liturgical* theology of work.

First Fruits in the Early Church

> The offering of the bread and wine . . . manifests the intrinsic relation between land and altar.
>
> —Matthew Philipp Whelan, "Prefiguring the Salvation of the World"

The *Didache*, possibly the earliest document discussing Christian worship, explicitly mentions the role and importance of the first-fruits offering

---

9. See Holman, *The Hungry Are Dying*, 31–63.

10. Arthur Geoghegan underlines the importance of the connection between work and charitable giving in early Christian communities:

> The Didache, the Epistle of Barnabas, and the Shepherd of Hermas directed the Christian worker to give alms from the fruits of his labor. In fact, so important was the role of labor in supporting the charitable program of the Church that the Apostolic Fathers taught the duty of labor only in connection with and as part of their teaching on the commandment of brotherly love. In practically every instance in which they enjoined the obligation of work, they urged Christians to labor so as not to be a burden on the community, but rather to be an active supporter of him who could not earn his living. The great motive for labor was almsgiving. The close connection between labor and almsgiving in the Apostolic Fathers shows the importance of labor for the practice of the corporal works of mercy and the predominance of working people in the Christian communities of that time. (Geoghegan, *The Attitude Towards Labor in Early Christianity*, 130)

in worship.[11] The document instructs the worshiping community to offer the best fruits of their labor to support the city's poor and its local prophets.[12] Aaron Milavec notes that a merchant or artisan who was catechized into this community would be "trained to regard everything he or she possessed as the Father's 'free gifts' (*Did.* 1:5) and to 'accept the deeds befalling you as good things, knowing that, apart from God, nothing happens' (*Did.* 3:10). In light of this understanding, undoubtedly the first and best products of the kiln, the loom, and the forge were set aside for first fruits and given to the prophets so that they could give thanks to God."[13]

The *Didache* clearly instructs workers to gather together with jars of oil or wine, dough from their kitchens, clothing from their shops, or grains from their threshing floors. If workers did not have these designated labor products to offer, The *Didache* simply instructs them to bring "whatever [else] you own as you think best."[14] Like the Israelite workers before them, Christian workers were given the liturgical freedom (and responsibility) to bring whatever represented the best of their daily labor, the cream of their crop. These first Christian offerings were extremely inclusive in terms of class, gender, and craft. Rich and poor, men and women, farmers and artisans, homemakers and merchants—all could offer something in service to the community and worship to God.

Likewise, the *Didascalia* also instructs early Christians to humbly offer the best and most honorable work of their hands. Echoing the Old Testament, workers are told that their holy labors emit a sweet aroma inhaled into God's nostrils. The document instructs workers to take "the fruits and the works of your hands" and "present" them to your priest. This offering will

> be acceptable to the Lord thy God for a sweet savour, in the heights of heaven before the Lord thy God. . . . Wherefore be constantly doing work, and be labouring and offering an oblation. For the Lord has lightened the weight from

11. Here is the instruction from the *Didache* 13.3–7:
   So when you take any firstfruits of what is produced by the winepress and the threshing floor, by cows and by sheep, you shall give the firstfruits to the prophets, for they are your high priests. If, however, you have no prophet, give [them] to the poor. If you prepare dough, take the firstfruits and give them according to the commandment. Likewise, when you open a jar of wine or oil, take the firstfruits and give them to the prophets. Take the firstfruits of money and clothing and whatever [else] you own as you think best and give them according to the commandment. (Niederwimmer, *The Didache*, 191)
   See also the discussion in Draper, "First-Fruits and the Support of Prophets, Teachers, and the Poor."
12. Draper, "First-Fruits and the Support of Prophets, Teachers, and the Poor," 239.
13. Milavec, *The Didache*, 80.
14. *Didache* 13.7, in Niederwimmer, *The Didache*, 191.

The Victory and Donor Panels in the Floor Mosaics at Aquileia's Basilica of Santa Maria Assunta. Photographed by Richard Stracke.

Figure 9.1. A donor brings a basket of bread.

you, and has loosed from you the collar-bands, and lifted from you the yoke of burden. . . . Likewise in the Gospel He said: *Come unto me, all ye that toil and are laden with heavy burdens, and I will give you rest. Take my yoke upon you, and learn of me; for I am gentle and lowly in heart: and ye shalt find rest unto your souls. For my yoke is pleasant, and my burden is light* [Mt 11.28–30].[15]

Jeremy Kidwell has written a careful historical study on the connection between craftsmanship and the first-fruits rituals in ancient Israel and the early church.[16] In fact, the cover of Kidwell's book highlights a portion of an ancient mosaic illustrating an early Christian offering ritual that dates to be-

15. *Didascalia* IX, in Connolly, *Didascalia Apostolorum*, 96–98.
16. Kidwell, *The Theology of Craft and the Craft of Work*, 147–99.

The Victory and Donor Panels in the Floor Mosaics at Aquileia's Basilica of Santa Maria Assunta. Photographed by Richard Stracke.

Figure 9.2. A woman holds a flower in her right hand and an offering of fruit in her left hand.

tween 313 and 333 AD (see figs. 9.1–9.4). This ancient mosaic was discovered along with several others under the floor of the Basilica di Aquileia not far from Venice, Italy. The mosaics represent some of the oldest surviving liturgical art in all of Christianity.

In these mosaics we witness scores of early Christian workers carrying baskets from all over the city that are filled with a variety of goods to be offered to both God and community.[17] Multiple mosaics in the basilica are filled with diverse images of daily life and labor in the city and the surrounding fields and seas. We see a wide assortment of merchants, farmers, and fishermen. We see animals both wild and domestic, men, women, and children. The Christ figure on one mosaic is portrayed working humbly as a shepherd. All four seasons of the city's economic life are depicted. The city's maritime economy

17. Kidwell, "Drawn into Worship," 162.

The Victory and Donor Panels in the Floor Mosaics at Aquileia's Basilica of Santa Maria Assunta. Photographed by Richard Stracke.

Figure 9.3. A fisherman brings an offering from his daily catch.

is reflected in the sanctuary's enormous mosaic depicting an incredible scene of fish, boats, fishermen, and a variety of sea animals.

A common theme depicted throughout these liturgical mosaics is processions of worldly gifts and offerings being carried into the church. The mosaics provide contemporary onlookers with a small but precious window into what must have been quite a sight: a host of workers nobly processing forward carrying baskets of fish, bread, flowers, grapes, and other wares to their God. *One of the oldest surviving worship spaces in all of Christendom is positively filled with images of work, workers, and workplaces.*

How to Gather Fruits

The ancient mosaics visually enable us to grasp the vocationally conversant nature of early Christian worship. The stirring scenes provide a vivid

The Victory and Donor Panels in the Floor Mosaics at Aquileia's Basilica of Santa Maria Assunta. Photographed by Richard Stracke.

Figure 9.4. A woman brings clusters of grapes for the Eucharist wine.

framing for the liturgical instructions that we find in the ancient texts of *The Apostolic Tradition*. Commonly attributed to Hippolytus, these canons provided early worship leaders with specific instructions on what to do when workers carried the work of their hands into church. The instructions read as follows:

> Whoever has the firstfruits of the earth is to bring them to the church, the first of their floors and the first of their presses, oil, honey, milk, wool, and the first of the produce of the work of their hands, all this they are to bring to the bishop, and the first of their trees. The priest who takes them is to give thanks to God for them, first outside the veil, he who has brought them remaining standing. The priest says: "We give thanks to you, Lord, almighty God, because you have made us worthy to see these fruits that the earth has produced this year."[18]

18. *Canons of Hippolytus* §36, in Bradshaw, Johnson, and Phillips, *The Apostolic Tradition*, 167.

Having presented the work, the worship leader calls out the worker *by name* and pronounces the following blessing over the work, the worker, and the workplace: "Bless, Lord, the crown of the year that is of your bounty, and may they satisfy the poor of your people. Your servant N. [name of the worker], has brought these things that are yours, because he fears you, bless him from your holy heaven, and all his house."[19] In the ancient world, to bless one's "house" was not simply to bless the place where one slept; one's "house" also often represented one's business affairs, fields, and labor.

The Apostolic Tradition is one of the earliest collections of worship instructions in the history of Christianity. It specifically mentions work, workers, and workplaces at multiple points. In the liturgy above, the worker's labor is received, named, honored, blessed, and distributed to the poor. The worker's workplace is named, prayed for, and blessed. Finally, the worship leader is clearly instructed to "name the name of the one who brought them in."[20]

These offering liturgies welcome both the labor and the laborer into the worshiping life of the community. More than that, they induct workers into a collaborative working relationship with God. Through offering, workers are reminded that they work on God's land, with God's gifts, through God's power, by God's grace.

The liturgy of Hippolytus simply assumes that if God is with the worker in the world, if God blesses the material matter of our work, than the worker can feel confident bringing that material work into spiritual worship. As one scholar points out, the liturgy of Hippolytus "is not gnostic but fundamentally incarnational and sacramental. In other words, for Hippolytus, work matters matter because *matter* matters!"[21] Worshipers should offer their worldly work proudly so that it can be blessed by God and be a blessing to others. As another scholar reflects, through their material offerings "the faithful bring their whole life to the altar and ask for its transformation."[22]

The ancient Christian Sahidic offering ritual provides workers with a succinct and powerful theology of work. God alone is origin, essence, and end of all human work. That much is made perfectly clear in the following prayer for workers: "We give thanks to you, Lord God, and we bring you the firstfruits of which you gave us to eat, having perfected them by your Word; and you commanded the earth to send forth every fruit, for profiting, gladdening, and

19. *Canons of Hippolytus* §36, in Bradshaw, Johnson, and Phillips, *The Apostolic Tradition*, 167.

20. See the Sahidic version of §31.2 in Bradshaw, Johnson, and Phillips, *The Apostolic Tradition*, 166.

21. Cummings, *Eucharist and Ecumenism*, 22.

22. Wannenwetsch, "Eucharist and the Ethics of Sacrifice and Self-Giving," 140.

"Call Me by My Name"

The work conditions of many factory workers in the Majority World are often dehumanizing. The factories identify workers as numbers, expendable resources in the industrial machine. The lyrics to this Singaporean song focus on the common practice of stripping workers of their names. As the oppressors seek to erase the workers' humanity and identity, the singer holds on to Jesus's promise of abundant life (John 10:10), knowing that the Lord will hear and call the worker by name (John 10:3).

> Alone I am yet not alone; there're people all around.
> I bear a name, yet I have none. I'm lost, can I be found?
> Just call me by my name, just call me by my name,
> just call me by my name, O my Lord, just call me by my name.
>
> To count the crowds that fill the street, statistics are the
>   measure;
> I am a tag without a name, a chest without a treasure.
> Just call me by my name, just call me by my name,
> just call me by my name, O my Lord, just call me by my name.
>
> Away from grave and nameless rut, a man for others came;
> Upon the lives of all he put a price, a soul, a name.
> Just call me by my name, just call me by my name,
> just call me by my name, O my Lord, just call me by my name.[a]

a. I-to Loh, *Hymnal Companion to "Sound the Bamboo": Asian Hymns in Their Cultural and Liturgical Contexts* (Chicago: GIA Publications, 2011), 188. Lyrics by Samuel Liew; Music: MY NAME; Samuel Liew. Copyright © 1990, Christian Conference of Asia, GIA publications, Inc. Used with permission.

the nourishment of the human race and all creation. We bless you, God, for these things, and all others with which you show kindness."[23]

Through worship, these workers are reminded that profit, joy, and nourishment are a part of God's design for human work. *Through worship*, these workers are reminded that the purpose of work is to bless not simply themselves but all of humanity and God as well. *Through worship*, these workers are reminded that God is intimately present with them in the fields and markets actively "perfecting" their work with his "Word." Laboring away at

23. See the Sahidic version of §31.3 in Bradshaw, Johnson, and Phillips, *The Apostolic Tradition*, 166.

their presses, looms, and kilns, workers are not alone; they are colaborers with God.

The lines of liturgical continuity between ancient Israel and the early church are striking (e.g., Deut. 26). In both communities workers enter worship and present the best of their work in an act of celebratory praise and thanksgiving. In both liturgies the craftsman does this in the presence of his priest, family, and community. In both liturgies the profits from his work are directly connected to the flourishing of the community and particularly the poor and vulnerable. In both liturgies the worker acknowledges God as the origin, essence, and end of work. In both liturgies it is the worker—not the priest—who selects, prepares, and provides the primary elements of worship. *The priest's role is to facilitate the worker's worship.*

Early Christians all around the Mediterranean did more than participate in these rituals; they began to reflect on them theologically. Origen, for example, noted that the regular observance of first-fruits offerings was a critical ingredient in helping ancient workers acknowledge and remember the presence of God in their everyday work. Origen specifically discusses a worker who fails to "offer the first fruits to the priests from the harvest of the lands, a harvest that God granted by producing his sun and by serving by his rains. A soul of this sort does not seem to me to have remembered God, nor does it seem to think or believe that God has given the harvest that he has taken in, which he stows away as if it had nothing to do with God."[24]

In the same vein, the Jewish writer Philo of Alexandria instructs first-century workers participating in the offering to remember this: "You do not possess the earth, or the water, or the air, or the heaven, or the stars, or any of the kinds of animals or plants. . . . Whatever from them you bring to offer to him as a sacrifice, you are bringing as the possession of God, and not as your own."[25]

Learning God's Economy through Worship

> From your labors that God has given you, give simply to all in need.
>
> —*Shepherd of Hermas*, Mandate 2, 27.4

Christian offerings invited workers to enter into a gracious economic exchange with both God and the world. These offerings redirected both work

---

24. Origen, §2.2 of "Homily 11: Numbers 18:8–32," in *Homilies on Numbers*, 52.
25. Philo, *On the Sacrifices of Cain and Abel* 97, in *The Works of Philo*, 106.

and the worker toward the poor, toward the mission of the church, and, ultimately, toward the worship of God. Through offering, work and workers were being practiced into God's alternative economy. Within the sanctuary the worker rejects the old economic life of anxious grasping and begins to practice the new economic life of gracious offering and reception. This new liturgical "exchange" involves God, workers, and creation. The threefold economy runs something like this:

In the world

1. God offers creation to workers.
2. Workers receive creation from God.
3. God and workers collaborate in creation through daily work.

In the sanctuary

4. Workers offer work back to God.
5. God receives work from workers.
6. God offers a greater Work back to workers. (Christ/bread and wine)
7. Workers receive that greater Work from God. (Christ/bread and wine)
8. God and workers are united through this Work. (Christ/bread and wine)

But the gracious exchange does not end here. When the corporate worship service ends, the liturgical collaboration does not. The liturgy is extended back into the world through the work of God and the worker.

9. God and workers continually offer work to each other in creation.
10. God and workers continually receive work from each other in creation.

The gracious exchange between God, workers, and all of creation goes on and on. This is the liturgical economy of God, and the offering ritual is how workers can become practiced into that divine economy.

Modern readers might understandably stumble over the language of "exchange" or "economy" being attached to divine-human relationships. These words invoke images of contractual or quid pro quo relationships. It is important to note that these are *grace-filled* and *covenantal* exchanges between workers and their God. Workers do nothing to deserve God's offerings; these are gifts of grace. Likewise, a worker's offerings are received by God not because they're perfect but because of God's grace. Finally, a worker's offerings do not emerge from a desire to settle a contract or to manipulate God into further economic action. Instead, a worker's offering emerges as a joyful response to the primary offering of God. The gracious exchange is initiated with God's gift of creation.

Anxious workers, be they ancient or modern, need to unlearn the economic habits of grasping and grinding. They need to learn to freely offer and freely receive in covenantal grace. Early Christian workers were initiated into this gracious exchange with God *through the offering rituals*. They did not study a book on the economy of God in the world, they practiced and habituated this gracious economy when they carried their work into worship.

Offerings afforded workers the opportunity to celebrate, remember, and practice the gracious economy of God. All three of these elements were critical to their spiritual formation. Workers had to learn to *celebrate* and enjoy the work of God in creation, in their daily work, and in Christ. Workers had to continually *remember* that they were not autonomous workers but rather deeply dependent participants in the greater work of God. Finally, workers had to *practice* this gracious economic exchange with their bodies through the repeated gestures of offering and receiving. Workers learned gracious economic gestures in the sanctuary so that they could continue them in the street.

Both offering and receiving were critically important (and interconnected) rituals for the early church. Cyprian, a third-century bishop, had harsh words for workers who thought that they could simply receive the works of bread and wine without offering any works of their own. Cyprian argues that it is extremely important that workers participate in the whole economy of God—both offering and receiving.[26] Therefore, "Cyprian criticized those 'who come without alms and [in communion] receive part of the sacrifice that a poor person has brought.'"[27] The call to worship was a gracious invitation to both offer and receive work. The liturgy was an opportunity to become an active laborer in the economy of God. Poor widows contribute what little work they have to the body of Christ, so would you, wealthy merchant, do nothing but receive?

This helps us understand a fascinating report that destitute orphans in some early communities were given glasses of water on the day of worship simply so they would have something of their own to offer to God in the sanctuary.[28] In the early church, poverty and unemployment were not simply

---

26. This statement requires careful theological nuance, which will be covered later in this chapter and the next.

27. Foley et al., *A Commentary on the Order of Mass*, 232 (brackets original).

28. Alexander Schmemann writes, "In the practice of the early Church, the eucharistic sacrifice was offered not only on behalf of all and for all, but *by all*, and therefore the real offering

an economic tragedy; they were a liturgical one as well.[29] No one could come to worship empty-handed (Deut. 16:16). Without employment, without bread, the orphans and widows would have no work to offer to God in worship. The charitable gift of bread to the poor was needed not simply to feed them but to enable them to offer something to God at the table. They needed to participate in the gracious exchange of offering and receiving, of entering into the gracious economy of God. By giving to the poor, one empowered them economically and liturgically.

What, then, is the "division of labor" between God and workers in the divine economy? Who is responsible for what? Origen's discussion of sailors working on a ship best captures the early Christian understanding of the gracious economy.

> So, when a ship has overcome the dangers of the sea, although the result be accomplished by great labour on the part of the sailors, and by the aid of all the art of navigation, and by the zeal and carefulness of the pilot, and by the favouring influence of the breezes, and the careful observation of the signs of the stars, no one in his sound senses would ascribe the safety of the vessel, when, after being tossed by the waves, and wearied by the billows, it has at last reached the harbour in safety, to anything else than to the mercy of God. Not even the sailors or pilot venture to say, "I have saved the ship," but they refer all to the mercy of God; not that they feel that they have contributed no skill or labour to save the ship, but because they know that while they contributed the labour, the safety of the vessel was ensured by God. So also in the race of our life we ourselves must expend labour, and bring diligence and zeal to bear; but it is from God that salvation is to be hoped for as the fruit of our labour.[30]

---

by each of his own gift, his own sacrifice, was a basic condition of it. . . . [Even] orphans who lived at the expense of the Church and did not have anything to bring participated in this sacrifice of love by bringing water." Schmemann, *For the Life of the World*, 107. See also Dix, *The Shape of the Liturgy*, 104.

29. Bernd Wannenwetsch underlines how the eucharistic liturgy emphasized inclusion of the poor:

> The stress laid on the participation of all communicants in the offertory is, once again, evident in a related practice in the church of Rome, which ensured that even the pro- verbial "have nots," the children of the papal orphan school, had something to offer: they were entrusted with the offering of the water which was to be mixed with the wine for the Eucharistic consumption. This concern for the complete representation of the community casts light on the ethical significance of the offertory, insofar as it beckons the acknowledgment of equality of all the faithful. In the light of the offertory rite, we can speak of a "Eucharistic equality," which even precedes the one that is experienced in the moment of consumption at the altar, where there is no "distinction of person" and everyone—prince or pauper—is made equal in the mode of reception. (Wannenwetsch, "Eucharist and the Ethics of Sacrifice and Self-Giving," 137–38)

30. Origen, *De Principiis* 3.18, in Coxe, Roberts, and Donaldson, *Ante-Nicene Fathers*, 4:322.

Origen describes the sailors as actors who both offer and receive within the much larger divine economy. In this narrative the sailors actively offer their professional knowledge, skills, and energy to the effort; at the same time, they are deeply reliant and dependent on God's constant provision for their active participation. Placed firmly within this gracious economy, the sailors recognize their vocational fragility, contingency, and dependence on God. The sailors also recognize that they are gifted, knowledgeable, and responsible agents. This helps us to understand the receiving and giving of offerings in our churches today as well.

Origin's helpful picture emerges from a liturgical imagination deeply informed by these offering rituals. The regular presentation of first fruits wove the work of God and the work of humanity into a seamless fabric. Through the offering the worker was invited to practice a twofold posture and practice. The worker learned both to offer and to receive, to act and to wait, to contribute and to partake, to work and to rest. The worker learned to delight in the works of God and also learned that God delighted in their work. Through the repetitive act of offering work in worship, workers could begin to see themselves as a part of the greater economy of God.

While the act of offering work was powerful and formative, *workers would receive a far greater work from Christ*. At the Lord's Table workers learned that all of their labors combined were radically dependent on a work that far surpassed their own. Here we begin a shift in focus from the act of offering human work to the act of receiving divine work; here we move from our first fruits into Christ's.

Irenaeus: Humanity's Fruits at God's Table

Of all the early church fathers, Irenaeus offers perhaps the most robust reflections on the ancient first-fruits rituals. He theologically binds early Christian understandings of human work directly to the celebration of the Lord's Table. At the time of his writing, Irenaeus was involved in a heated debate with a group of Gnostic teachers who denied the inherent goodness of creation, materiality, and human work. Far from being a coherent or organized religion, ancient Gnosticism was a diverse collection of worldviews that—broadly speaking—sought to transcend material life through the acquisition of spiritual knowledge. Within Gnosticism, mundane work in the material world was obviously not sacred, holy, or spiritual. Spirituality was a tool for celestial transcendence, something you practiced to escape the material prison of life and labor.

In his response to Gnostic cynicism about life in the world, Irenaeus formulates a theological defense of the goodness of God's creation, material life, and human labor. His defense of materiality, however, was not simply theological, it was liturgical as well. Irenaeus points directly to two worship practices, the first-fruits offering and the Lord's Supper, to make his case. Irenaeus argues that *Christ himself* commanded his disciples to lift up the material and collaborative work of creation at his holy table in a sacred act of spiritual worship and celebration. Irenaeus writes,

> Our Lord commanded his disciples to offer to God the first fruits of his own creation, not because God was in need of them, but to enable the disciples to bear fruit and show gratitude. He took a piece of creation—bread—and gave thanks, saying, "This is my body." Similarly with the cup, also a part of the creation to which we belong—he declared that it was his blood.[31]

> For an offering must be made to God. We must show ourselves grateful to the Creator in everything; and when we offer him the first-fruits of his own creation we must do it with a pure intention, in sincere faith, in firm hope and in fervent love. This offering, this pure offering, is presented to the Creator by the Church alone, as she offers him with thanksgiving a portion of his own creation.[32]

According to Irenaeus, orthodox Christianity will not abandon Israel's practice of offering creational work as worship. "Offerings, as a general class, have not been abolished. There were offerings then, and there are offerings now. The people of God had sacrifices and his Church has sacrifices."[33] Christian workers will continue this practice, in part, for *pedagogical* reasons: "[God] asks for these things, not because he needs them, but for our sake, in order that we may not be unfruitful. Similarly the same Word [Christ] commanded the people of God to make offerings, not because he needed them, but to teach them to serve God—just as it is his will that we too should unceasingly offer our gift at the altar."[34]

This helps us understand Irenaeus's strict liturgical instructions that workers carry offerings to worship "frequently and without intermission,"[35] for it is through the *frequency* of offering that workers are practiced into the

31. Irenaeus, §17.5 of *Against the Heresies* IV, in Wiles and Santer, *Documents in Early Christian Thought*, 183.

32. Irenaeus, §18.4 of *Against the Heresies* IV, in Wiles and Santer, *Documents in Early Christian Thought*, 186.

33. Irenaeus, §18.2 of *Against the Heresies* IV, in Wiles and Santer, *Documents in Early Christian Thought*, 185.

34. Irenaeus, §18.6 of *Against the Heresies* IV, in Wiles and Santer, *Documents in Early Christian Thought*, 187.

35. Irenaeus, §18.6 of *Against Heresies* IV, in Coxe, Roberts, and Donaldson, *Ante-Nicene Fathers*, 1:436.

economy of Christ. Workers offer themselves to God in the sanctuary so they might learn to continually offer themselves to God in the streets (Rom. 12:1).

Frequent participation in first-fruits rituals offered the pedagogical power needed to redirect a Christian's working life away from personal enrichment and empowerment and toward the ultimate purpose of their craft: holy service to both God and neighbor—both the heavenly city and the earthly city. Reflecting on early first-fruits processionals, liturgical scholar Josef Jungmann remarks that these practices may have "contributed a great deal towards making the faithful understand . . . more clearly that *the* holy Sacrifice was *their* Sacrifice which they should offer together with Christ. . . . The faithful must have been keenly alive to the fact that their entire lives belonged to God and that they all were one in the Sacrifice of Christ."[36] Their whole lives and whole labor were lying there on the Lord's Table.

For Irenaeus, the overly spiritualized world-escapism of the Gnostics is inimical to the earthy gospel celebrated at the table. Emmanuel did not come to rescue humanity from his creation; he came to reside with, work alongside, and restore humanity to a renewed creation and a renewed work within his world. "For God so loved the world that he sent his only son" (John 3:16). Around the earthy and aromatic table of the Lord, Christians taste the incarnational work of God in the world. Here they see with their own eyes that Christ is "the Son of the Creator of the world, that is, his Word, through whom wood bears fruit, springs gush out and the earth puts forth 'first the blade, then the ear, then the full grain in the ear' [Mark 4:28]."[37]

For Irenaeus, the twin liturgies of offering and table reject the Gnostic divorce between heaven and earth, adoration and vocation. As Irenaeus writes, "When the bread, which comes from the earth, receives the invocation of God, it is no longer ordinary bread; it is eucharist—composed of two elements, one earthly and one heavenly. Similarly, when our bodies partake of the Eucharist, they are no longer corruptible; they have the hope of resurrection."[38]

In the offering and the Eucharist, materiality and spirituality are one. "Our way of thinking is in harmony with the eucharist, and conversely the eucharist confirms our thinking. We offer [Christ] what is his own, and thereby proclaim the harmonious fellowship and union of flesh and Spirit."[39]

36. Jungmann, *The Early Liturgy*, 172 (emphasis added).
37. Irenaeus, §18.4 of *Against the Heresies* IV, in Wiles and Santer, *Documents in Early Christian Thought*, 187.
38. Irenaeus, §18.5 of *Against the Heresies* IV, in Wiles and Santer, *Documents in Early Christian Thought*, 187.
39. Irenaeus, §18.5 of *Against the Heresies* IV, in Wiles and Santer, *Documents in Early Christian Thought*, 187.

A Dancing Offertory: African American Catholics

Offering and receiving are two critical liturgical movements in the life of a community. Bruce Morrill, a white Catholic theologian, had the opportunity to visit St. Augustine's Church in New Orleans and participate in their worship. He observed as a group of African American Catholics demonstrated the power of *bodily* movement toward the altar in the acts of offering and receiving. Struck by the experience, Morrill recalls

> an exuberant two-hour liturgy combining the Mass of Paul VI with the music, bodily and vocal prayer styles, and preaching patterns of African-American Christianity. Most arresting and memorable for me were the two processions of the entire assembly framing the liturgy of the eucharist, which began with every member—old and young, women, men and children—coming up the main aisle to deposit their donations in a large basket at the foot of the altar, singing and dancing with the choir's anthem. Bringing up the rear were elders and children bearing bread and wine. I was deeply affected, especially as I experienced the impact on the second procession for [receiving] communion, how much more communal and consecratory and empowering it felt because of its mirroring the first corporate movement.[a]

As one, their bodies dance forward to offer their work to Christ; as one, their bodies dance forward to receive the work from Christ.

a. Morrill, "Holy Communion as Public Act," quoted in Kidwell, "Drawn into Worship," 224.

Awakening to the Scandal of Worldly Work in Heavenly Worship

Imagine watching your hard work distributed to the poor, celebrated in worship, or feasted on in community. Imagine watching the fish you caught and the cheese you cured being passed around and enjoyed by your elders and spiritual mentors. Imagine watching the red robe that you fashioned walk out of worship on the back of a poor widow on your street. Finally, imagine watching bread from your home oven and wine from your backyard vines offered in the worship of almighty God.

The scandalous Christian belief that ordinary work participates in the extraordinary work and worship of God was not theoretical for ancient Christians. It was embodied on the table in front of them. They could see the theological doctrine in the grains they had planted, watered, harvested, ground, mixed, kneaded, and baked. They could taste the complex ecclesial dogma in the grapes they had cultivated and crushed. The fusion of human worship and work was enacted right there at the table. God had taken the humble work of their hands and transformed it into a cosmic and world-changing work of divine action.

The scandalous nature of this practice is captured poignantly in an exchange between Pope Gregory and an unnamed woman in the sixth century. We have only a thirdhand account, but the story is illustrative of our point. In the sanctuary a woman processes forward to receive Communion from Pope Gregory. Giving her the bread, Gregory declares it to be Christ's body broken for her. The woman responds in a most unusual way: she laughs.

According to the account, when the woman looked down, she recognized that the body of Christ came from her own kitchen. She had kneaded that body with her own hands. The idea that her work in her kitchen had participated in any way with the work of God was too absurd a concept for her to fathom.[40] In one account, the woman confesses, "I recognized the fragment to be of the same oblation-loaf which I made myself with my own hands and offered to you; and when I understood you to call it the Lord's Body, I smiled."[41] Worship, it appears, had taught this humble baker something critically important about her kitchen and the holy work that went on there.

Work Is Worship, in Christ Alone

That we can give at all rests on what we have been given, on the sense of receiving our very selves as gift.

—Rowan Williams, *Eucharistic Sacrifice*

Am I worthy to approach God with the work of my hands? My daily labors are often selfish and sin-stained. My work is implicated in a global economic system that includes moral corruption, economic injustice, and environmental devastation. Are these feeble and fallen offerings worthy of a holy and righteous God? Modern workers who initiate an electronic transfer of tithes

40. Borenstein, *Medieval Christianity*, 92.
41. Atchley and Cuthbert, *Ordo Romanus Primus*, 87.

to their local church rarely, if ever, ask themselves questions like these. They seldom ask, "By what audacious magic do I dare approach God's holy altar with the sordid fruits from my fallen labor?" These are not live questions for us today, but they should be.

Early Christians, like the ancient Israelites, considered these questions to be critical, and for good reason. In this final discussion of offering we will see that early Christians argued again and again that workers—on their own— should not dare to approach God with the fruits of their labor. They give several reasons for this. First of all, God does not *need* human work—or human workers, for that matter. God's economy can run just fine without them. Moreover, God does not desire rebellious work or wicked workers to be offered up at his holy table. Sinful workers and unjust fruits—on their own—are absolutely disqualified and unworthy of admittance. On its own merits, sin-stained work can never be worship; on their own merits, sin-stained workers can never be worthy priests. *In order for work to become worship, a greater work must be accomplished; in order for workers to become priests, a higher priest must ordain them.*

In the New Testament and within early Christianity we see a strong emphasis on Christ as the sole high priest. Christ's priesthood alone can transform a sinful group of workers into a holy priesthood. It is only through Christ's work on the cross that humanity's work in the world can be transformed into holy sacrifices of worship. Christ's work makes humanity's work worship. Christ's work alone makes workers worthy to approach the altar (Heb. 4:14–5:10). The *secondary* work and worship of humanity can be declared holy only because of Christ's *primary* acts of worship and work in our place. *The plural self-offerings of workers are made worthy (and delightful) to God through the singular self-offering of Christ* (Heb. 10:1–10; 13:15).

More than presenting a representative portion, early Christians were called to offer their whole lives as a sacrifice to God.[42] Throughout the New

---

42. This was quite literal for the early martyrs, who often described themselves as sacrificial self-offerings. In this way martyrdom was not simply a political act but a liturgical act as well. Ignatius of Antioch, pondering his own impending martyrdom, declares, "I am the wheat of God, and by the teeth of the beasts I shall be ground, that I may be found the pure bread of God. . . . Entreat of our Lord in my behalf, that through these instruments I may be found a sacrifice to God." Ignatius, *Epistle to the Romans* 4.1–2, in Coxe, Roberts, and Donaldson, *Ante-Nicene Fathers*, 1:103. For some early Christians, the process of martyrdom was actually understood to be a sacred liturgy enacted in the city square before both God and the world. According to Robin Darling Young, martyrdom "functioned as a public liturgical sacrifice in which the word of Jesus and his kingdom was confessed and acted out, and an offering made that repeated his own." Young, *In Procession before the World*, 11. Through their sacrificial death, martyrs led a public worship service in the city streets using their body as the primary instrument of holy worship.

Testament, the Apostolic Fathers, and early Nicene Christianity we find repeated examples of early Christians describing the whole of their lives, labor,
gifts, and their very bodies as instruments of holy sacrifice, offering, and
praise (Acts 20:35; Rom. 12:1; 15:14–17; 1 Cor. 16:1–2; 2 Cor. 9:5–15; 1 Tim.
6:17–19; Heb. 13:16).

Some modern Protestants have a habit of claiming that, because of the ultimate sacrifice of Christ, Israel's practices of sacrifice are now irrelevant—they
have been superseded. The early church fathers complicated these overeager
dismissals. Jeremy Kidwell argues that, in the early church, Israel's "practice
of burnt offerings is not discarded by Christians *but intensified*."[43] Christ's
sacrifice did not end our human responsibility to engage in sacrifice; instead,
it radicalizes and spreads God's sacrificial calling into every aspect of life and
work. As Gregory of Nazianzus entreated his congregation, "Let us become
reason-endowed whole burnt offerings."[44]

Edward Kilmartin, exploring the earliest theologies of sacrifice and offering, argues that for the early church, "Self-offering is the primary category:
the surrender of the whole of human existence to the will of God in order to
receive from him the meaning of one's life. The paradigm is the self-emptying
of Jesus (Heb 9:14). . . . The self-offering of Christians committed to the way
of Jesus embraces the whole range of human activity (Rom. 12:1–2; 15:16)."[45]
Note, for example, the apostle Paul's comment on his body "being poured
out like a drink offering on the sacrifice" (Phil. 2:17). Irenaeus adds that, in
offering, the worshiper should imitate "the poor widow who threw her whole
livelihood into the treasury of God [Luke 21:1–4]."[46] Augustine says that in
this liturgical action the worshiper must come to learn a scandalous truth:
"She herself is offered in the very offering she makes to God."[47]

Having noted the all-encompassing nature of early Christian sacrifice, let's
return to our primary questions: By what audacious magic are sinful works
and sinful workers transformed into holy sacrifices of praise? What right do
we have to call our work "worship"?

Cyril of Alexandria sheds important light on this question as he explores
Christ's active involvement in a disciple's humble offering at the altar. For

43. Kidwell, "Drawn into Worship," 185 (emphasis added).
44. Quoted in Kidwell, "Drawn into Worship," 186.
45. Kilmartin, "Offerings," 827.
46. Irenaeus, §18.2 of *Against the Heresies* IV, in Wiles and Santer, *Documents in Early
Christian Thought*, 185.
47. "This is the Sacrifice, as the faithful understand, which the Church continues to celebrate
in the sacrament of the altar, in which it is clear to the Church that she herself is offered in the
very offering she makes to God." Augustine, *City of God* 10.6, quoted in Cardó, *The Cross
and the Eucharist*, 44.

Cyril, Christ does not passively wait at the altar to receive the worker's offering. Instead, Christ actually accompanies her as she stands up and makes
her way to the altar. More than that, for Cyril, Christ appears to actually
carry her (and her offering) to the throne of God. According to Lawrence
Welch, "For Cyril, there is no other way the baptized can come to the Father
except through the prayers and sacrifice of Christ. This insight is liturgically experienced and inspired. Christ as high priest and mediator unites
the baptized to himself by making them one with his ecclesial body thereby
uniting them to the Father."[48] Instead of sinful workers trying desperately
(and fruitlessly) to purify their sinful work on their own, Cyril demonstrates
how the atoning work of Christ sanctifies their fallen work and readies it
for worship.

Just as Christ took up our humanity and presented it to the Father, now
also Christ takes up our work (present in the bread and wine) and lifts it
up to God in an act of thanksgiving and praise. Cyril of Alexandria helps
us to see that when a worker brings her daily work forward, she does not
offer it alone. It is actually Christ who is offering not only her work but
also her very body to God as worship. Welch argues that for Cyril, Christ
carries "worship to the Father that sinful humanity cannot offer."[49] He
continues, "Cyril insists that the risen Christ, 'who is still one of us' after
the resurrection, continues to present himself to the Father on our behalf."[50]
Christ alone, Cyril argues, can offer "the worship which fallen humanity
owes to the Father."[51]

What is the relationship between our self-offering and Christ's? Rowan
Williams's commentary on the early church fathers is helpful here.[52] Williams
affirms the Protestant reading that Christ alone is *the* sacrifice and *the* high
priest, that Christ alone reconciles all things to God (Col. 1). No further
sacrifice needs to be made to restore the world to God; no human work needs
to be done (Heb. 10). Protestants everywhere cheer.

However, Williams offers a challenge (and an invitation) to Protestants
as well. He argues that voices within the early church compel us also to
recognize that God's primary sacrificial move toward humanity invites and

---

48. Welch, *Christology and Eucharist*, 38.
49. Welch, *Christology and Eucharist*, 113.
50. Welch, *Christology and Eucharist*, 90.
51. Welch, *Christology and Eucharist*, 112.
52. In *Eucharistic Sacrifice*, Rowan Williams provides a particularly robust historical and
theological exploration of this theme of sacrificial self-offering in the worship and theology of
the early church. He explores the insights of Justin Martyr, Irenaeus of Antioch, Irenaeus of
Lyon, Ephrem the Syrian, and many other voices on precisely this point. His reflections form
the conceptual backbone of this section, as is laid out in subsequent notes.

enables humanity to offer a secondary *sacrificial response*. As Williams observes,

> The effect of Christ's sacrifice is precisely to make us "liturgical" beings, capable of offering ourselves, our praises and our symbolic gifts to a God who we know will receive us in Christ. Because of the cross we are now . . . offered to the Father: *what we are is redefined in sacrificial terms*. . . . We bring ourselves near to the altar of the cross as we come and offer our gifts—and we are encouraged to do so because the way is open through the flesh of Christ.[53]

Because of Christ's priestly work, workers can enter into his holy priesthood. Within Christ's priesthood, workers can engage in their own priestly acts of worship and work. Their small creations can enter into Christ's new creation. As Williams notes, Christ's "sacrifice wins a holy people, a praising people, who actualize their priestly task in a uniquely concentrated and fruitful fashion when they offer bread and wine as a memorial and a thanksgiving."[54] Therefore, Williams argues, "Christians are priests entirely in a derivative sense: They 'offer,' which is the characteristic priestly act, but only because they are being offered by the eternal high priest, and because they have been made a worthy offering by the atonement."[55]

In worship, Christ lifts workers up, having redeemed them and their work, and Christ offers them to the Father in an act of worship. In the sanctuary, Christ graciously gathers a multiplicity of diverse work and workers from all over the city and offers them up—plumbers, nurses, architects, and teachers—to the Father as an offering of praise. *In his priesthood*, they are made priests; *in his work*, their work is worship.

In closing, we find Augustine deftly weaving all of these themes from the early church together. Here we watch as he threads together the work of our hands, the work of Christ, and the liturgical celebration of the Lord's Supper into a single fabric.

> A true sacrifice is every work which is done that we may be united to God. . . . For, though made or offered by man, sacrifice is a divine thing. . . . Thus man himself . . . is a sacrifice. . . . Our body, too, is a sacrifice. . . . True sacrifices are works of mercy to ourselves or others, done with a reference to God. . . . This also is the sacrifice which the Church continually celebrates in the

53. R. D. Williams, *Eucharistic Sacrifice*, 27 (emphasis added).
54. R. D. Williams, *Eucharistic Sacrifice*, 32.
55. R. D. Williams, *Eucharistic Sacrifice*, 16.

sacrament of the altar . . . in which . . . *she herself is offered in the offering she makes to God.*[56]

The Death (and Resurrection) of the Modern Offering

Sadly, the ancient practices of first-fruits offerings would slowly die out in the Christian liturgy. Numerous factors played a role. The growing size of congregations made gathering and distributing all of these diverse workplace products difficult. The use of currency was simply more efficient for the laity to offer and the priesthood to collect and distribute. Josef Jungmann remarks that soon enough "it was felt to be less fitting that all sorts of things . . . be brought into the church. Already in the fourth century regulations were issued that in the future bread and wine and other things necessary for worship be brought to the altar as heretofore, but that all other gifts be handed in elsewhere. It was understood through the gifts of bread and wine, all other things which the faithful wanted to give were symbolically represented and conjointly offered up."[57]

Today, our work within the twenty-first-century global marketplace is "symbolically represented" as worship leaders give thanks for the bread and wine on the people's behalf. Our daily labors are "symbolically represented" when we place currency in the offering plate or transfer our funds electronically.

In many ways this liturgical evolution makes perfect and practical sense. It is difficult for a deacon to effectively gather computer chips, financial spreadsheets, ad campaigns, or shipping manifests. How would a deacon distribute such things to the poor? It is also rather impractical to ask some workers to carry their products into worship. Where would they put a garbage truck, a cargo ship, or a jumbo jet? Moreover, making offerings so public and visible might encourage feelings of jealousy and pride—better to keep offerings anonymous and secret.

While these liturgical challenges are real, modern practices of "symbolic representation" often lack the pedagogical force needed to bridge the modern divide between faith and work. In the modern church's desire for efficiency, practicality, and anonymity, something critical has been lost.

Compare the pedagogical potency of three different offering experiences. First, an ancient Israelite farmer is feasting on his harvest fruits outside King

---

56. Augustine, *City of God* 10.6, in Dods, *The Works of Aurelius Augustine*, 1:390–92 (emphasis added).

57. Jungmann, *The Early Liturgy*, 172.

David's Jerusalem in the presence of God, his coworkers, his family, and the poor. Second, an early Christian baker is carting his bread through second-century Jerusalem. He carefully displays his loaves at his table in the marketplace. He sets the most beautiful loaves aside to bring to the church for the feeding of the local poor. And third, a modern Christian is flying in a jetliner 35,000 feet above Jerusalem at 700 miles an hour. A flight attendant, she is missing her Sunday church service in Atlanta because she's serving on a flight to Dubai. This flight attendant can't be physically present at church, but her bank will automatically transfer a portion of her paycheck to the church's account. The transfer goes through at 1:00 a.m. just as her 787 passes over Jerusalem. While she offers drinks in coach, her work is offered to God in Atlanta. Here we have three different acts of offering, three different pedagogies for the offerer.

Jeremy Kidwell argues that modern offering rituals fundamentally lack "social context, festivity, or explicit material reference to the work of the offerer."[58] The purpose of the preceding example is certainly not to pick on a flight attendant but rather to raise a series of questions about what has happened to the offering and what it means for Christian disciples today. The flight attendant gave money to both God and the church at 1:00 a.m., during the drink service. That much is clear. And yet, while the bank is capable of offering money on her behalf, *is the bank capable of offering her work, her body, her very life?* The questions only proliferate. How will the flight attendant learn to stop, celebrate, and remember the goodness of God in her work? How will she learn to examine, select, and offer the very best of her work to God? How will she learn to vocationally offer and receive, act and wait, speak and listen with God? Where will she practice these postures of offering and sacrifice? Who will say her name out loud in worship? Who will bless her work? How will she come to see her work as participating in God's?

Our purposes here are not Luddite in nature; we don't wish to simplistically resurrect the ancient liturgies of the past. We live and labor within the twenty-first-century global marketplace, and we have many reasons to be thankful for our current age. Our purpose, rather, is to point out the dangerously widening gap between our practices of offerings and our practices of work. There is a desperate need for a new liturgical imagination when it comes to the offering—one that is fed by these ancient and embodied sources of wisdom that show us how work and worship become one through the practice of offering.

---

58. Kidwell, *The Theology of Craft and the Craft of Work*, 209.

PART 3
PRACTICES

10

Work at the Lord's Table

Communion is the perfect embodiment of the mystery of human work. Communion shows dramatically the indissoluble link between the bread for which we all must toil and the bread from which God gives as a gift. . . . Christ nourishes our souls with the very things we bring to him—things he first gave to us.

—Ben Patterson, *Serving God*

The liturgy of the Eucharist is best understood as a journey or procession. It is a journey of the church into a dimension of the Kingdom. . . . It is not an escape from the world, rather it is the arrival at a vantage point from which we can see more deeply into the reality of the world.

—Alexander Schmemann, *For the Life of the World*

For many, the Lord's Table feels a million miles away from their daily work in the world. What does this measly cracker have to do with my monthly sales record, my upcoming performance review, my cruel boss? What does this tiny cup have to do with air-conditioning repair, petrochemicals, or a lesson plan for third graders? How on earth does my church's Communion table connect to my company's conference table?

This chapter explores a wide variety of ways in which the bread and the cup can inform, impact, and intersect with a worker's daily life and labor.

Rather than focusing our attention on the priestly officiant at the table, we've built this chapter around the lived experience of a worker visiting the table.[1]

As the chapter proceeds, we will explore how the Lord's Supper can invite a worker to remember, participate in, and practice the work and economy of God. Briefly stated, here is what we mean by this. At the table the worker can pause and *remember* a divine work that provides meaning and direction for her work in the world. At the table she can *participate* in the work of God by actively offering, sharing, consuming, and enjoying the divine work with others. Finally, at the table she can *practice* the economic patterns of God's gracious economy and make those patterns her own. Throughout this chapter we will explore how memory, participation, and practice all play a role in the formation of workers at the Lord's Table.

Throughout the entire worship service workers have been invited to sing, pray, and dance their way into God's gracious economy. But here at the table— in actually consuming the bread and wine—God's economy is now entering into the body of the worker. At the conclusion of the Lord's Supper the worker will depart. She will return to her daily labor not by her own strength but by the strength that lives within her.

Contemporary theologies of work are in constant danger of falling prey to the twin dangers of economic optimism and economic pessimism. Some theologies of work romanticize the power and potential of human industry and free markets, while other theologies of work demonize them as spaces of pure evil, corruption, and greed. We hope to demonstrate that this theological tension of economic optimism and pessimism finds a liturgical resolution in the embodied practice of the Lord's Supper. At several points, the table celebration will honor and uplift human work and industry by including it and sanctifying it through the work of God. At other points, the table will profoundly challenge and even subvert human work and industry by placing it in a secondary relationship completely dependent on the primary work and industry of God. In the end, we hope to demonstrate how worship at the table enables workers to avoid the Scylla and Charybdis of economic optimism and pessimism.

This chapter will not provide an in-depth biblical, theological, or historical analysis of the Lord's Table. Those foundations have already been laid in earlier chapters. Our task here is to build on those foundations and reflect on the worker's journey through the Lord's Supper. We hope to demonstrate that

---

1. This is not a systematic or comprehensive theology of the Lord's Supper. Such a project would focus primarily on the theocentric work of the Father, Son, and Holy Spirit at the table. Here we are focused on workers and work at the table. We are interested in exploring how God's table engages workers and work.

in and through the supper the disparate parts of a worker's life—faith, work, and worship—find their unity. As Evelyn Underhill so beautifully puts it,

> The Eucharist is an action which binds visible and invisible in one service. It takes natural and ordinary things, the food of our temporal existence, won by our own labour from the natural world, and makes these things holy by offering them with thanksgiving to God. . . . Each brings what he can; probably not the best bread and the finest vintage; but the best possible in the circumstances. Real grapes, grown, picked and pressed out by our own efforts, real flour that we have ground and baked.[2]

Preliminary Cautions

Any discussion of worship and work at the Lord's Supper immediately encounters several substantial challenges. Three deserve mention from the outset.

The first challenge is the vast global diversity of workers who approach the Lord's Table on any given Sunday. An executive in Tokyo, a waiter in London, a strawberry picker in California, a shop owner in Nairobi, and a software developer in Buenos Aires will each bring very different workplace experiences to the table. Their differences of profession and gifting, class and culture, power and privilege present themselves at the table in unique ways. Obviously, no author could address all of this vocational diversity in a single chapter. Rather than speak for all workers everywhere, we thought it might prove more helpful to walk with a single worker as she participates in the Lord's Supper. Therefore, throughout this chapter the reader follows a semifictional businesswoman as she journeys through the Lord's Supper. "Natalie" represents an amalgamation of a variety of workers we have met and learned alongside of over our years of research and teaching in cities such as New York, Seattle, Houston, Los Angeles, Phoenix, and San Francisco. The reader should assume that "Natalie" is an educated mid-level manager working for a large corporation in an American city.

The second challenge concerns the liturgical diversity of the global church and its varied celebrations of the bread and the cup. Some workers will call it "Communion," others the "Lord's Supper," and still others "the Eucharist." Some will consume wheat, others rice, and still others millet. Some drink juice, others wine. Some will experience a holy act of remembrance, others a holy act of transubstantiation. In light of this diversity, we've attempted

2. Underhill, *The Mystery of Sacrifice*, 18.

to describe the table in ways that are more accessible, diverse, and ecumenical. Our language is limited and imperfect—but stay with us. Readers who celebrate the Lord's Supper with little formality will likely have a more challenging time in this chapter. We ask these readers to pause and slow down. Consider this an opportunity to reflect on the rich and complex flavors of a new dish you might just be eating too quickly. While there is a lot that divides our diverse table practices, we believe that there is at least one important point of commonality: *all over the world, in every denomination and in every culture, workers arrive at the table hungry and thirsty for the work of Christ.*

The final challenge is the complexity of the table itself. No matter how simple the ritual might appear on its face, there is a lot going on every time we approach the table. A baseball metaphor may prove helpful on this point. If a batting coach were to break down the swing of a baseball bat into its separate elements (grip, setup, torque, step, swing, and follow-through—not to mention the ball, bat, muscles, bones, tendons, eyes, brain synapses, etc.)—it would quickly become clear that a simple baseball swing is *anything but* "simple." Indeed, the single event that we call "a swing" quickly becomes overwhelmingly complex when you slow it down to consider its many moving parts.

In this chapter we break down the Lord's Supper into seven actions and consider a variety of ways in which those actions intersect with our working lives. The following are seven verbs, seven particular actions a worker might engage in at the table.

To examine	To share
To approach	To hold
To thank	To consume
To receive	

As we will see, these seven actions taken at the table can directly engage both work and workers in a complex multiplicity of ways. The many intersections between faith, work, and worship at the table may well be overwhelming. In a way, the complex fruits of the Lord's Table *should* overwhelm us. The diverse gifts of God for the diverse people of God are purposefully rich and complex.

To be sure, during any single trip to the table no flesh-and-blood worker will ever encounter all of the intersections between work and worship that we outline here. Our level of detail is meant to illustrate the vast riches available at the table whenever a worker approaches the table of their Lord. With these notes firmly in mind, we can begin to follow Natalie, the middle manager, as she makes her pilgrimage through the great feast.

The Worker Examines

> The old Adam will ask "What do I have to sacrifice?" meaning, what am I re-
> quired to give up? . . . But the new Adam will ask "What do I have to sacrifice?"
> meaning, what do I possess that I may offer up to his glory?
>
> —David Fagerberg, *Consecrating the World*

Workers must carefully examine their work and their week before they approach the table. As we demonstrated earlier, Israelite workers were repeatedly
warned not to approach the altar with hands stained by marketplace sins.
Likewise, the early church was deeply concerned with examining the ethical
quality of the workers and workplace fruits offered at the altar. Both ancient
Israel and the early church provided workers with a variety of mechanisms
for marketplace atonement and restoration. Ancient workers were instructed
to examine their workplace sins and seek reconciliation *before* presenting
themselves and their work at the altar.

In a similar manner, before contemporary workers approach the Lord's
Table, churches can occasionally offer them a moment of vocational examination and confession. As Natalie prepares for her approach, she can ask
herself: Is there a rancorous battle with a coworker that needs to be confessed
or resolved? Has a customer been cheated? A report fudged? Did I offer the
Lord my best this week—my *first* fruits?

This moment of examination should not be skipped over or taken lightly.
After all, soon enough Natalie will be moving toward that table; she'll be offering herself and her work up to a holy God. She is about to lay down her
schedule, her projects, her meetings, her career ambitions, her whole labor
and life—all of it. Likewise, Christ himself is about to offer his whole life and
profound work to her. Is Natalie going to receive Christ's work with *these*
dirty hands? Before workers offer or receive, they need some liturgical space
to conduct a vocational "audit."

Beyond confessions, Natalie can also be prompted to examine any workplace laments or tears she might need to carry to Christ's Table. She is,
after all, about to visit a table that takes suffering, pain, and injustice rather
seriously. This particular table, stained with blood, will never put a rosy or
romantic glow on what it means to walk faithfully through a fallen world.
Natalie can carry the sexism in her office, her unfulfilled career ambitions,
the guilt she feels about dividing her time between her boss, her young children, husband, and parents—not to mention her unfair pay, her boredom,
and her stress. All of these vocational pains can be carried to the Lord's
Table. Through carrying these vocational laments forward, Natalie can fight

against her own unsustainable habit of attempting to carry her tears and anger on her own.

But the Lord's Table is not simply a place for sorrow-filled laments and confessions; it's also a place of great victory and celebration. If Natalie has received a promotion, a commendation, or perhaps a new academic degree, there will soon come an opportunity for her to come to the table in thanksgiving and praise. Natalie needs time to prepare for this moment. She needs space to examine her work for God's good gifts of beauty, goodness, and fruitfulness that need to be offered up in praise.

For all of these reasons, an examination of work should occur *before* approaching the table. Sins need to be examined, forgiveness sought, anger expressed, praises readied. The worker's hands, heart, and body need to be examined before they hold the work of God. All of it, her vocational trumpets, ashes, tears, petitions, and fruits can be gathered up and brought to the table of her Lord. Obviously, no single worker will engage all of this during a single trip to the table, but all are dimensions of the meal that can and should be experienced over time. A worker's complex pains and praises should be directed to Christ, and this is the opportunity. As Alexander Schmemann explains, "Only when this preparation is completed, when all is *referred* to the sacrifice of Christ and included in it, and our lives, 'hid with Christ in God,' . . . can we begin the liturgy" of the Lord's Table.[3]

The Worker Approaches

> Like children in the nursery, we are taught generosity by the making of little gifts; and so prepared for that total and mutual gift in which alone our lives are made complete.
>
> —Evelyn Underhill, *The Mystery of Sacrifice*

> The time has come now to offer to God the totality of all our lives, of ourselves, of the world in which we live. This is the first meaning of our bringing to the altar the elements of our food.
>
> —Alexander Schmemann, *For the Life of the World*

Having examined her work, Natalie approaches the table to offer up her life, her family, her work, her city to God in an act of worship. Strictly speaking, Natalie will never be fully prepared or worthy—in and of herself—to

3. Schmemann, *For the Life of the World*, 111.

approach the table. As we discussed earlier, work and workers who are fallen are only allowed to approach Christ's table when they come clothed in Christ himself. He is the high priest who enables their priestly offerings.

Christ alone can carry a worker to the table. Christ alone can make the worker new. Christ alone can turn Natalie's work into worship. As Alexander Schmemann explains, "It is Christ himself who takes all of us and the totality of our life to God in His eucharistic ascension."[4]

Natalie is called by God to approach the table. *This* is her first "calling." This is her primary vocation. Every other calling in Natalie's life is second-ary to this calling. Businesswoman, wife, mother, neighbor, friend, citizen, sister, and volunteer—all of these callings are relativized by her call to Christ's table. Christ bids her to come. He has called her by name. He has made her his holy priest.

Natalie's diverse callings are holy. They're all sacred spaces of priestly ser-vice, work, and worship. However, like all good things, each of these callings can claim supremacy in her life. Each of these callings can become an idol. In responding to the table's call, Natalie can remind herself on a weekly basis that Christ's call comes first. He has made her a daughter and priest of God. This is her primary identity, her primary title, her primary call. As Natalie approaches the table, she reminds herself that all of her other roles, titles, and callings are given meaning and direction from this singular calling. This calling in Christ directs all the others, not the other way around.

On occasion, workers can be encouraged to carry a physical object, a fruit from their work, to the table—something representative of their vocational life in the world. As we learned earlier, the *physical* presentation of unique and peculiar gifts played an important pedagogical role in the formation of workers in ancient Israel and the early church—not to mention the global church as well.

As Natalie approaches the table, she looks around and notices that she's not alone. Other workers are approaching as well. In her office, Natalie is the only Christian on her particular team. This reality often leaves her feeling lonely and isolated. Approaching the table, Natalie can watch as her broth-ers and sisters, faithful workers from all over the city, gather around a single table. The table visually reminds her of a theological truth she easily forgets while at work: she is not alone.

The approach of other workers to the table offers Natalie some private comfort, but it carries some public obligation as well. If these workers stand with Natalie, she must stand with them as well. In Christ they are one body,

4. Schmemann, *For the Life of the World*, 36.

united by the table. What happens to these workers in the marketplace happens to her as well. In fact, the table connects Natalie to a global body of workers who are struggling all over the world. In light of this, Natalie can no longer live and labor as if she's an autonomous free agent in the marketplace out to "get hers." Watching these workers approach the table and stand at her side, Natalie must awaken to the fact that she was never alone, never autonomous, never free to simply advance herself in the global marketplace. The ultimate purpose of Natalie's work is not her own flourishing, it's the flourishing of others. *She works so that others might work, worship, and flourish within God's gracious and just economy.*

Watching others approach the table, Natalie notices that blue-collar and white-collar workers are queuing up in a rather haphazard way. There is a CEO waiting behind a migrant worker; there is a professor behind a preschool teacher; over there is an investment banker behind a homeless person.[5] On Monday, the economy of the world will quickly sort and rank these people according to their education, age, ability, race, appearance, gender, and productivity. An invisible hand will assign them a value. Soon enough these "human resources" will be monetized. But here, on Sunday, the economy of the table forces rich and poor, high-tech and low-tech, into a single-file line. There is nothing these workers can do to earn a spot at the front, nothing they can do to get a larger portion of bread. No amount of hustle, no networking prowess, no family connection—nothing will get them to the table any faster. Here workers slowly and clumsily begin to practice and participate in an upside-down economy in which—sometimes, at least—the last go first.

As Natalie watches her fellow workers approach the table, she ponders one last thing. These workers are, on the whole, terribly ordinary, terrifically mundane. None of them, as far as she can tell, is "changing the world." In fact, Natalie has been listening to their workplace stories for years now, and those stories are, for the most part, spectacularly dull.

While the mundane and monotonous details of their jobs bored Natalie in the past, on this particular morning they fill her with comfort. Why? Natalie has been troubled all week by an alumni magazine she received in the mail from her alma mater. The magazine featured a select group of her former classmates who were all working in a variety of exotic and fascinating careers all around the world. Reading the magazine over her lunch break, Natalie pondered her mid-level management position, at a mid-level company, in

---

5. We are well aware that it is rare to have such a broad range of economic diversity in one congregation, but one of the many benefits of working toward this biblical vision of a socio-economically diverse church is that it can teach workers to serve and wait in line behind people whom the economy dismisses, dehumanizes, or ignores.

a mid-level suburb, in what feels like a mid-level life. Flipping through the pages, she wondered to herself, "Does my mid-level career matter?" To make matters worse, earlier in the worship service Natalie struggled with feelings of inadequacy as she watched a video about a missionary doing inspiring church planting work in Haiti and an urban activist heroically fighting for racial justice in St. Louis.

A Song of Offering

The mystery of how God transforms the labor of workers into the sacraments is filled with beauty and power. In this song by the Porter's Gate collective we see this sacred exchange between workers and their God.

"God the Maker"

Verse 1
We bring our time, we bring our treasure,
we lay them down before Your throne.
You will make them something greater,
more than we could ever know.

Chorus
Glory be to God, the Maker
glory be to God, Creator
take our time, use our treasure
turn them into something greater:
Glory be to God, the Maker.

Verse 2
We bring our gifts, we bring our power
place them in Your sov'reign hand.
You will take what we have given,
You will use it for Your plan.

Verse 3
Though our hearts are weak from failure,
broken dreams and failed attempts,
show us that in ev'ry season,
You will fill our emptiness.[a]

a. Lyrics and music by Paul Zach, David Gungor, and Isaac Wardell, featuring Latifah Alattas, from *Work Songs* (Porter's Gate Publishing, 2017), available at https://theportersgate.bandcamp .com/track/god-the-maker-feat-latifah-alattas. Used with permission of Porter's Gate Publishing.

And yet, as Natalie watches her fellow "ordinary" and "mundane" workers approach the table, she catches herself. She's reminded that their ordinary work is processing into the extraordinary work of Christ. She remembers that Christ the common carpenter took ordinary mud and made a blind man see. She remembers that Christ took ordinary fish and fed five thousand people. She remembers that Christ took ordinary women and men, fishermen and tentmakers, and began a movement that would overturn an empire. Finally, arriving at the table, Natalie remembers that the carpenter took ordinary bread from an ordinary servant coming out of an ordinary kitchen and began to work the extraordinary.

The Worker Thanks

> Through your goodness we have this bread to offer, which earth has given and human hands have made. . . . Through your goodness we have this wine to offer, fruit of the vine and work of human hands. . . . Be present, be present, make yourself known in the breaking of bread.
>
> —Anglican Offertory, in *Anglican Eucharistic Liturgies 1985–2010*

Having examined their work and approached the table, workers are now engaged in an act of thanksgiving. Bread and wine, the handcrafted products of human industry, are lifted into the air. The pastoral words of thanksgiving are being said. The workers gaze on the bread and wine, the mysterious amalgamation of mortal and immortal labor—"the gifts of God for the people of God."

The simple act of elevation and thanksgiving can intersect with a worker's daily labor in a number of ways. In giving thanks for the bread and wine, Natalie can acknowledge that God alone gave her hands to work, a mind to think, and a creation to order, craft, fill, and enjoy. She can remember that it was God who provided her with a family, an education, and an internship. It was God who provided her with coworkers with whom she can learn and collaborate. It was God who provided her with protection from that disastrous merger. Natalie is not simply giving thanks for a loaf of bread or a cup of wine; she is giving thanks for her daily work and, more importantly, for the work of God in her office.

With bread and wine lifted high, Natalie can give thanks that her imperfect work can, in Christ, be included in the economy of God. Lesslie Newbigin captures the chastened thanksgiving of the worker: "We can commit ourselves without reserve to all the secular work our shared humanity requires of us, knowing that nothing we do in itself is good enough to form part of that [heavenly] city's building . . . and yet knowing that as we offer [our work] up to the Father in the name of Christ and in the power of the Spirit, it is safe with him and—purged in fire—it will find its place in the holy city at the end."[6]

The Worker Receives

> Feasting at the table is both a summons for our work . . . and a reassurance that [the great] work has already been done.
>
> —David Jensen, *Responsive Labor*

Teaching a modern worker to receive is a more difficult challenge than one might initially suspect. After a long week of striving and scratching in the marketplace for every economic fruit she can, Natalie enters the sanctuary. Now she is being told that she can *do nothing*. After a week of striving, she is being told to stop, to rest, and to receive. The transition is jarring. At this strange table there is nothing she can do to earn these fruits. Her only task now is to open her hands and accept them. There, placed in her palm, is a profit she cannot earn. A great project has been completed on Natalie's behalf, *and she can have no part whatsoever in its completion.*

In humbly receiving bread and wine, the worker encounters a perplexing and beautiful paradox at the intersection between faith, work, and worship. Two messages are being communicated to Natalie at once. First, her work is good and can participate in the mighty work of God. And yet, second, here, in the moment of reception, she is in a position of total dependence and total reliance. The worker can do nothing. She can participate in no way. Standing there, Natalie is forced to admit, "Here is a cross I cannot carry, a hill I cannot climb, a work I cannot do. My task is only to receive."

In the moment of reception, Natalie must actively practice reliance and rest. She must rest in a work that is already finished, in a task already complete. The work of Christ, embodied in bread and wine, actively demands that Natalie stop her professional strivings. Week after week, workers have to practice resting in the gracious economy of God at the table.

Natalie will have to remember this gift (and this practice) when she leaves the table and returns to work. She will need to work within the "practiced knowledge" that the great work is already finished. Going forward, Natalie's work should be marked by a profound *restfulness*. Her work patterns should

---

6. Newbigin, *Foolishness to the Greeks*, 136.

emit an unhurried calm; they should evoke a profound peace. Natalie's habits of striving and grasping are now out of bounds. Receiving God's work, she must cease her hurried work. As she moves through her office, she no longer can "carry the weight of the world" on her shoulders. That weight was already lifted; it is no longer hers to bear.

A single trip to the Lord's Table does not a restful worker make. The practice of reception, of resting and relying, must be *practiced*. Through the power of the Spirit, Natalie is going to have to habituate her rest in Christ. Again and again she will need to return to the table to practice opening her tight fists and receiving this great work accomplished on her behalf.

Here at the table, before they return to a world that ritualizes economic patterns of striving, self-sufficiency, and exhaustion, workers have an opportunity to rest and receive. Here at the table, workers are given an opportunity to ritualize a Sabbath economy, one of rest and restoration.

The Worker Shares

> If bread is not broken, it cannot be distributed. Good work, too, bears the traces of these seams—broken open so that others are invited in.
>
> —David Jensen, *Responsive Labor*

Having received, workers now have an opportunity to share the work of God and humanity with others. In sharing bread and wine, Natalie can practice extending the gracious economy of God to those beyond herself.

Natalie watches persons from a variety of professions, who might otherwise be at odds, sharing the work of Christ with one another. A defense lawyer is serving a prosecutor; a union worker is serving a CEO; a doctor is assisting a nurse; the owner of a local bookstore is serving an Amazon delivery driver. In the economy of the world, these workers might very well be drawn into a Darwinian struggle. And yet here, at the table, they're invited to practice a strange economy of mutuality and solidarity.[7] At the table, God's work is

---

7. Michael Rhodes comments on the centrality of God's economy in the early church's observance of the Lord's Supper:

> The failure to embrace this unity across class boundaries drives Paul to say that the Corinthians are in fact not celebrating the Lord's Supper at all. In Corinth, the Lord's Supper meal was apparently shared unequally among rich and poor, and such lack of concern for the poor totally invalidated worship. . . . Because their liturgy reinforced economic distinctions it would have been better had they not gathered at all. . . . But when celebrated rightly, this liturgy fuelled a counter-cultural economic imagination in the early church that nurtured the radical economic sharing of Acts 2 and 4; the liturgy

not being hoarded; it's being broken open, poured out, and shared. The final purpose of God's work is not individual profit but the freedom and nourishment of all. Could Natalie's work have a similar purpose?

In sharing, workers do not listen to a theological lecture about economic ethics. Instead, at the table they have an opportunity to physically practice a gracious economy with one another. Here workers share the fruits of hard labor *before* they consume it for themselves. Rather than grasping out of self-interest, they try out the rather unfamiliar economic gestures of sharing.

In sharing, Natalie enacts a theology of work that embodies two critical truths about the ultimate meaning and purpose of profit. First, there is nothing inherently evil about the profits that Natalie earns. In fact, Natalie's profits (her fruits) are *so good* that they are being lifted up, sanctified, broken, and shared with the community right here at God's holy table. Natalie should take righteous joy and pride in the profits she earns and presents. Second, as Natalie passes her cup to others, she is reminded that her profits ultimately exist not for herself but for the flourishing of her neighbors and the glory of her God. The final purpose of Natalie's work is not her own independence, security, or self-sufficiency; it's a deeper communion with others and with Christ.

John Chrysostom, an early church father, deeply understood this eucharistic economy. He argues in a sermon on 1 Corinthians 3 that good work must be continually shared or "communicated" with others.

> For the smith, if he chose to impart his craft to no one, ruins both himself and all other crafts. Likewise the cordwainer, the husbandman, the baker, and every one of those who pursue any necessary calling; if he chose not to communicate to anyone the results of his art, will ruin not the others only but himself also with them . . . . For in everything to give and receive is the principle of numerous blessings: in seeds, in scholars, in arts. *For if any one desire to keep his art to himself, he subverts both himself and the whole course of things.*[8]

He writes, when it comes to wealth, "If you enjoy it alone, you too have lost it. . . . But if you possess it jointly with the rest, then will it be more your own."[9] In sharing at the table, the worker can watch as "the curse of human labor is transformed into a blessing."[10]

---

undergirded the Jubilee practice, just as the Deuteronomic tithe-meal undergirded the OT economic legislation. (Rhodes, "'Follow Us as We Follow Moses,'" 188–89)

8. John Chrysostom, *Homilies on First Corinthians* 10.7, 57 (emphasis added).

9. John Chrysostom, *Homilies on First Corinthians* 10.7, 57.

10. Henderson, Quinn, and Larson, *Liturgy, Justice, and the Reign of God*, 99.

The Worker Holds

> God . . . is not far away from us, altogether apart from the world we see, touch, hear, smell and taste about us. Rather he awaits us every instant in our action, in the work of the moment. There is a sense in which he is at the tip of my pen, my spade, my brush, my needle—of my heart and of my thought.
>
> —Pierre Teilhard de Chardin, *The Divine Milieu*

> There is a danger in a very word-oriented service on the theme of work . . . work is experienced . . . and so, for most people, it is rarely put into words.
>
> —Cameron Butland, *Work in Worship*

Holding real bread and real wine in their hands, workers can meditate on the work of Christ in their lives and labor. Natalie's mind, of course, could go in a million different directions. What follows are just a few things on which she might ponder while she holds the work of Christ.

Natalie could consider that resting in her hands is a confounding amalgamation of Christ's faithfulness and her own rebellion. On the one hand, the bread reminds her of the curse of her own work. Like her own company, this bread's industrial production is bound up in a sinful global economy filled with economic injustice, environmental degradation, greed, racism, sexism, and everything else that is sinful and broken in the world. Natalie shudders at the unjust structures of the global economy and her own complicity in them.

But that is not the end of it. There is another side. The bread in her hands can also remind Natalie of the goodness of God moving through the global economy as well. Bound up in this small piece of bread is the divine miracle of seed, soil, and grain. Bound up in this bread is the divine miracle of a hardworking farmer, his cultivation, care, and agricultural wisdom. Bound up in this bread is the craftsmanship, diligence, and coordination of a whole team of bakers.

Here, with this bread in her hands, Natalie can ponder the mysterious mixture of brokenness and beauty in her work and in the world. Both Natalie and her work are a messy amalgamation of faithfulness and rebellion, creativity and corruption, a complex mess that Christ, in his mysterious grace, has decided to work within.

While Natalie holds the bread, her mind might wander elsewhere. Running her fingers over the sharp edges of the crust, she might be reminded that, like this bread, Jesus is profoundly—even uncomfortably—close. Christ is near, not simply in the sanctuary but in her daily labor as well. Christ's raw and real presence is made clear to her, right here in the rough edges of this bread.

Holding and pausing, the worker is given some of the most precious gifts available in the modern global economy—time, space, and silence. Moreover, in many worship services, the worker has been constantly spoken to, given directions, lessons, and answers. Here, just for a moment, workers like Natalie are given a sacred silence to ponder the work of Christ in their lives.

The silence may not give workers clear or crisp answers to all the questions they bring to the table. However, standing there, holding her bread and wine, Natalie will receive something more precious than answers. She will receive a presence—the same presence that will be with her tomorrow at her desk.

The Worker Consumes

[Your bread and wine] must invade my life. My life must become, as a result of the sacrament, an unlimited and endless contact with you.

—Pierre Teilhard de Chardin, *The Divine Milieu*

Having held the bread, workers now begin to consume it—a gastronomical reminder that Christ is in them and they are in Christ. Nourished by the work of God, one with him, disciples can work in the world, not by their strength but by Christ's strength in them.

Consuming the wine, Natalie allows it to linger on her tongue for an extra moment—savoring the flavor, depth, and beauty. Rich and robust, *this* is the work of Christ, she thinks to herself—delight-full. Tasting the wine, she celebrates Christ's complex goodness in her life and labor. She enjoys him. She delights in him. Like the feasting Israelites of old, Natalie stops and celebrates the goodness of God's abundant work in her life; she recalls the many harvests God has brought into her storehouses.

John Calvin considered food and flavor, color and aroma to be the gracious gifts of a lavish creator. They represented a divine superabundance that the faithful must stop and savor. Within the divine economy, color and flavor are not purely utilitarian. Good food and good drink are more than vitamins and minerals, proteins and calories. They were created for the joy and delight of humanity. Calvin writes, "Now if we ponder to what end God created food, we shall find that he meant not only to provide for necessity but also for delight and good cheer."[11] Elsewhere Calvin writes that the "addition of wine is

---

11. Calvin, *Institutes of the Christian Religion* 3.10.2, 720–21.

owing to God's superabundant liberality. . . . His liberality appears still more conspicuous in giving us dainties."[12]

Obviously, it would be ideal if the Lord's Supper were *an actual supper*. As we learned from the festive meals of ancient Israel and the early church, feasts matter. Workers gain something important in preparing, gathering, and feasting together on the Lord's harvest. Likewise, something important is lost when the table is divested of flavor and feasting. Something is lost when a worker is given little else but a single-serving cracker and a chaser of juice.

Savoring the flavors of the feast, Natalie can begin to develop not only a sense of gratitude but a sense of responsibility as well. She can ask herself: Does my work add flavor, depth, color, or beauty to my workplace? When people receive my work, do they receive it as a superabundant blessing that gladdens their hearts? My work may be ethical, but does it emit a pleasing aroma?

Conclusion

> I carry thee as food on my journey.
>
> —The Maronite Liturgy,
> quoted in Evelyn Underhill,
> *The Mystery of Sacrifice*

While the rest of worship has invited the worker to enter into God's economy, at the table, God's gracious economy has actually entered into the worker. Christ and the worker are now one. Natalie can now work *in Christ*. Christ will be her grace at work. Christ will be her offering at work. Her strength. Her peace. Natalie's work will be worship, through Christ's work in her.

---

12. Calvin, *Commentary on the Book of Psalms*, 155–56 (on Ps. 104:15).

11

Worship That Gathers Workers

But what might "worship for workers" actually look like in contemporary practice? How might a worship leader implement these pages of biblical, historical, and global insight on a Sunday morning? In these final chapters we provide readers with tangible principles and practices for developing worship that is vocationally conversant.

Once again, this is not a "how-to" book. We're not interested in prescribing a one-size-fits-all solution for diverse worshiping communities. Every church, culture, and local marketplace is distinct. Gathered worship should be responsive to the particular workforce that it serves. The praises and petitions of rural dairy farmers in Canada will differ from those of urban software engineers in Hong Kong. An aged industrial city that has just closed its last factory and a youthful metropolis whose tech sector is booming will each require a different set of congregational prayers. When it comes to developing worship for workers, we cannot and should not prescribe a singular approach.

That said, we don't want to leave the reader empty-handed. Throughout the final two chapters we provide a variety of practical examples and guiding principles for developing worship that engages workers. *We hope that these chapters serve as a generative starting point, a lens through which diverse leaders can imagine their own creative and responsive liturgies for workers in their midst*. Worship leaders looking for work-focused congregational songs, prayers, and confessions should consult the resources in the footnotes.[1]

The many ideas, practices, and resources explored below might seem overwhelming to exhausted pastors and worship leaders who are simply trying to recover from the last Sunday and prepare for the next. We encourage those who feel this way to initially select one or two places where they would like to start. Don't try to do everything at once.

Pastors and worship leaders from less formal worship traditions should not be turned off by the more formal congregational prayers that we provide below. They need not be dictated as written. Pay attention to the prayers' structure and purpose—make them your own. In the same way, musicians should not limit themselves to the rural or industrial work songs of the past. They should feel empowered to write new vocationally conversant songs for the future. Our songs should find inspiration in the theological and vocational wisdom of the past while being ever responsive to the new work of God and the people in the world today.

In this chapter we outline and discuss a variety of resources and models for *gathering* workers and work into the sanctuary. In the next chapter we explore the inverse, worship practices for *scattering* workers meaningfully back into the world. In all, these principles and practices are meant to serve as an opening invitation for the modern Western church to join its ancient brothers and sisters in connecting their faith and work through worship.

How to Gather Workers in Worship

As we learned in our examination of ancient Israel and the early church, workers should never appear before God empty-handed. Workers need to carry their lives (and their labor) with them into God's presence. Corporate worship, therefore, must be intentionally designed to encourage workers to humbly offer their work and their whole lives as sacrifices—holy and pleasing—to God. It is important here to call to mind our discussion from

---

1. Excellent liturgical resources can be found in Fanucci, *To Bless Our Callings*; Butland, *Work in Worship* (rev. ed.); McKelvey, *Every Moment Holy*; The Porter's Gate Worship Project, *Work Songs*, https://theportersgate.bandcamp.com/releases; Theology of Work Project, https://www.theologyofwork.org/work-in-worship; Calvin Institute of Christian Worship, https://worship.calvin.edu/resources/resource-library/worship-resources-about-faith-and-work.

chapter 1. There we discussed five elements that workers need to carry with them into the sanctuary: vocational laments (tears), vocational praises (trumpets), vocational confessions (ashes), vocational requests (petitions), and vocational offerings (fruits). In this chapter we will discuss *how* a worship service can actually invite workers to carry in (and lay down) their vocational lives before God.

Before we do this, we need to briefly address three preliminary issues: (1) how a worker *prepares* for vocationally conversant worship, (2) the *space* in which vocationally conversant worship occurs, and (3) the pastoral *welcome* that will invite these workers to begin vocationally conversant worship. These elements of preparation, space, and welcome are important factors in effectively gathering workers into worship.

Preparation: A Worker's Journey to Worship

Whether they walk, ride, or drive, what happens during the workers' journey into corporate worship actually matters. "Bringing your work to worship" is not natural for modern Western worshipers. It takes intentionality and practice. Workers need to actively prepare *during their journey* to bring their work into the sanctuary.

Workers can learn a lot here from the ancient "psalms of ascent" (Pss. 120–134). These ancient songs and prayers were designed specifically to serve the Israelites as they left their fields and markets and began ascending the mountain of Zion to participate in worship in the Jerusalem temple.[2] The psalms of ascent actively encouraged Israelites to carry their daily lives up the mountain to the Lord. Their experiences of war, famine, injustice, harvest, toil, economic distress—all of it could be carried into worship. In Psalm 122 worshipers carry a variety of petitions to the temple. They climb, wanting to intercede for their city, to plead with God for its shalom, its security, and its economic prosperity. In Psalm 126 worshipers carry their tears and sorrow up the mountain in the hopes that, on their returning descent, they will carry joy and find laid out before them a fruitful harvest. Nothing is out of bounds; everything can be carried to Yahweh.

Contemporary workers have much to learn about liturgical honesty and dialogue from the psalms of ascent. A worker's journey into corporate worship is an opportunity for honest vocational examination. As a modern family

---

2. We are focusing in this section on the ways in which these psalms have been used by God's people over the centuries. We see that they played a formational role as "commuter liturgies" or pilgrim prayer psalms, preparing worshipers for the communal liturgies of the temple. See Goldingay, *Psalms*, 1:26; Kidner, *Psalms 1–72*, 19–20, 58.

travels to worship, they can discuss and prepare together. A simple reflective question for the journey might be "What from your week do you need to bring to God today?"[3] Prayerful conversations on the bus or the walk can prepare worshipers to inhabit the sanctuary differently. They can enter mindful of the things they need to honestly bring before God.

Some worshipers might need to carry physical items in their pockets that remind them of specific trumpets, ashes, tears, petitions, or fruits that need to be carried in. Pastors and worship leaders can provide a simple exercise, a family conversation prompt, or a written psalm to help workers prepare for an honest dialogue with God on Sunday.

Space: Art and Architecture That Gather Workers

Is a person's working life welcome in this sanctuary? Do workers truly matter in this place? Worship spaces can visually encourage worshipers to bring their weekly experiences into worship. They can accomplish this through art, architecture, and a variety of other powerful visual signals.

Unfortunately, the inverse is also true. Worship spaces also can visually *discourage* workers from truly showing up. Pastors and worship leaders should consider the visual signals they send to workers about *what* and *who* is truly welcome in worship. What images, for example, are most prominent on your walls and projector screens during your songs and sermons? Images of pristine rural meadows and starry skies? Or images of the city and streets that your people pray for and work in on a daily basis? Which vocations are visually represented on center stage? Are workers invited to visually lead the community in prayers and readings, or is center stage reserved for church staff alone? What visual signals is your worship space sending week in and week out? Is the priesthood of all believers visually welcomed? Are their parishes acknowledged?

The temple in ancient Israel was filled with vivid images of Eden, nature, and the world of agriculture (e.g., the flowers, gourds, and palm trees described in 1 Kings 6). These images reminded the people that God was the creator and sustainer of their lands, their crops, and their herds. God was the crafter and cultivator of Eden. The art and architecture of the temple pointed worshipers to their own creative calling to cultivate the earth. For, if Adam and Eve were "garden priests" called to worship God through work in the garden-temple, the Israelites were called to be a nation of priests, worshiping

---

3. Parents of younger children might adapt this question to "What are the highs or lows—things that made you sad or smile this week—that you want to speak to God about today?"

and glorifying God through the cultivation of Canaan. Offering the fruits of God's garden back to God was an act of worship. *This theological and vocational truth was visually reinforced through the agricultural images surrounding the worship space.*

We remember also the early Christian art and architecture of the Basilica di Aquileia near Venice (see chap. 9). The beautiful mosaics on the floors and walls of the ancient sanctuary are filled with earthy images of fishing, cultivation, and work: Christ working as a shepherd; boats and fishermen; workers carrying their fruits and flowers, their fish, grapes, and bread joyfully into worship. All of these images surrounded workers as they worshiped in the sanctuary—the great economy of God manifest in nature and the city visually enveloped them.

The earthy art and architecture of Israel's temple and the great Basilica di Aquileia prompt contemporary readers to ask, "How might our worship spaces visually encourage workers to connect their faith and work while they worship?"

Temple Beth Am is a beautifully constructed synagogue in Los Angeles. It is a visually powerful worship space to engage for a wide variety of artistic and architectural reasons. We wish to highlight one facet of its visual power: aesthetic honesty. The sanctuary space is profoundly honest about the beauty and brokenness of life in the world. Its visual depiction of truth, as we will see, invites all those who enter to be honest with God about the praises and the pains they carry inside. Rather than providing an escape from the world, the sanctuary encourages worshipers to actively connect God's word and

Figure 11.1. The sanctuary at Temple Beth Am.

Figure 11.2. The front right side of the sanctuary of Temple Beth Am.

work in history (the Torah) to their community's public lives of both praise and lament.

At the center of the sanctuary stands a replicated ark of the covenant, in which the scrolls of the Torah are kept. The wall to the right contains triumphant images and phrases from traditional Jewish harvests, festivals, and Scriptures reminding the people of the goodness of God. The menorah recalls the nearness and faithfulness of God, even in times of trouble. These visuals are designed to alert worshipers to God's steadfast presence and power in their communal history, their daily lives and world.

If the right side recalls the beauty and goodness of life in the world, the wall on the left side calls to mind its ugliness and evil. Here a light fixture of gnarled metal and razor wire casts dark shadows on the wall like tears staining a cheek. This six-piece fixture memorializes the six million Jews murdered in the Holocaust. The wall visually evokes the losses and laments of the Jewish community, including the Shoah, the medieval pogroms, and the destruction of the Second Temple.

The walls hem in the worshipers, not allowing them to ignore either the faithfulness of God or the violence of the world. Worshipers are made to

Figure 11.3. The front left side of the sanctuary of Temple Beth Am.

sit with two realities: divine blessing and gnawing heartbreak—six lights of horror, seven lights of hope. From either side the trumpets and tears of real life *visually* inform their spiritual songs and prayers. Sugary and saccharine prayers that romanticize life in the world have no place next to a Holocaust memorial. The walls joyfully declaring the harvests and feasts of God's faithfulness will not abide a cynical or hopeless message from the rabbi.

The aesthetic design of the synagogue can aid the congregation in developing honest habits of worldly reflection in worship. The architecture of Temple Beth Am speaks to the community (and to us) about how joyful praise and honest lament can both find their place in holy worship. Its art and architecture facilitate not an escape from the world but rather a deeper and more honest engagement with it.

Again, we emphasize that pastors and worship leaders should carefully consider the visual signals they send to workers about *what* and *who* is truly welcome in worship. What visual signals is your worship space sending to workers week in and week out? What visual changes can be made to gather work and workers in?

A Welcoming Opening Prayer

Father, Son, and Holy Spirit,
We gather this morning from all over your city;
  we gather from the places you've called us to serve.
We come with hearts, minds, and hands that are full, Lord,
  full of stories to tell:
  stories of praise and thanksgiving,
  stories of sadness and confession.
Some of us carry urgent requests for you, Lord;
  we need you to move quickly in our lives and our world.
We carry these things before you, Lord,
  openly and honestly
  as an act of love for you and our neighbor.
May all of our offerings
  be a sacrifice of praise to you this day.
Gather our stories into your story,
  gather our work into your work,
  bring our lives into your life.
For you have called us here, Lord,
  you have carried us,
  and all these things, to you.
And so we gather, Lord, for worship,
  not by our power, but by the power of your Spirit;
  not in our name, but in the name of your Son.
May we, today, be a sacrifice of praise to you. Amen.[a]

a. Prayer by Matthew Kaemingk. Other examples of opening prayers can be found at the Theology of Work Project website: https://www.theologyofwork.org/work-in-worship/prayer-material-for-services/opening-prayers.

Welcome: The Pastoral Invitation

The pastoral welcome at the beginning of a worship service plays a vital role in bridging the gap between the world of work and the world of worship. This welcome and prayer can *acknowledge* that workers have had a week full of diverse and complex experiences in the world. It can *invite* those diverse experiences into the sanctuary. Your vocational trumpets and fruits are welcome here, as are your vocational tears, ashes, and petitions. Finally, the pastoral welcome can *submit* the people's week and work to the work of God. The language employed here is critical. Pastoral welcomes should avoid any hint of a hierarchy between clergy and laity, worship and work. The priestly calling of *all* worshipers needs to be reinforced. (For an example of an opening prayer that actively welcomes workers and their work, see the sidebar "A Welcoming Opening Prayer.")

Gathering Workplace Tears

> Please, Lord, the load of slavery is so heavy
> it's about to destroy us all.
> The grass in the cotton field is so high.
> The sun is so hot.
> We almost perish in the middle of the day.
> Do, Master, have mercy and help us please.
>
> —Slave minister's prayer,
> quoted in Frederick C. Knight,
> *Working the Diaspora*

Every Sunday, many workers will arrive at church feeling stressed, bored, angry, or heartbroken about their various callings in the world. While their emotions are palpable, they often don't know how to communicate their vocational frustrations to God. Tears—in their minds—are not welcome in the sanctuary. Anger—in their minds—can't be a form of worship. Some fear that God can't handle their rage. Others imagine that God is interested only in festive praise or humble confession.[4]

---

4. It may seem counterintuitive to begin our discussion with pain as opposed to praise. It is true that praise is the bedrock of the Christian life. It is the foundation from which all prayer begins and the *telos* that we are oriented to in seeking the glory of God. We must never forget this truth. And yet in many churches in North America, distorted forms of praise have arisen that drown out the voicing of suffering and sorrows of life. "If we just sing our praises louder, perhaps the pain will go away" is the mentality that rules the day. This approach to praise is antithetical to the spirituality of the psalms. Praise arises from experiences of pain and not just from joy (compare Ps. 40 and Ps. 150). The psalms do their formative work by embracing workers in the midst of their tangled experiences of despair, anxiety, and hope and involving them in a dialogue with God.

When worship focuses on praise to the exclusion of sorrow and suffering, the spiritual vitality of workers withers. This is true for both blue-collar workers and white-collar workers. Praise can function to transform pain by keeping hope alive on the horizon. And even more importantly for workers, pain can keep our praise honest rather being an act of pretending. *"The praise has power to transform the pain. But conversely the present pain also keeps the act of praise honest"* (Brueggemann, *Israel's Praise*, 133).

Unemployment Service Offertory Prayer

Some congregations have organized special lament services for the unemployed. The following is an example of a prayer that might be offered.

Lord Jesus, we bring before you the impoverishment of
unemployment:
the waste of human potential,
the undermining of relationships,
the devastation of communities.

We bring before you the great injustices of our industrial society.
We bring before you our nation,
with all its divisions between rich and poor,
powerful and powerless,
north and south,
employed and unemployed.

Lord Jesus, we bring before you all these weighty concerns.
We offer them with these our gifts of bread and wine,
praying that as the bread and wine are transformed into your
Body and Blood,
so our nation may be transformed,
so that your grace may flow into our world,
bringing hope and healing, reconciliation and peace,
joy and understanding. Amen.[a]

a. Cameron Butland, *Work in Worship: A Treasury of Prayers, Readings, and Hymns* (London: Hodder & Stoughton, 1985), 192. Reproduced by permission of Hodder & Stoughton Limited.

In previous chapters we uncovered multiple examples of ancient workers being invited to bring their workplace tears and laments to God. In their slavery, the ancient Israelites cried out loudly to God in prayer. God not only

---

There is a challenge for pastors serving workers in contexts where the habits of praise are misshapen. The task is to help workers pray their way down to the source of the hurt and hold it before God. This approach to worship may not be popular with everyone in the church, especially with those accustomed to liturgies that anxiously reassure workers that the world is not such a bad or painful place after all (Brueggemann, *Israel's Praise*, 159–60). But in every church we have encountered we have found a contingency of workers who are hungry for honest conversations about the raw realities of work. What they long for are expressions of worship in which lament and praise are not experienced as mutually exclusive.

heard but also actively responded to their vocational groanings with delivering power (Exod. 1:6–14; 2:23–25; 3:7–10). Likewise, the psalmist cries openly to God that the "wicked man" in the marketplace always seems to get ahead while faithful workers are left behind (Ps. 10). In African American spirituals we witness oppressed workers crying out for God to deliver them from their cruel masters. In these gut-level groans we learn that God gives ear to the laments of workers. God saw their tears in the past and sees ours today as well.

Those who plan and lead worship have a responsibility to remind worshipers that it is both right and good for them to carry their vocational tears before God. Worship leaders can offer workers more than a mere verbal reminder of this fact. They can create intentional spaces within worship to encourage

Guided Prayer Exercise for a Service of Lament

Reflect and Write: Think of a situation in your working life that might warrant lament. If nothing comes to mind, think of someone close to you whose experience of work requires lament. Write out the circumstances of this situation following these steps:

- Read two lament psalms. (Some possibilities are Pss. 13; 22; 44; 88; 89.)
- Think through the emotions that you (or the psalmists) are feeling in the workplace. Be as descriptive and specific as possible. Good poetry communicates emotion and experience, not just facts.
- Identify images and metaphors that capture the experience of these vocational emotions and circumstances. You want your metaphors to evoke empathy in the one hearing your lament (which in this case is God). This is a difficult step, for it's at this point that the depth of your grief is beginning to be articulated.
- Finally, gather these reflections and write your own psalm of lament to God. Make sure that you're addressing God and writing this as a prayer to him. You might include a plea for God's attention; an articulation of your circumstance; expressions of pain, shock, anger, frustration that you have felt through words and metaphors; questions to God; and pleas for deliverance.
- Once you have written your lament, pray your way through it.

them to do so. For example, some congregations conduct services of prayer and lament for those who are unemployed (see the sidebar "Unemployment Service Offertory Prayer").

One simple practice is to invite workers to write down a sentence or two describing a specific longing for God's healing and justice in their working lives. These prayers can be placed in the offering plate or carried forward to the table. A group of leaders can covenant to both carry and pray through these laments in the coming week. With permission of the writers, a few of these laments might be projected onto the walls of the sanctuary the following Sunday.[5] The visual projection of the people's vocational heartbreaks might ground their prayers the following week.

A second option is that during a dedicated service of lament pastors can lead their community through a guided prayer exercise. (For an example, see the sidebar "Guided Prayer Exercise for a Service of Lament.") Specific psalms of lament can be read aloud, and workers can even be invited to write their own.

A third option might appeal to leaders interested in providing visual and physical prompts. Pastor Jen Rozema wanted to find a creative way of helping her congregation prepare for Lent through the practice of lament. Inspired by the architecture of Temple Beth Am, she created an inviting space at the front of the sanctuary for people to bring forward laments from their daily lives. Congregants were invited to come forward during songs and prayers and write their laments on a piece of paper. A rock wall was constructed where they could insert their prayers into the cracks.

At first, Rozema was uncertain about her liturgical experiment, even a bit skeptical. She wondered if the congregation would come forward and truly engage. She wondered if the practice would have staying power throughout the multiple weeks of Lent. Rozema was surprised by the response. After the first week of instruction and invitation, people began to come forward week after week without any pastoral prompting or invitation.

These illustrative examples of vocational lament can be used to stimulate creative pastoral responses that are appropriate to your own context. No matter the form, the central focus should be to find meaningful ways of equipping the priesthood of all believers to articulate their own vocational laments to God.

---

5. Discernment is needed about what should and should not be projected on the walls. Some laments may be too specific and indicate who is voicing the prayer. If it is known who wrote the lament, then permission should be sought before including it. If not, and the lament is sufficiently broad and the author indecipherable, then it may be included.

Figures 11.4. and **11.5.** These photos are of the lament wall at the front left side of the sanctuary of Park Christian Reformed Church in Holland, Michigan.

Gathering Workplace Trumpets

> Then Samuel took a stone and set it up. . . . He named it Ebenezer, saying, "Thus far the LORD has helped us."
>
> —1 Samuel 7:12

After a great military victory, the prophet Samuel recognized the people's need to pause and physically mark the great work God had accomplished in their midst. Likewise, people today need to regularly stop and praise God for his providential care, protection, and provision in their lives. When the harvest is gathered safely inside, the community needs to blast its trumpets of praise.

As we emphasize in previous chapters, there are two noteworthy reasons workers need to offer praise and thanksgiving. First, God is the worthy object of our vocational praises. God alone is the creator and sustainer of our daily work. Therefore, it is right, good, and even commanded that we give God praise for our vocational harvests. Second, in the physical act of offering vocational praises to God, workers learn something important about themselves and their work. Blowing trumpets of praise toward God (not toward ourselves) reminds us of the proper object of workplace praise. In times of great harvest, workers need to be reminded that they are not self-sufficient, self-made men and women. Their boom crops, bonuses, and promotions are thanks to the *unmerited* favor of God. Workers, both ancient and modern, are prone to lapses in economic memory. They're prone to forget that, without God, they would still be slaves in Egypt.

Finally, whenever a worker encounters a great professional blessing, a lavish and festive period of celebration is needed. Parties matter. Feasts are critical. According to the Old Testament, faithful workers require festive diversions in which God can be praised, good food enjoyed, coworkers acknowledged, and the marginalized blessed. After their harvest, the Israelites were commanded to stop their work, buy their favorite food and drink, and throw a lavish feast of both worship and celebration. Around the feasting table, these workers could remember not only the source of their profits (God) but also the ultimate end of their profits (the joy and flourishing of the whole community). Israel's joy-filled theology of work was developed *through the feast*. The God of the harvest is worthy of our workplace praises, trumpets, and parties. This theological truth needs to be liturgically practiced in the congregation and habituated in its feasts. (For an example of a prayer for liturgical use, see the sidebar "Thanks and Petition to God for Work and Workers.")

Beyond the sanctuary, congregations need to develop their own informal patterns of celebration for vocational triumphs among their members. Pro-

Thanks and Petition to God for Work and Workers

The following responsive prayer welcomes in the thanksgiving and petitions of workers and blows their trumpets of praise.

For the riches of your creation, giving us the materials of the earth:
We thank you, Lord.
For the labour of our hands and minds, developing invention and skill:
We thank you, Lord.
For agriculture, industry and commerce, providing work and wealth and goods for the world:
We thank you, Lord.
For all who work in transport and distribution, service industries and local government, that in giving service they may find reward:
Hear our prayer.
For those in management and the trade unions, that mutual respect and good relations may always be maintained:
Hear our prayer.
For the unemployed and the handicapped, that they might not lose hope, and may find a positive role in life:
Hear our prayer.
For young people at work and those who educate and train them, that they may find promise and aspiration fulfilled:
Hear our prayer.
Lord the Creator, whose great goodness has provided for our needs; help us so to use, develop and preserve the resources of the earth that, through our industry, the needs of all may be fulfilled, human dignity enhanced, and our people live in true prosperity and peace; through Jesus Christ our Lord. **Amen.**[a]

a. Cameron Butland, *Work in Worship: A Treasury of Prayers, Readings, and Hymns* (London: Hodder & Stoughton, 1985), 57. Reproduced by permission of Hodder & Stoughton Limited.

fessional harvests must be marked, God praised, and the poor blessed. Care must be given that these celebrations not become opportunities for professional boasting or comparison. The focus must be on the power of God, not the worker. In the light of Israel's witness, God's generosity to one group of workers must be shared with the marginalized and celebrated in community.

Blessing God through Daily Work

The following prayer stimulates a vocational imagination within workers for their own callings to bless God through their daily work.

Let the health authority bless you, great God,
the local surgeries sing your praise.
May the hospitals and hospices bless you, Beloved,
praise your name and glorify you for ever.

Let those who work with computers bless you, great God,
those who sweep offices sing your praise.
May those who keep guard and those in charge bless you,
*   Beloved,*
praise your name and glorify you for ever.

Let the shopping malls and leisure centres bless you, great God,
the swimming pools sing your praise.
May the sports grounds and stadiums bless you, Beloved,
praise your name and glorify you for ever.

Let the cinemas and theatres bless you, great God,
the concert halls sing your praise.
May the pubs and cafes bless you, Beloved,
praise your name and glorify you for ever.

Let the police and the courts bless you, great God,
the firefighters sing your praise.
May the ambulance drivers bless you, Beloved,
praise your name and glorify you for ever.

Let the taxis and buses, the trains and trams bless you, great God,
the drivers and conductors sing your praise.
May the mechanics and engineers bless you, Beloved,
praise your name and glorify you for ever.[a]

a. Jim Cotter, *Out of the Silence . . . Into the Silence: Prayer's Daily Round; An Unfolding of Prayers, Psalms, and Canticles for Daily or Occasional Use.* © Jim Cotter. Published by Cairns Publications 2006. Used by permission, Hymns Ancient & Modern Ltd. rights@hymnsam.co.uk. Our thanks to Gideon Strauss for this reference and material.

How might workers bless God through vocational praise? Several psalms call out for various parts of creation to praise God (Pss. 69:34; 98:8; 148:7–14). Culture, the work of human hands within God's creation, should also reflect

God's glory as an act of praise. (See the psalm-like prayer in the sidebar "Blessing God through Daily Work.")

Some gatherings of vocational praise and celebration might fit more appropriately in the homes of workers rather than during worship on a Sunday morning. Invariably, there are significant events like graduations, promotions, retirements, or other important milestones in the life of a worker or a work community. Creative thought should be given to helping people make major vocational transitions well. See, for example, the sidebar "Prayers for People in Their Transitions and Callings" and consider how the prayers there might inspire similar prayers in your community. These major milestones are critical junctures in the lives of workers. In these vocational moments, workers need their community to be present to celebrate, bless, and journey alongside of them.

Failing to give God praise for his provisions in our professional lives can lead to a functional atheism. Workers come to believe that they are self-made successes—begotten of their own professional brilliance, willpower, and grit. Workers must stop and name the goodness of God in times of profit. They need to publicly raise an Ebenezer.

The Israelite farmer in Deuteronomy 26 publicly displayed his professional wealth in front of the whole community and declared aloud the glory of God. Some modern workers may claim that they don't want to publicly name or boast about their vocational triumphs and harvest. While this desire for privacy and secrecy is understandable, it is also spiritually dangerous. Avoiding explicit public acts of celebration might actually be an unconscious effort to deny our deep vocational dependence on God. Public acts of thanksgiving can cultivate professional humility and gratitude, whereas acts of professional privacy and secrecy can cultivate professional pride and hoarding.

Whatever form these public expressions of vocational praise and thanksgiving take, it is important to involve the community, and especially those on the margins, in a meaningful way. A commitment must be made to reach out to the marginalized, not out of condescending pity but to rightly honor and bless all members of the economy of God. We will say more about this when we get to our discussion of "fruits."

Gathering Workplace Ashes

> By your many sins and dishonest trade you have desecrated your sanctuaries.
>
> —Ezekiel 28:18

Prayers for People in Their Transitions and Callings

A Blessing at College Graduation

May God, who is present in sunrise and nightfall
and in the crossing of the sea,
guide your feet as you go.

May God, who is with you when you sit
and when you stand,
encompass you with love
and lead you by the hand.

May God, who knows your path
and the places where you rest,
be with you in your waiting,
be your good news for sharing,
and lead you in the way that is everlasting.[a]

Petitions for the Callings of Young Adults

For young people growing in wisdom, and for the persistence to listen for the voice of God amid many other voices clamoring for their attention.

For all who mentor younger generations—for the wisdom of educators and employers to teach, and for the openness of young adults to listen.

For young adults burdened by student loan debt and other financial stresses, that their commitment to their callings may still find ways to flourish.

For young people struggling to hear God's voice in their lives, especially those who suffer from depression, anxiety, or other mental health concerns.

Workers enter the sanctuary guilty. All week long they've participated in and contributed to a fallen marketplace that is rebelling against the economy of God. The stain of sin marks their hands and hearts. Gathered worship must name, confront, and contend with the marketplace evil we carry inside.

For couples discerning marriage, that they might invite God into their dreaming and planning.

For professionals starting out in their careers and for all those searching for work.

For couples trying to conceive and all those who feel frustrated in their callings.

For young adults in transition: for veterans returning from deployment, for recent graduates, for expectant parents, and for those beginning new work.

For those who are single by choice and for those who are searching for a partner, that our community may welcome their gifts and pray for their needs, no matter where they are on their journey.[b]

A Blessing for Retirement

To everything, Lord, you have given a season,
Calling each thing good in its time.
In the years of our lives,
You call us to work,
You ask us to play,
You command us to rest,
And by your grace, you weave our days together in peace.
We pray for our brother [or sister] N., who comes to the end of his [her] season of work.
Thank you for friends made, challenges met, and growth enjoyed,
And for all he [she] has learned and accomplished.
Help him [her] now let the old work go,
To take up the new life for which you have also given him [her] gifts;
Through Christ the Worker, in whose love is our eternal rest and joy. Amen.[c]

a. Shane Claiborne and Jonathan Wilson-Hartgrove, *Common Prayer: A Liturgy for Ordinary Radicals* (Grand Rapids: Zondervan, 2012), 71, quoted in Fanucci, *To Bless Our Callings*, 37. Used with permission.
b. Fanucci, *To Bless Our Callings*, 44–45. Used with permission.
c. Episcopal Church, *Changes*, 53, quoted in Fanucci, *To Bless Our Callings*, 70. Used with permission.

Worship leaders must graciously provide guilt-stricken workers with the ashes they need to repent and be reconciled once again.

Faithful worship in ancient Israel and the early church could not turn a blind eye to the dirty hands of workers, nor could it accept their sin-stained

Corporate Prayers of Vocational Intercession and Confession

David Welbourn has compiled a wonderful book of congregational prayers, litanies, and liturgies on work in worship. Here are illustrative examples of corporate prayers of vocational intercession and confession.

Prayer of Intercession

O God the Father, Creator of all things:
Have mercy upon us.
O God the Son, Redeemer of the world:
Have mercy upon us.
O God the Holy Spirit, Giver of life:
Have mercy upon us.
O Holy, blessed and glorious Trinity, three Persons and one God:
Have mercy upon us.
From envy, avarice and status-seeking, from covetousness which is idolatry; from wanting more than is our fair share:
Good Lord, deliver us.
From ruthlessness in making money, and from irresponsibility in spending it:
Good Lord, deliver us.
From unwillingness to know the cost to others of our own standard of living:
Good Lord, deliver us.
For financiers and politicians, industrialists and trade unionists, and all who wield economic power; that they may have grace, wisdom and compassion:
Lord, hear our prayer.

marketplace offerings. These worshiping communities developed liturgical practices to name and confront economic and vocational evil. Their liturgies enabled workers to confess, repent, and ultimately become reconciled to both God and their economic neighbor.

Contemporary calls for vocational confession and repentance should be filled with a deep pastoral compassion. Pastors need to empathize with the moral fragility and vulnerability of workers laboring in the global marketplace.

For the bewildered and those who cannot cope with a budget or with filling in forms or with the pressures of modern life:
Lord, hear our prayer.
For the victims of inflation, pensioners, people on small fixed incomes, and all who have been robbed of their savings:
Lord, hear our prayer.
For those who cannot find jobs, or homes they can afford, for people made redundant for whatever reason:
Lord, hear our prayer.
For the increase of the fruits of the earth, that all may enjoy them:
Lord, hear our prayer.
Lord, when we are deciding how to make money, how to steward it, and what to do with it; help us to look hard at our motives, our aims and our prejudices—honestly, as in your sight.
O Lord Jesus Christ, who for our sake became poor; grant us grace to forsake all covetous desires and inordinate love of riches, and to seek first the kingdom of God and his righteousness. For your name's sake. Amen.

Prayer of Confession

Gracious Lord, we bring before you our personal failures in our daily work. We have been poor stewards of your gifts; we have not given you the glory, nor laboured in your love. We confess, too, the faults of our industrial society: continuing injustice, lack of harmony, the inability—and worse—the unwillingness to seek the paths of reconciliation. Have mercy upon us, and grant that, as the workshop at Nazareth was blessed through the labour of the Christ, so the workplaces of this land may be enriched by the work of those who call him "Lord." We ask this in his name. Amen.[a]

a. Theology of Work Project, "From Ruthlessness in Making Money and Irresponsibility Spending It, Lord, Deliver Us" (Prayer), compiled by David Welbourn. https://www.theologyofwork.org/work-in-worship/prayer-material-for-services/intercessions/from-ruthlessness-in-making-money-and-irresponsibility-spending-it-lord-del. Used with permission.

Ancient or modern, work is hard, workers are weary, and idols are all around. In times of economic desperation and drought ancient Israelite farmers regularly turned to other gods to secure their professional futures. Modern Christians, working in the undulating ocean of the global economy, often feel vulnerable and fragile as well. They're constantly tempted to seek economic security, status, and salvation in other gods. In light of this economic vulnerability, worship leaders need to provide intentional time and space for workers to prayerfully examine their lives and carry their vocational confessions to a holy and gracious God.

The vocational ashes that workers carry into confession can't simply be individualistic; they need to be corporate and structural as well. Workers need to consider their own moral complicity in twisted economic structures that demean their neighbors, destroy the earth, and dishonor the beauty and craftsmanship of God. Public confessions should reflect both the personal and the public nature of economic evil (for examples, see the sidebar "Corporate Prayers of Vocational Intercession and Confession"). This type of discipling takes time and the involvement of the entire leadership of the church, not just the worship leader. Yet the liturgy can slowly help cultivate a sanctified imagination for confessing structural injustices and sins.

Confessions that sheepishly ignore the realities of vocational evil do not serve workers at all. The guilt remains. It festers and destroys. Providing spaces for vocational confession graciously allows workers the opportunity to offer their burdensome debts to Christ. It is only through repeated acts of honest confession that workers can exchange their heavy burdens for a yoke that is easy and a burden that is light (Matt. 11:28–30).

Gathering Workplace Petitions

> The winds are in Thy hand,
> bridle them and bind them,
> that they may not come forth
> to destroy the labours of the ploughman,
> nor to defeat the husbandman of his hopes.
> —Free Church Book of Common
> Prayer, quoted in Kevin Lowe,
> *Baptized with the Soil*

Corporate worship can and should gather workers' vocational requests and petitions. Having welcomed them in, worship can direct these requests to God. Through prayers and petitions offered in the sanctuary, workers can slowly begin the practice of dialoguing with God about their work.

Vocational requests brought to God in worship should not be narrowly self-focused. Workers are ordained members of the priesthood of all believers. This means that they are called to the ministry of intercession. They need, therefore, to regularly practice interceding before God on behalf of their coworkers, clients, and supervisors. The task of worship is to develop a holy priesthood capable of fulfilling their ministry of intercession in both the sanctuary and the workplace. Through corporate prayer, workers can slowly learn to pray for the Holy Spirit's renewal and restoration of their economic neighbors and their particular industry. *As priests, they must practice praying for their vocational parish.*

In some church traditions it is customary for individuals to offer personal "testimonies" during corporate worship. Through these testimonies, individuals sometimes share their personal stories, needs, and requests with the larger community. Offering testimonies *from the marketplace* can be a powerful way to connect individual workers to their community and their God. When a vocational testimony is offered—honestly and vulnerably—the walls separating the sanctuary and the marketplace become increasingly porous. Through testimony, workers can carry real vocational struggles, requests, and petitions into the sanctuary. Whole congregations can begin to carry one another's vocational petitions together.

Some traditions actively respond in real time to personal testimonies with forms of spontaneous prayer. In the chapter on Psalms we described the Korean ritual of *tong-sung ki-do*. Inspired by this method, one could imagine a worker sharing a difficult professional experience of what Koreans call *han* (deep suffering, frustrated hope, bitter resentment, and loss). The community can then respond by petitioning God—out loud—to move in the marketplace on the worker's behalf. Witnessing this exchange between a suffering worker and a prayerful community can be both powerful and formative. Workers who regularly witness this practice can begin to develop a sanctified understanding of their own vocational longings and petitions that need to be voiced.

One worship leader longed for his weekly "prayers of the people" to emerge directly from the real lives and labors of his people. Rather than composing the congregational prayer by himself in his office, he solicited the people's help. Two weeks prior to the service, the following email was distributed to a number of congregants.

Dear _____:

I have been asked to lead the prayers of the people on Sunday Oct 5th and I would love to get your input in crafting this prayer.

Part of my prayer will name specific areas where we need to see God's kingdom to come and His will to be done in our city and world through our daily work. Would you mind sending me 2 or 3 sentences from your daily prayers that . . . voice the longings and needs for God's kingdom shalom to be established in lasting ways? If the words came from your own prayer life it will help inform how I pray and how our congregation prays as well.

I really appreciate your input. You are helping me shepherd our congregation on how to pray specifically for God's kingdom to come and his will to be done in our workplaces as it is in heaven!

Thank you in advance.

Several congregants responded and contributed to the prayer. Respondents included a warehouse worker recently laid off, a social worker for at-risk youth, a doctor at a community clinic, an FBI agent, a lawyer, and a grant writer. The responses were then synthesized and placed within a responsive prayer based on Psalm 90:17. Wherever possible, the original phrasing of the people's prayers was included to help paint an honest picture of their lived reality in the city. Here is that prayer:

Leader
Eternal God made known to us in Jesus and who through the Holy Spirit bends low to hear the cries of your people: open your eyes and look upon us your people and upon your world.

Every week we gather together from our neighborhoods and places of work where people are inundated by the busyness of life leaving little opportunity to experience true community, let alone the love of Jesus.

In many places in our city: race, ethnicity, age, sexual orientation, mental ability, income, or immigration status impede us being seen as your true image bearers. In too many places it seems that justice is only for the privileged. The cycles of poverty, addiction, and violence are so powerful that those whose work it is to assist struggle to hold out any hope for change.

We long for your will to be done on earth as it is in heaven, so we pray:

Congregation
May the favor of the Lord our God rest on us; establish the work of our hands for us—yes, establish the work of our hands.

Leader
For those working in companies with poor leadership or unethical practices, open their eyes to both the brokenness and your heart for redemption.

We pray for creativity and collaboration among the business community to form strong businesses, create new jobs, and help establish a stable economy in our city.

For those who protect our society: bring your peace to the turbulence and violence of their work. Fill them with wisdom that they may be shrewd yet innocent, just and yet merciful to all they meet.

Give attorneys the opportunity to represent you well in their work. Cause them to be patient with those they encounter, regardless of what they may spitefully hurl at them.

Let judges who preside over the care of foster and adoption cases not be tired emotionally and physically. Let them take seriously their positions and know that every single decision they make each day will affect generations and generations that follow.

For those who work in community health clinics: help them to imitate your compassion toward their patients.

Grant teachers and administrators the wisdom and grace to love their students the way you love them.

Give grace to social workers to be opened afresh to each case, and grant them wisdom to use their power to help those who are so vulnerable.

We long for your will to be done on earth as it is in heaven, so we pray:

Congregation
May the favor of the Lord our God rest on us; establish the work of our hands for us—yes, establish the work of our hands.

Leader
Jesus, it is into your resurrected and resurrecting hands that we bring our prayers.

For yours is the kingdom and the power and the glory forever and ever. Amen.

The "prayers of the people" can involve workers in a wide variety of ways.[6] Some pastors have even come alongside workers to help them craft specific prayers focusing on their respective industries. Scott Calgaro, at the Center for Faith and Work in New York City, reported that the following practice had a tremendous impact on their approach to discipling urban professionals. The following prayer was composed by a young urban planner who works daily with New York City's built environment. Note how his prayer is set on fire by his deep understanding of his industry and the specific role it plays in both the flourishing of New York City and the glory of God.

A Petition for Urban Planning

Father, you delight in your creation, in your people and in the urban environments we build. So essential is the built environment to our growth as beings uniquely created in your image that you command us to build cities, seek their peace and prosperity, and to pray for them.

As wondrous as our present city may be, it is also broken, revealing and compounding our sinful natures. As broken as our present city may be, it is also a place of wonder and grand inspiration. You have not abandoned us in our city. Instead, you are active in renewing us. We pray now for those who create the physical city:

For our urban planners and government agents: May they be inspired with a compelling long-term vision for the robust growth of the physical city and its infrastructure. Grant them a curious spirit to seek out and listen. And may they use wisdom when creating and refining city codes and regulations to promote health and foster positive growth and equality.

For the real estate developers, investors, and lenders: Lead them in the stewardship of their resources so that each project would result in financial and civic returns. Allow them to delight and take pride in the authenticity of what they build while guarding their hearts and egos against greed and self-boasting.

---

6. For several examples of the prayers of the people, see the "Intercessions about Work" resources on the Theology of Work Project website: https://www.theologyofwork.org/work-in-worship/prayer-material-for-services/intercessions.

For the architects, designers, and engineers: Grant them creativity to imagine and push the boundaries of design, form, functionality, and efficiency for the spaces where we work, live, play, and travel. May they exercise wisdom and provide clear counsel to their clients.

For the builders, contractors, and tradespeople: Strengthen their bodies as they construct the seen and unseen parts of our city. Strengthen their minds to perceive, understand, and make known any potential faults that would impact the integrity of our city.

For the real estate brokers and agents: May they work diligently with perseverance on behalf of their clients. Help them to discern fact from fiction, to negotiate boldly, to speak of others with high esteem, and to be excellent stewards of the relationships you have given them. And when a deal falls apart, keep them from becoming bitter and jaded.

Father, you are the perfect creator, beautiful builder, and eternal sustainer. In your Son alone do all things hold together. By your Spirit, these physical spaces of infrastructure, buildings great and small, and open spaces where we, as communal beings, live, work and flourish together, are being created and renewed.

Finally, our God, you know full well the joys and struggles of each of us. Would you meet us in our particular needs and show us your goodness? Thank you for giving us the promise for a fully redeemed future city, one that you will have established, will have made safe, and will have made wondrously beautiful.

In the name of Christ. Amen.[7]

Gathering Workplace Fruits

Bless, Lord, the crown of the year that is of your bounty, and may they satisfy the poor of your people. Your servant N. [name of the worker], has brought these things that are yours, because he fears you, bless him from your holy heaven, and all his house.

—*Canons of Hippolytus* §36

7. Johnathan Agrelius, Center for Faith and Work Gotham Fellow, class of 2014. Used with permission.

The fruits of our labor must come before the Lord in corporate worship. In both ancient Israel and the early church we see a consistent emphasis on the need to bring the products and profits of labor forward for the flourishing of the community and the glory of God. Without first-fruits ceremonies that are tactile, communal, and contextual, the integrity of work and workers can begin to break down.

Sadly, modern practices of offering have fallen on hard times and are facing several headwinds in the Western church.[8] The fruits of our labor are increasingly transferred across digital platforms without any human action or interaction at all. No song is sung. No careful selection of the finest or first fruits. No basket presented before the community. No public declarations of the goodness of God. No celebratory feast. No public naming of the worker or the work. As Jeremy Kidwell remarks, contemporary offering rituals lack "social context, festivity, or explicit material reference to the work of the offerer."[9] A comprehensive reimagining of the offering is clearly needed.

We need not despair. With the advent of digital transfers, a moment of creative opportunity has arrived. The "time for offering" no longer needs to be focused narrowly on the mere transfer of currency. That period of three-to-five minutes during a worship service is suddenly free to take on a new—or rather, very old—focus. Offering can return to its ancient focus whereby the community renders its whole life and whole labor to God in worship. The guiding liturgical question can suddenly be that of holistic worship and holistic discipleship: *How can this time of offering encourage and enable workers to offer their whole lives to God as a living and working sacrifice?* (Rom. 12:1).

In light of our investigations of Scripture, history, and the global church, there are four principles that can inform the future of the offering rituals.

---

8. In examining the offering practices of the Old Testament and the early church, we found that ancient offering ceremonies were slow, intentional, physical, and vocationally specific. By the fourth and fifth centuries, offering practices were increasingly monetized into a singular currency. Now, in the twenty-first century, offerings are increasingly digitized. Today, workers involved in diverse industries engage in the same ritual of disembodied offering as money is transferred electronically in the blink of an eye while they sleep. The dissonance between ancient and contemporary practices is breathtaking and requires careful reflection and a creative response.

The slow, intentional, physical, and vocationally specific offerings of the ancient world had a formative impact on workers. Workers had to select this animal and not that one, this fruit and not the other one, this bunch of grapes, that loaf, this clothing. Workers carried the best of their work, the first fruits, before the watching eyes of their priests and their community in worship. The crafter was named and the craft was blessed. Unjust or ill-gotten products were turned away by the religious leaders.

We are not naive Luddites. The digitization offerings of the contemporary world will not be stopped in most worshiping communities. But that doesn't mean that transformation of the offering cannot take place even in these churches. All is not lost.

9. Kidwell, *The Theology of Craft and the Craft of Work*, 209.

Offerings need to strive to be more *embodied, creational, vocational,* and *communal.* By this we mean that offerings need to engage our bodies, our material world, and our daily work, and they need to actively connect worshipers to one another and their city. What follows are a few practical examples of offering prayers and ceremonies guided by these four principles. On occasion, workers can be invited to carry symbolic items from their work forward during the offering on Sunday. These offerings can be piled up at the front of the sanctuary and offered up to God. We have already given several examples of offering practices from Scripture, history, and the global church today. Readers can refer also to our illustrative story and liturgy at the opening chapter on the early church. Finding songs fitting for such a service can be challenging.[10]

During a time of professional harvest, pastors can offer workers opportunities to share their vocational testimonies—stories of God's fruitful provision in their vocations. A service where workers share their testimonies can be fairly simple. The goal is to create space for workers to reflect on God's work in their lives and to connect with others through their stories. Here is a simple structure for preparing testimonies:

- Tell us about your work.
- Describe a specific challenge you or your particular industry have faced this year.
- How have you seen God move and produce fruit through this workplace challenge?

Workers should be encouraged not to force their story to have a happy ending. Often God's presence is felt amidst dark and difficult times. The fruit of their testimony may be a story of God's deliverance, but it might also be a story of God's presence through a coworker or friend amidst a period of God's silence.[11] When possible, workers should be encouraged to bring a visual artifact or product with them when they offer their testimony. Tangible

10. The song "Bring to God Your Gifts for Harvest" by Heather Pencavel is one example of an offertory song that connects different times of "harvest" with various industries and occupations. It encourages worshipers to "worship God in home and office, boardroom, classroom, factory." Cited on the Theology of Work Project website: https://dev.theology ofwork.org/work-in-worship/hymns-psalms-poems/hymns/less-familiar-hymns-related-to -work/bring-to-god-your-gifts-for-harvest.

11. It is also important to not overlook what we learned from the medieval blessing of the plow festival: *embedded within these offerings are petitions for God's continued blessing in the next season.* Celebratory offerings are also petitions that form workers to live lives of dependence on God.

artifacts help the community see and connect with the worker's story. Photos can also be used creatively in testimonies. PhotoVoice[12] is one effective tool developed by sociologists that helps guide storytelling and facilitate community engagement and learning. The visuals capture key components of the vocational experience and connect the congregation to the fruits of God's faithfulness.

In chapter 5 we described a traditional harvest festival in Zimbabwe. This annual rite embodies a form of praise that shifts the community's focus away from an individual's work and toward the work of God in the communal economy. During the festival some workers bring their harvest crops. Others transform their crops into bread, wine, and other foods for the communal meal. White-collar workers from urban areas use their wages to buy decorations to adorn the sanctuary for the harvest festival. Neighboring households pool their offerings and bring them forward collectively during the worship service.

Urban churches detached from agricultural economies will need to use their imagination here. Instead of piling up harvest crops at the front of the sanctuary, *urban professionals might gather together to creatively identify ways in which their professional fruits might directly benefit the broader community*. Here are a few examples:

- Seasoned business leaders might celebrate God's economic blessing to them by turning around and training, mentoring, and funding young entrepreneurs serving more economically distressed communities.
- Mechanics in a congregation might band together a few times a year to celebrate God's goodness, eat pizza, and fix cars for single mothers in their community. The mechanics could even restore broken-down cars and, in an act of vocational celebration, offer them to people in need.[13]
- Real estate agents, city planners, and home builders might host a dinner party where they discuss how their vocational skills, political connections, and financial offerings might produce more low-income housing options in their city.

12. PhotoVoice is a form of participatory action research that flips the roles of teacher and student so that each person has an opportunity to educate others about their lived experience. Using a combination of photographs, small-group discussion of these images, and facilitated critical dialogue, participants are given space to discuss personal experiences with people with whom they normally don't engage. See R. R. Williams, "Engaging and Researching Congregations Visually."

13. Our thanks to the mechanics at Bellevue Presbyterian Church for inspiring this idea. See Vargas, "Auto Angels Repair Cars for Qualifying Low-Income Families."

- Parents might host collective graduation parties for students that intentionally praise God for his goodness and faithfulness in their studies.

These diverse examples illustrate a creative combination of vocational festivity, thanksgiving, and communal blessing.

Conclusion: Vocational Dialogue

Corporate worship should invite workers into a transformative dialogue with their God. Being a dialogue, it should invite workers to both speak and listen, offer and receive, act and rest. If worship is going to be an honest dialogue, workers will need to carry their whole lives, work included, into the liturgical discourse. They will need to be vulnerable and forthright. And they will need to practice.

Workplace petitions and laments won't always come easily. After all, many professionals have little to no practice dialoguing with God about their work on a Sunday morning. To make matters worse, many pastors have little to no practice leading dialogues about work in worship. *This means that worship is going to be awkward for everyone for quite some time.* That's okay. Both pastors and professionals need to be gracious with one another as they clumsily begin this dialogue about faith and work in worship. God can handle clumsy dialogues. God is used to it. According to the Scriptures we've examined, what God cannot abide is the separation and disintegration of faith, work, and worship.

Finally, in any healthy dialogue both parties have things to offer and things to receive. In this chapter we've focused more on how one dialogue partner (the worker) can speak to God. In the final chapter we will focus more on how God replies to the worker with his Word, his Spirit, and his very life. And it is through this divine response that workers are sent out from the sanctuary—scattered as salt, light, and leaven back into their daily work.

While we will discuss the shaping and sending of workers in the next chapter, it is important to note that the formation of workers is already well underway. Gathering workers into worship is, in and of itself, a formative practice that directly contributes to mission. The diastolic momentum of workers *toward* the sanctuary can directly contribute to their systolic movement *toward* their work. Put another way, worshipers who regularly carry their life and work to God in the sanctuary are being formed to carry God's life and work back into their workplaces.

12

Worship That Scatters Workers

May the God who dances in creation . . .
who shakes our lives like thunder
bless us and drive us out with power.

—Janet Morley, quoted in Hannah
Ward and Jennifer Wild, *Human Rites*

The sanctuary has a gathering responsibility to graciously welcome work and workers in. That said, it cannot hold the priesthood of all believers there indefinitely. The sanctuary also has a *scattering* responsibility. Corporate worship must actively push and propel worshipers back into their work in the world. It must bless and send the priesthood out to extend their worship into their vocational parishes. Gathered worship in the sanctuary must become scattered worship in the streets.

A healthy heart's systolic pressure will disperse (or scatter) freshly oxygenated blood throughout the body. It will do so with great force. In the same way, a healthy sanctuary must produce a strong systolic push to send workers into the world. The sanctuary's ability to shape and scatter workers is critical to the health and mission of the church.

In this chapter we explore how Sunday morning worship can *orient*, *pray*, *commission*, and ultimately *send* workers toward their vocations in the world. Once again, this is not a "how-to" manual. Worship leaders should use these principles and practices as a generative starting point from which they can imagine and create their own worship services.

Orienting Workers toward Monday

> Often Jesus, whom you sought at the memorials of the altars . . . came to meet you in the way while you were working.
>
> —Guerric of Igny (twelfth-century abbot), *Liturgical Sermons*

Maps orient wandering travelers. They remind them where they are going, how to get there, and what they can expect along the way. Workers wandering through the world's economy often arrive in worship asking *geographical* questions—questions of orientation. Where is God at work? Where am I called to serve him? Where should I go next?

Like a good map, corporate worship can orient a worker who is wandering. It can plant them within the larger context of God's life and work in the world. Put another way, worship can orient the priesthood of all believers *toward* their parishes, their specific missions within the city. As worship sends workers out into the city, it can offer workers a compass—a sense of true north—for the vocational pilgrimage ahead.

Here are two rather straightforward ways corporate worship can alert, orient, and direct workers toward the larger work of God in the city. First, worship leaders can invite congregants to submit photos of themselves in their respective places of work, study, or service. They can develop these photos into a slideshow or art piece to be displayed during a worship service. During a quiet time of reflection, leaders can call attention to the images. They can ask worshipers to give thanks for these diverse callings scattered throughout the city. They can invite worshipers to prayerfully intercede before God on their behalf and encourage them to quietly reflect on the many ways in which God is at work *in and through these vocations in the city*. This simple liturgical exercise can orient workers toward their city and their vocations. Their eyes can be slowly trained to see the profound power of God that is present and active within the priesthood and their diverse vocational parishes.

A second example orients workers through the liturgical use of an actual map. When we, the authors, were children, our respective churches had "mission maps" displayed prominently just outside the sanctuary. Imagine a map of the world and a map of the local city. The world map illustrated, with the help of a few tiny flags, the specific locations of various missionaries whom we supported. The city map illustrated the location of our church building and various nonprofit ministries that we supported around the city. These maps were meant to orient the laypeople, to remind them where and how they could join in the mission of God throughout the city and the world. If you wanted to know where you could participate in the mission of God, these mission maps could orient, connect, and send you. Big red letters above the city map declared "God is on the move!" Unfortunately, God was only "on the move" in four buildings across the city: the homeless shelter, the food bank, the thrift store, and, of course, the church building.

Although these mission maps were created with the best of intentions, they were rather *disorienting* for the laity. A reliable map that truly oriented people to God's complex presence, power, and mission in the city would need to be far more full and complex.

Often, when a mission map is designed by a church staff, it will cleanly and crisply orient people toward the organized ministries of the institutional church. However, when it is designed by the people of God, it might just orient people toward the disorganized ministries of the organic church throughout the city. We will illustrate.

If you want to create a more accurate mission map for your community, one that can truly orient the church toward its complex mission in the city, don't let the pastoral staff create the map; have the laity do it. Take a large map of your city and place it at the front of the sanctuary. During worship, invite the laity to process forward and place pins on the map where they work, serve, study, or play. This simple liturgical exercise can orient worshipers to the complex mission of the church in the city. On Monday morning the people of God will be on mission at the hospital, the playground, the gas station, the coffee shop, the home, and the real estate office. Where is "God on the move" through this church? Wherever you see a pin.

If your church is too large to accomplish this mapping exercise during corporate worship, place the map in the foyer and invite people to place their pins on the map over the course of a month. At the conclusion of the month have elders proceed into worship carrying the map. During the benediction, point to the map to orient the worshipers toward their city and their mission within it. Bless them and send them out to extend Christ's economy of grace into their specific communities. Point to the map and remind them where they are going. Remind them where they are called, where God will meet them. Orient the priesthood toward their parishes, not your church grounds.[1]

---

1. It is important to keep in mind our discussion in chap. 3 of priests and parishes and their complexity.

Praying Workers toward Monday

> Since it has pleased Our Lord to give you the sort of life which involves con-
> stant distractions, you must get used to making your prayers short, but also so
> habitual that you will never omit them.
>
> —Francis de Sales, *Selected Letters*

Beyond orientation, the sanctuary can actually pray workers toward their vocations in the city as well. The power of congregational prayer to send workers into Monday is directly connected to its theocentric character. God—not the worker—is the origin, essence, and end of prayer.

The principle is this: pray regularly for God's faithful work in your city. Pray for God's beauty, craftsmanship, justice, and care to be made manifest in its streets. Pray for God's presence and power to be made known in its factories, markets, and shops. Allow the prayer's theocentricity to awaken the congregation not only to God's presence and power in the city but also to their own presence and power there. As we witnessed in Psalms, the prayers of Israel were primarily filled with phrases concerning the work, care, and craftsmanship of God—not the worker. Through theocentric prayer, *workers were prayed into (conformed to) the peculiar patterns of God's work in the world*—God's creativity, service, justice, and care shaped their own. Vocational prayers that are focused primarily on God's work will ultimately provide worshipers with a pattern for their own work. Obviously, a distinction needs to be carefully made between the immortal work of God and the finite and fallen work of humanity. However, the kingdom patterns of Christian work—of creativity, service, and justice—can and should be established in theocentric prayer.

Workers regularly find their minds wandering toward thoughts of work during worship. Rather than trying to beat back these "intruding" thoughts, worship leaders can invite workers to bring these vocational "interruptions," these ordinary tasks and deadlines, *into their prayers to God*.

One way of doing this is to make time at the end of worship for people to prayerfully reflect on the coming week. Invite them to physically pull out their digital calendars in the middle of the sanctuary and ask them to reflect on questions like these: What do you see in this coming week that gives you anxiety or fear? Which meetings or tasks excite you? When will you especially need God's gracious power to break in? Give people time to prayerfully examine their coming week. Give them time to offer their calendars to God. Here leaders can even invite the congregation to recite the Lord's Prayer aloud as they scroll through their calendars. With the coming week firmly at the forefront of their minds, the prayer orients the congregation toward God—and the week ahead.

Leaders might engage in a "TTT ritual." Where will you be at *this time tomorrow*? Take some time to visualize Monday at 10:00 a.m. What will you be working on? Who will you be working with? Offer this specific place, this specific task, and these specific people to God. This is your priesthood; this is your parish. A regular practice along these lines can add critical detail, purpose, and direction to what can often be overly vague congregational prayers. Workers may have a difficult time grabbing hold of abstract spiritual language about "the world." Raw specificity gives them a prayerful foothold in the rough edges of their real lives.

Another option is to ground congregational prayers in images from work. Once again, solicit photos from the congregation from the concrete places where they work, serve, parent, and play. During the traditional "prayers of the people," encourage the worshipers to visually pray their way through the images—the vocational spaces within which they've been called to serve. The priesthood of all believers can be asked to intercede for one another's vocations—for God's power to be made manifest within these specific parishes.

These expressions of prayerful solidarity are not insignificant. The worshipers' knowledge that they are not alone, that the community prays with and for them, can have a profound impact as they disperse toward Monday. It is from a prayer-filled community that they move toward a prayer-filled vocation.

In the deeply secular and modern West an integrated life of work and prayer is not automatic, easy, or straightforward. That said, a life of *ora et labora*—pray and work—can be practiced. And the sanctuary can play a role in turning the practice of prayer and work into a habit. Put another way, if marketplace work is going to be prayer-filled, sanctuary prayers need to be work-filled.

Commissioning Workers toward Monday

Corporate worship can ordain and commission worshipers toward their work in the world. Theologically speaking, the commissioning of workers is rooted in Adam and Eve's original ordination to priestly work in the garden-temple. That "cultural mandate," that original commissioning, was (and still is) central to God's mission in the world. Human beings, both in Eden and today, are called to creative, sustaining, and redemptive work in the world.

These workers are called to be priests, and their small work can participate in God's larger work through Christ. Therefore, it is both right and good for the church to commission the priesthood of all believers toward their priestly work in the world.[2]

Traditionally, when congregations ordain and commission pastors, elders, and missionaries, they often articulate how their vocations reflect and participate in God's *redemptive* work in the world. Congregations that commission workers should do the same. They should carefully articulate how specific workers' vocations reflect and participate in God's *creative, sustaining*, and *redemptive* plan.

Commissioning rituals root workers in God's mission and reinforce their primary calling within God's kingdom economy—not the world's. Through the commissioning service, workers are reminded that it is God who has gifted and called them to serve as a holy priesthood in the marketplace. As they take their vocational vows they bind their lives and labor to God's patterns of life and labor. Workers will not carry the weight of these vocational vows alone. The church community surrounds and stands with them. The Holy Spirit together with the communion of saints sends these workers out, not as free agents but as members of a larger body at work in the world.

When commissioning workers within a specific industry, pastors should take time to learn about the unique cultural character of the industry in question. This learning process need not be lonely work for pastors. They should ask the laity for help. After all, if you want to learn about a local parish, you normally ask the local priest. Pastors should ask workers about their industry's virtues and vices, its challenges and opportunities, its beauty and heartbreak. Having listened to them, pastors might choose to create a series of industrial prayers and vows that reflect what the workers have told them. Like a good missionary, pastors should listen and pay attention to the people they hope to serve, allowing the "locals" to take the lead wherever possible.

The commissioning of a specific industry (education, medicine, law, technology, etc.) should reflect the culture of the local community and industry in question. That said, it might be helpful to consider a paradigmatic structure. Some combination of these five elements might prove useful in designing a commissioning service.[3]

2. See our biblical and theological discussion in chap. 3 of the creational priesthood of Adam, Eve, and all believers.

3. At the Theology of Work Project website, you can read how one pastor describes a commissioning service with health care workers: "Commissioning Our People for the Workplace," https://www.theologyofwork.org/resources/commissioning-our-people-for-the-workplace.

1. *Testimony:* Identify a representative from the industry and ask them to give a short testimony. Ask them to speak about the unique opportunities and challenges facing Christians serving in the industry. Ask them to testify, to give witness to, the ways the living God is actively working in their field.

2. *Affirmation:* Affirm those being commissioned for responding to God's leading in their lives. Affirm that God is with them, that God delights in the aroma of their work. Affirm their priestly calling to their industrial parish.

3. *Framing:* Frame their work within the creative, sustaining, and redemptive work of God. Frame their work as integral to both the mission of God and the witness of the local church.

4. *Vows:* Invite workers to vow, God helping them, that they will
   - work according to the patterns of God's good work in the world;
   - avoid unjust, evil, and idolatrous patterns of work;
   - prayerfully intercede for their industry, clients, and coworkers;
   - support other disciples serving in the industry;
   - offer their work as worship to God.

5. *Blessing and Charge:* At the end, invite the congregation or elders to stand and surround the workers. Bless both the workers and their work in the name of the Father, Son, and Holy Spirit. Charge them to go out and work in ways that are honoring and responsive to God's work in the world.

Whenever possible, industrial vows, prayers, and blessings should be developed *with* the people who actually work in the industry. This pastoral practice honors the workers' spiritual insight, wisdom, and priesthood. It's vital that industrial prayers move beyond spiritual generalities and moral platitudes. They should be rooted in the raw and rough edges of the industry's lived reality.

For a more general commissioning service, one that is inclusive of all vocations, see J. Fletcher Lowe's model in the sidebar "A Commissioning to Vocation in Daily Life." In general, the call-and-response pattern in that model enables workers to be active participants in the commissioning.[4]

---

4. For an example of a commissioning service that enlists the participation of the entire congregation, see the Center for Faith and Work at LeTourneau University's "Commissioning Service for Christians in the Workplace," https://centerforfaithandwork.com/article/commissioning-service-christians-workplace.

A Commissioning to Vocation in Daily Life

Leader: My Brothers and Sisters in Christ Jesus: we are all baptized by one Spirit into one Body, and given gifts for a variety of ministries for the common good. In the ministry of your daily life and work, will you proclaim by word and example the Good News of God in Christ?
Answer: I Will
Leader: In your daily occupation, will you seek and serve Christ in all persons, loving your neighbor as yourself?
Answer: I Will
Leader: In the vocation to which God has called you, will you strive for justice and peace among all people, and respect the dignity of every human being?
Answer: I Will
Leader: Name the occupation for which you seek God's blessing.
(Each person names their occupation.)
Leader: Let us pray. Almighty God, whose Son Jesus Christ in his earthly life shared our toil and made holy our labor: be present with your people where they work. Deliver us from the service of self alone, and grant that we, remembering the account that we must one day give, may be faithful stewards of your good gifts; for the sake of him who came among us as one who serves, your Son our Savior Jesus Christ. Amen.
In the Name of God, I recognize and affirm your commitment to follow Christ in the vocation to which God has called you. May the Holy Spirit guide and strengthen you to bear faithful witness to Christ, and to carry on his work of reconciliation in the world.[a]

a. Lowe, "A Commissioning to Vocation in Daily Life." Used with permission.

The Catholic liturgy below prescribes the use of oil to anoint and bless newly commissioned workers. A bowl of oil is placed in the center of the group, and the liturgy runs as follows:

God blesses our work, the work of human hands, to make the land fruitful and to provide food for us. Let us ask God to mark our hands and our labors with a blessing this day.

(Invite all to extend their hands over the bowl of oil to be used for the blessing.)

Blessed are you, Lord God, for through your goodness this oil is the fruit of the earth and the work of human hands. By your mighty love, it carries your blessing to us and to all that we do. Let it be a blessing to all who labor with their hands and to all who work with the land.

Blessed be God forever.

(All are invited to bless each other's hands, tracing the oil on the palms in the shape of a cross.)[5]

Sending Workers toward Monday

> The word "Mass" is derived from the Latin, *mitto miss*, meaning, "you are sent."
>
> —Constance Cherry, *The Worship Architect*

Worship that shapes and scatters workers will close with two critical elements: a blessing and a charge.[6] The *blessing* boldly reminds workers of God's imminent presence and power before, beside, and within their working lives. The *charge* boldly reminds workers of the public implications of God's blessing. Workers now have an active responsibility to labor in ways that are responsive to the blessings and work of God in their lives.[7] As Constance Cherry explains, the pastoral charge "is the 'so that' of the blessing; we are blessed for a purpose."[8]

In the book of Numbers, Israelite farmers, herdsman, and merchants are blessed with the following words: "The LORD bless you and keep you; the LORD make his face shine on you and be gracious to you; the LORD turn his face toward you and give you peace" (6:24–26). Psalm 67:1 invokes this blessing but, instructively, goes on to say that the blessing's purpose is "that [God's] ways may be known on earth, [God's] salvation among all nations" (67:2). The

---

5. "Blessing All Who Work the Land," Catholic Rural Life, https://catholicrurallife.org /resources/spiritual/calendar-of-blessings/5-may-blessing-of-all-who-work-the-land.

6. "The two primary parts of the sending are known as the 'benediction' and the 'charge.'" Cherry, *The Worship Architect*, 113.

7. "A blessing without a charge lacks the connection to service; a charge without a blessing lacks the sense of power needed for service." Cherry, *The Worship Architect*, 115.

8. Cherry, *The Worship Architect*, 115.

Benedictions for Sending Workers toward Monday

Benediction 1

God of goodness,
Your Son called his disciples to follow
in the midst of their daily work.
So, too, you call each of us today to give our lives:
to love, to work, and to serve your people.
As we go forth from this place,
let our callings be joined in response to your call:
our "yes"—at home, at work, and at play—
to the fullness of life that you offer.

May we give the whole of ourselves and our lives
to the redeeming work of your Spirit in our world,
and may our homes and workplaces
be changed by the vision of your hope and love.
We ask this through Christ our Lord. Amen.[a]

Benediction 2

God of our callings, we ask you to bless these men and women
gathered here today. Fill them with your strength, guide them

Aaronic blessing is joined to the Abrahamic charge, when God declares, "I will bless you . . . so that you will be a blessing" (Gen. 12:2 NRSV).

The book of Hebrews echoes this blessing-and-charge structure: "May the God of peace, who through the blood of the eternal covenant brought back from the dead our Lord Jesus, that great Shepherd of the sheep, equip you with everything good for doing his will, and may he work in us what is pleasing to him, through Jesus Christ, to whom be glory for ever and ever. Amen" (13:20–21). Blessing and charge go hand in hand as people disperse *to continue* their worship through their vocations. Three good examples of benedictions that express this pattern are given in the sidebar "Benedictions for Sending Workers toward Monday."

The benediction must repeatedly remind workers that they are called not to a "moment" of worship but rather to a life of worship.[9] The benediction

9. "The way in which we part answers questions of how we will be in relationship while apart and what we will do until we meet again." Cherry, *The Worship Architect*, 112.

with your love. Let them know of our prayers and support for their daily work. Lead all of us to work together toward your vision of flourishing for creation. We ask that you bless each one of us in our labors, and send us forth to serve your name.
(Stretch out your hands in blessing or bless the hands of each person in turn.)
May God bless you and the work of your hands, now and forevermore. Amen.[b]

Benediction 3
O God, our Father, in Jesus Christ your Son you have called us to true discipleship and service. Help us to be always watchful of our attitudes, so that when Christ comes in glory to receive us we may be prepared to enter with him into his Kingdom. Help us to be faithful in all our relationships and diligent in all our work, so that we can be trusted to be and to do what you expect of us. Help us to be peacemakers wherever we are, so that as we strive for truth and justice we may do so with humility as children of your Kingdom. Help us to be so Christ-like on earth, that finally we may reign with Christ in heaven. Amen.[c]

a. Fanucci, *To Bless Our Callings*, 123–24. Used with permission.
b. Fanucci, *To Bless Our Callings*, 161. Used with permission.
c. "Biddings and Blessings from the Methodist Church in the Caribbean and the Americas." Used with permission.

marks not the end of worship but its beginning. The movements and practices of Christlike grace and service, habituated in the sanctuary, must now spill out into the streets.

Worshipers can prepare their bodies to receive this benediction. They can open their hands to receive it, or, better yet, they can turn their bodies and face the exit—the world outside. The pastor's blessing can then be voiced over their shoulders and into the city. In the turning of workers' bodies, the sanctuary can then release its full systolic force into the world. The benediction can scatter worshipers into their vocations for a week of work, worship, and service (Hebrew, *avodah*). Embodied movements like these allow the words of blessing and charge to be received with missional power and focus. Here is one brief example of what this looks like for a worker we interviewed.

Jean spends her week working with stroke patients as a speech therapist. Her work is rewarding but also demanding and stressful. She practices a unique ritual during the benediction to prepare herself for the challenges of

Monday. Jean closes her eyes and pictures the faces of her patients as the pastor declares, "May the blessing of God Almighty, the Father, Son, and Holy Spirit, be upon us and through us with all those to whom he sends us, now and forever. Amen."[10] In stillness, Jean hears God respond, "Go out and serve *these people* on my behalf."[11] Now begins her worship in the world—"the liturgy after the liturgy."

---

10. This benediction is used at Grace Brethren Church of Long Beach in California. It is allegedly based on part of a lecture given by N. T. Wright.

11. Willson, "Shaping the Lenses on Everyday Work," 243–44.

Epilogue

Rethinking Monday

Rethinking Sunday in the light of Monday. That has been the focus of the book. How can Sunday worship faithfully engage work and workers? *But what about Monday?* Clearly, Sunday morning is not enough. A single hour in the sanctuary cannot possibly sustain workers on its own. The daily churn is too much, the challenges and idols too many. The dialogue between workers and their God must continue throughout the week.

This book is admittedly incomplete. Focused on Sunday, it does not venture out to rethink the practices of professionals on Monday. Daily spiritual practices of prayer, worship, and liturgy *for Monday* are clearly critical. Workers need to learn how to practice the presence of God on a daily basis as they move through their workplaces.[1] Moreover, much more work needs to be done to analyze how modern workplaces shape, form, and discipline workers on a daily basis in ways that are both honoring and dishonoring to their creator.

Furthermore, we've discussed how the institutional church needs to rethink how it gathers, equips, and sends the workers on Sunday morning. But we've not discussed how the church needs to rethink its ministries to disciple workers throughout the week. We've not discussed how the church's institutional structures, its education systems, and its discipleship programs need to be redesigned to empower the priesthood of all believers and *their* vocational mission in the world.

Rethinking Sunday morning is a strategic place to begin, but by itself, gathered worship is simply not sufficient for cultivating the priesthood of all believers for God's mission in the world. The liturgy, education, and

---

1. See Daniels and Vandewarker, *Working in the Presence of God*; T. Warren, *Liturgy of the Ordinary*.

discipleship efforts of the church need to work together; they need to reinforce one another.

In the introduction we argued that the modern divorce between faith, work, and worship is an extremely powerful cultural force. It is a gusting cultural wind that constantly threatens to pull our lives apart. Sunday morning cannot confront these powerful realities alone. Sunday rituals are not the only rituals that need to be rethought; *Monday rituals need to change as well.* Workers need spiritual guidance on how to habitually draw near to God, listen to God, and faithfully worship God in and through their daily work. This requires spiritual wisdom and practice. Workers need to understand how their *everyday* practices, rituals, and habits in the workplace direct them either toward or away from God and God's gracious economy. Everyday liturgies for the workplace are needed to guide not simply workers' minds but their hearts and hands as well.

The pastoral vocation throughout the week must change as well. Cultivating the priesthood of all believers must become integral to a pastor's week. *The pastor's role is that of a servant; pastors exist to serve the servants of God—the holy priesthood in the world.* Empowering the vocational mission of the laity in the city through the ministry of the word and sacrament is the pastor's mission. This obviously means that rethinking Sunday morning is not enough; pastors need to rethink their discipleship throughout the week as well.

In order for church leaders to serve the priesthood of believers, they will need to become *more conversant* with the working lives of people in their communities. They don't need to become experts in each vocational domain, but they do need to become conversant. They must do this because the mission of their church will be embodied in the everyday working lives of its priests.

New practices for pastoral ministry are needed to reorient church leaders around equipping the priesthood for work and worship. The traditional practices of preaching and teaching remain important facets. However, if equipping the lives of the laity is considered central, a pastor's approach to preaching and teaching will need to change as well.

All of this change may well sound exhausting to pastors, but it shouldn't. The heavy weight of holy worship and work is no longer carried by one priest in the congregation. The heavy weight of God's mission and glory is now graciously spread out. It is now carried by a whole community of priests. The pastor does not bear the work of God alone. And, to be truthful, not even the whole priesthood could or should attempt to bear its full weight. Their high priest, Jesus Christ, carries their work and worship to the Father on their behalf. He carries both the pastor and the professional forward. Their work becomes worship through Christ's strength alone.

The centrality of the priesthood of all believers is not a new or innovative idea. It did not begin with the modern faith and work movement. Nor did it even emerge with Martin Luther or the Reformation movement. Its deep roots can be found in the early church and Scripture itself.[2] The priesthood of humanity can be heard in the creational call of Adam and Eve. It can be seen in Cain and Abel's primal desire to offer their humble work in priestly worship to God. The priesthood of all believers is anything but new.

That said, new work does need to be done. Pastors, professionals, and theologians together need to unearth and make actionable this biblical vision of priestly work. *In too many churches the "priesthood of all believers" remains an abstract theological doctrine without a lived (or liturgical) reality.*

Fortunately, we are not without a witness. There are many capable individuals and institutions ready to lend a hand. For decades now the steady, insightful work of leaders such as Steven Garber, R. Paul Stevens, Katherine Leary Alsdorf, Robert Banks, and Richard Mouw has provided rich theological and pastoral insights for workers and church leaders alike. Recently, several institutions have taken up this important work as well. Made to Flourish Network, the De Pree Center for Christian Leadership, the Theology of Work Project, and the Center for Faith and Work in New York City are just a few of the many organizations deeply engaged in providing church leaders with resources for equipping the priesthood of all believers.

Seminaries and theological scholars have a long way to go in terms of contributing actionable academic resources on these issues. This can begin only when theological scholars humbly listen to and learn from the priesthood at work in the marketplace. This will require scholars to learn new modes of ethnographic research that theologically attends to workers on the front lines of God's mission in the world. This ethnographic attentiveness must inform their theological, liturgical, and pastoral reflections on this doctrine that we call "the priesthood of all believers." With that, we close with the wise embodied witness of Brother Lawrence:

> As he proceeded in his work, he continued his familiar conversation with his Maker, imploring His grace, and offering to Him all his actions. When he had finished, he examined himself how he had discharged his duty; if he found well, he returned thanks to GOD; if otherwise, he asked pardon; and without being discouraged, he set his mind right again, and continued his exercise of

2. Eastwood, *The Royal Priesthood of the Faithful.*

the presence of GOD, as if he had never deviated from it. "Thus," said he, "by rising after my falls, and by frequently renewed acts of faith and love, I am come to a state, wherein it would be as difficult for me not to think of GOD, as it was at first to accustom myself to it. . . . The time of business," said he, "does not with me differ from the time of prayer; and in the noise and clutter of my kitchen, while several persons are at the same time calling for different things, I possess GOD in as great tranquility as if I were upon my knees at the Blessed Sacrament."[3]

3. Brother Lawrence, *The Practice of the Presence of God*, 9.

Acknowledgments

Matt and Cory are slow learners. A variety of individuals and institutions have been inexplicably patient with us. This project is the end result of a gracious network of generous friends and colleagues, schools and churches, students and family members. A great cloud of witnesses, they contributed to every page in this book. Cory and Matt's communal debts are deep and broad. And, while we cannot repay these debts, we can name a few.

We are grateful to our doctoral mentor, Richard Mouw, for his steadfast friendship, wisdom, and support over this past decade. We also thank our faithful theological guides in the Netherlands: Cornelis van der Kooi and George Harinck; our senior colleagues from whom we have learned so much over the years: John Witvliet, Nicholas Wolterstorff, Denise Daniels, James K. A. Smith, Gideon Strauss, Katherine Leary Alsdorf, and Steven Garber; our peers who have offered their continued encouragement, guidance, and friendship: Bob Covolo, James Eglington, Scott Calgaro, and David Kim; our research assistants, Zack Ellis and David Park, for their enthusiasm and hard work organizing our diverse sources and building the references for this book; and our colleagues who helped us gain a richer understanding of the global church and its witness on worship and work: Ruth Padilla DeBorst, Tomoko Arakawa, Juan Martinez, Daniel Ramirez, Emmanuel Bellon, Richard Gardner, and Doug McConnell.

We are also mutually indebted to a number of generative institutions that have supported our research over the years: Fuller Theological Seminary; the Max De Pree Center for Leadership; Calvin Theological Seminary; Calvin Institute of Christian Worship; Made to Flourish Network; the Christian Reformed Church; *Comment* magazine; Cardus; Baker Publishing; the Center for Faith and Work at Redeemer Presbyterian Church; Porter's Gate Sacred

Arts Collective; KIROS Business Fellowship; Gotham Fellows; Oikonomia Network; the Center for Business Integrity at Seattle Pacific University; Vrije Universiteit Amsterdam; M. J. Murdock Charitable Trust; and Theologische Universiteit Kampen.

I (Matt) am deeply grateful to all the pastors, professionals, and churches who contributed to the Cascade Fellows faith and work ministry in Seattle, Washington. I am particularly indebted to my staff and pastoral partners in that effort, so thank you Shannon Sigler, David Arinder, Shannon Vandewarker, Jennifer Hill, Ryan Beattie, Lauren Pattie, Allyson Darakjian, and Mark Mohrlang. Working and serving alongside all of you was a truly formative education in faithful work and worship. Every page of this book bears the marks of the years we spent learning together. I'm grateful for them and you.

Several business leaders and Christian professionals have patiently taught, mentored, and befriended me along the way: Uli Chi, Steve Bell, Jessica Hsieh, Teri Howe, Jennifer Porter, Steve Aeschbacher, Nancy and Al Erisman, Bob Richards, Ryan Moede, Jeffrey Riddell, Natalie McElroy, and all the members of Grace Presbyterian's business fellowship (the NBSB).

My thanks as well to Mark Roberts for his ever-faithful support, feedback, and encouragement. I'm grateful to his whole team at the De Pree Center and his doctoral students within Fuller Seminary's DMin program in faith, work, economics, and vocation. I'm particularly thankful for their thoughtful engagement with my trial lectures on work and worship.

I'm also appreciative of my colleagues and friends who graciously agreed to read sections of the book and offer substantive feedback: Noel Snyder, Luke Hyder, John Goldingay, Andy Dearman, Matthew Whitney, Scott Cormode, Steve Young, Stewart Graham, Brian Dijkema, Luke Bobo, Matt Rusten, Porter Taylor, David Taylor, Brian Turnbow, and Todd Johnson. Thanks to Dan Carter, who went the distance and offered extensive pastoral feedback throughout.

And thanks to my family. To my three rambunctious and joy-filled sons, Calvin, Kees, and Caedmon, for helping your dad build a tiny shed in our backyard where I could write this book. That little shed and this (not so little) book took me away from our games far too often. I'm glad that you invaded my workspace and interrupted me as often as you did. Your demands for play were a divine interruption that I'm truly grateful for. To our parents, Donna and Gary, Wendy and Stewart, I'm grateful for the steadfast love, support, and encouragement you freely give to our family.

And finally, gratitude to my beloved wife, Heather—a worship leader and liturgical theologian in her own right. Your friendship and feedback, your love and encouragement, saw me through the longest and hardest days of this project. You were a consistent and stabilizing hand as I wearied and wavered. I'm continually grateful for the ways in which Christ makes his grace known to me through you. My gratitude grows.

I (Cory) am deeply indebted to a group of pastors, worship leaders, and chaplains who have influenced my thinking over several years and who offered thoughtful feedback on this project: Beth Balmer, Jessica Garcia, Wil Rogan, Ryan Bestelmeyer, Steven Gros, Daniel Long, Jesse Krohmer, Josh Swanson, Christina Rea, Jen Rozema, Jack Droppers, Derek Zeyl, Matt Postma, and Margriet van der Kooi. Your seasoned pastoral wisdom grounded this project in the lived realities of workers and pastoral ministry. I am well aware that my ability to connect with the lived experiences of church leaders is due to your influence.

A special thank you is in order for Bill Hoehn for his support and belief in this research project. In the early stages of my research he introduced me to his corporate chaplain, Roy Inzunza. Roy's friendship and wisdom on being a priestly presence among workers have been priceless. Bill and Roy, thank you for your support and enthusiasm for this project.

I am indebted to a group of pastors who introduced me to an amazing collection of workers who shared with me about their experiences of work, worship, and church: Tyler Johnson, Jim Mullins, Riccardo Stewart, Jonathan Gundlach, Eric Marsh, and Lou Huesmann. The trust you showed in me opened doors for me to interview several diverse groups of workers in your churches. These interviews proved to be an education of their own to me. The questions I ask, the way I approach my work as a theologian, and my own habits of inhabiting gathered worship have been deeply impacted by these workers.

Ruth and Jim Padilla DeBorst, thank you for your hospitality at Casa Adobe. The hospitality your community showed me and the Resonate Mission Innovation Team was formative on several levels. Our daily prayers and night of worship exposed me to numerous prophetic prayers and songs from a variety of countries in Latin America. These songs and prayers embodied what had, to that point, largely been an interesting theoretical idea in my head. My imagination was enlarged by the images and language of daily work evoked in songs of lament and of praise. A special thank you to Heidi Michelson for granting us permission to use her addition to the song "Vos Sos el Dios de los Pobres."

My thanks as well to Roel Kuiper, George Harinck, Jos Colijn, Hans Schaeffer, and the community at the Theologische Universiteit Kampen for your warm hospitality during the fall of 2018. Being in the city of Herman Bavinck while researching for this book was an inspiration, and your friendship is a gift.

Thank you to my students at Calvin Theological Seminary who persistently asked for lived examples of prayers and liturgies that empower the priesthood of believers. The creative ways in which you have taken this vision of the liturgy providing an intensification of life in the world have been inspiring and instructive to me. Hearing you compose prayers of praise, lament, confession, and petition for your parishes gives me hope for the next generation of pastors and worship leaders. Kristy Bootsma and Nicole Romero, thank you for your bold prophetic prayers in the seminary chapel during the fall of 2019. Anthony Vander Schaaf, thank you for your thoughtful and candid reflections on the book in light of your experiences. You helped keep my theology grounded in the raw realities of work. Jason Crossen, Christopher Bouma, and Zach DeBruyne, thank you for your helpful questions and feedback on the ideas of this book. Your excitement for this project and for ministry organized around the priesthood of believers encourages me to keep striving for ways to serve ministry leaders.

All good theology is grounded in relationships. A special thank you to my colleagues at Calvin Seminary who share a passion to form leaders to serve Christ in their diverse contexts around the world. Mariano, David, Geoff, Danjuma, and John, thank you for checking in on me throughout this writing project. I want to thank a group of people whose friendship has directly and indirectly shaped this book: Jana and Andrew Mead, Hannah and Alison Kummer, Jordan Bremer, Breanna Vander Schaaf, Chris and Jane Klein, Todd and Katharine Broberg, Albert and Carolyn Strydhorst, and Moses Chung. Without your companionship here in Grand Rapids I would not be in a position to undertake this research project. To my parents, David and Anita, thank you for your faithful love and consistent, practical care for our family and home. Your visits have helped us joyfully welcome a new child into a loving and safe environment.

To my wife, Monica, and my son, Warren. Thank you for your consistent love and embrace. Warren, you entered into this world in the last stage of this project. You have no idea how much your big brown eyes fill my heart with joy and spur me on to worship. You train me to enter more fully into the materiality of my life in this world, and it is there that I grow in my knowledge of God and myself. As I enter into the sanctuary, I offer up an offering of thanksgiving for you and your mother—two testimonies of God's surprising grace in my life. Monica, we have sowed with many tears and have found a song of joy (Ps. 126). I am forever grateful for the tangible love and wisdom God has given me through your friendship and companionship.

Bibliography

Adeyemo, Tokunboh, ed. *Africa Bible Commentary: A One-Volume Commentary Written by 70 African Scholars*. Nairobi: Zondervan Academic, 2006.

Agamben, Giorgio. *The Omnibus Homo Sacer*. Stanford: Stanford University Press, 2017.

Alford, Henry. "Come, Ye Faithful People, Come." Lyrics: 1844. Tune: George J. Elvey, 1858. Hymnary.org, https://hymnary.org/media/fetch/139853.

Allen, O. Wesley, Jr. "Between Text and Sermon: Isaiah 58:1–12." *Interpretation* 73 (2019): 191–93.

Altmann, Peter. *Festive Meals in Ancient Israel: Deuteronomy's Identity Politics in Their Ancient Near Eastern Context*. Beihefte zur Zeitschrift für die alttestamentliche Wissenschaft 424. Berlin: de Gruyter, 2011.

———. "Making the Meal Sacred in the Old Testament: Complexities and Possibilities for Christian Appropriation." In *Sacrality and Materiality: Locating Intersections*, edited by Rebecca Giselbrecht and Ralph Kunz, 115–27. Göttingen: Vandenhoeck & Ruprecht, 2016.

———. "Sacred Meals and Feasts in the Old Testament/Hebrew Bible and Its Environment: A 'Treasure Chest' for Early Christian Reflection." In *The Eucharist—Its Origins and Contexts: Sacred Meal, Communal Meal, Table Fellowship in Late Antiquity, Early Judaism, and Early Christianity*, edited by David Hellholm and Dieter Sänger, 1:23–41. 3 vols. Wissenschaftliche Untersuchungen zum Neuen Testament 376. Tübingen: Mohr Siebeck, 2017.

Ambrose, Gill, ed. *Together for a Season: All-Age Resources for Feasts and Festivals of the Christian Year*. London: Church House Publishing, 2009.

Ammerman, Nancy Tatom. *Sacred Stories, Spiritual Tribes: Finding Religion in Everyday Life*. New York: Oxford University Press, 2014.

Anderson, Bernhard W. *Out of the Depths: The Psalms Speak for Us Today*. 3rd ed. Louisville: Westminster John Knox, 2000.

Anglican Eucharistic Liturgies 1985–2010: The Authorized Rites of the Anglican Communion. Edited by Colin Buchanan. London: Canterbury Press Norwich, 2011.

Anizor, Uche, and Hank Voss. *Representing Christ: A Vision for the Priesthood of All Believers*. Downers Grove, IL: InterVarsity, 2016.

"Apple Spas Is the Most Important of Three Savior Days." *ItsUkraine.Com* (blog), August 19, 2015. http://itsukraine.com/events/apple-spas-is-the-most-important -of-three-savoir-days.

Armerding, C. E. "Festivals and Feasts." In *Dictionary of the Old Testament: Pentateuch*, edited by T. Desmond Alexander and David W. Baker, 300–313. Downers Grove, IL: InterVarsity, 2003.

Atchley, E. G., and F. Cuthbert. *Ordo Romanus Primus*. Edited by Vernon Staley. Library of Liturgiology and Ecclesiology 6. London: De La More, 1905.

Atkinson, Tyler. *Singing at the Winepress: Ecclesiastes and the Ethics of Work*. New York: Bloomsbury T&T Clark, 2015.

Augustine. *City of God*, books 8–16. Translated by Gerald Walsh and Grace Monahan. The Fathers of the Church: A New Translation, vol. 14. New York: Fathers of the Church, 1952.

———. *On the Psalms*. Translated by Scholastica Hebgin and Felicitas Corrigan. 2 vols. Ancient Christian Writers 29, 30. Westminster, MD: Newman, 1960.

Averbeck, R. E. "Sacrifices and Offerings." In *Dictionary of the Old Testament: Pentateuch*, edited by T. Desmond Alexander and David W. Baker, 706–33. Downers Grove, IL: InterVarsity, 2003.

Baldovin, John F. "Eucharistic Prayer." In *The New Westminster Dictionary of Liturgy and Worship*, edited by Paul Bradshaw, 192–99. Louisville: Westminster John Knox, 2002.

———. *The Urban Character of Worship: The Origins, Development, and Meaning of Stational Liturgy*. Orientalia Christiana Analecta 228. Rome: Pontifical Oriental Institute, 1987.

Balentine, Samuel E. *The Torah's Vision of Worship*. Minneapolis: Fortress, 1999.

Banks, Robert. *God the Worker: Journeys into the Mind, Heart and Imagination of God*. Eugene, OR: Wipf & Stock, 1992.

Barna Group. "Is the Gap Between Pulpit & Pew Narrowing?" Report published for the Center for Faith and Work at LeTourneau University, 2015. https://centerfor faithandwork.com/node/804.

Barowski, Oded. *Agriculture in Iron Age Israel*. Winona Lake, IN: Eisenbrauns, 1987.

Barram, Michael. "Between Text and Sermon: Isaiah 58:1–12." *Interpretation* 69 (2015): 460–62.

Bavinck, Herman. *Sin and Salvation in Christ.* Vol. 3 of *Reformed Dogmatics.* Translated by John Vriend. Edited by John Bolt. Grand Rapids: Baker Academic, 2006.

Bayly, Lewis. *The Practice of Piety: Amplified with Notes by the Author.* Edited by C. Matthew McMahon and Therese B. McMahon. Coconut Creek, FL: Puritan Publications, 2012.

Beal, Lissa M. Wray. *1 & 2 Kings.* Apollos Old Testament Commentary 9. Downers Grove, IL: InterVarsity, 2014.

Beale, G. K. *The Temple and the Church's Mission: A Biblical Theology of the Dwelling Place of God.* Downers Grove, IL: InterVarsity, 2004.

Beckett, John D. *Mastering Monday: A Guide to Integrating Faith and Work.* Downers Grove, IL: InterVarsity, 2006.

Begbie, Jeremy S. *Resounding Truth: Christian Wisdom in the World of Music.* Grand Rapids: Baker Academic, 2007.

Benedict. *The Rule of St. Benedict.* Edited by Timothy Fry. Collegeville, MN: Liturgical Press, 1982.

Benson, Bruce Ellis. *Liturgy as a Way of Life: Embodying the Arts in Christian Worship.* Grand Rapids: Baker Academic, 2013.

Berry, Priscilla. *Fostering Spirituality in the Workplace: A Leader's Guide to Sustainability.* New York: Business Expert, 2013.

Berry, Wendell. *The Farm.* Berkeley: Counterpoint, 1995.

Blenkinsopp, Joseph. *Sage, Priest, Prophet: Religious and Intellectual Leadership in Ancient Israel.* Louisville: Westminster John Knox, 1995.

Bliney, Moses O. *From Africa to America: Religion and Adaptation among Ghanaian Immigrants in New York.* New York: New York University Press, 2011.

Boff, Leonardo. *Church, Charism and Power: Liberation Theology and the Institutional Church.* Translated by John W. Diercksmeier. New York: Crossroad, 1985.

Boniface-Malle, Anastasia. "Numbers." In *Africa Bible Commentary: A One-Volume Commentary Written by 70 African Scholars,* edited by Tokunboh Adeyemo, 169–208. Grand Rapids: Zondervan, 2006.

Borenstein, Daniel, ed. *Medieval Christianity.* A People's History of Christianity 4. Minneapolis: Fortress, 2009.

Boylston, Tom. "The Shade of the Divine: Approaching the Sacred in an Ethiopian Orthodox Christian Community." PhD diss., London School of Economics, 2012.

Bradshaw, Paul. *Daily Prayer in the Early Church: A Study of the Origin and Early Development of the Divine Office.* Eugene, OR: Wipf & Stock, 2008.

———. "Difficulties in Doing Liturgical Theology." *Pacifica* 11, no. 2 (1998): 181–94.

———. *Early Christian Worship: A Basic Introduction to Ideas and Practice.* Collegeville, MN: Liturgical Press, 2010.

———. *Essays on Early Eastern Eucharistic Prayers.* Collegeville, MN: Liturgical Press, 1997.

————. *Eucharistic Origins*. London: SPCK, 2004.

————. "Gregory Dix and the Offertory Procession." *Theology* 120, no. 1 (2017): 27–33.

————. "Harvest Thanksgiving." In *The New SCM Dictionary of Liturgy and Worship*, edited by Paul Bradshaw, 233–34. London: SCM, 2005.

————. *The Search for the Origins of Christian Worship: Sources and Methods for the Study of Early Liturgy*. 2nd ed. Oxford: Oxford University Press, 2002.

————. *Two Ways of Praying: Introducing Liturgical Spirituality*. 2nd ed. Maryville, TN: OSL Publications, 2008.

Bradshaw, Paul F., and Maxwell E. Johnson. *The Eucharistic Liturgies: Their Evolution and Interpretation*. Collegeville, MN: Liturgical Press, 2012.

Bradshaw, Paul F., Maxwell E. Johnson, and L. Edward Phillips. *The Apostolic Tradition: A Commentary*. Edited by Harold W. Attridge. Hermeneia. Minneapolis: Fortress, 2002.

Bradshaw, Paul, and Bryan Spinks, eds. *Liturgy in Dialogue: Essays in Memory of Ronald Jasper*. London: SPCK, 1993.

Brock, Brian. *Christian Ethics in a Technological Age*. Grand Rapids: Eerdmans, 2010.

Brooke, George J., ed. *Studies on the Texts of the Desert of Judah*. Boston: Brill, 2012.

Brother Lawrence. *The Practice of the Presence of God*. Edited by Donald E. Demaray. New York: Alba House, 1997.

Brown, Colin, ed. *The New International Dictionary of the New Testament*. Grand Rapids: Zondervan, 1978.

Brown, Peter. *Through the Eye of a Needle: Wealth, the Fall of Rome, and the Making of Christianity in the West, 350–550 AD*. Princeton: Princeton University Press, 2012.

Brown, William W., ed. *Anti-Slavery Harp: A Collection of Songs for Anti-Slavery Meetings*. 3rd ed. Boston: Bela Marsh, 1851.

Browning, Elizabeth Barrett. *Aurora Leigh*. New York: Oxford University Press, 1993.

Brueggemann, Walter. "The Book of Exodus: Introduction, Commentary, and Reflections." In *The New Interpreter's Bible*, vol. 1, *General Articles on the Bible, General Articles on the Old Testament, the Book of Genesis, Book of Exodus, Book of Leviticus*. Nashville: Abingdon, 1994.

————. *Deuteronomy*. Abingdon Old Testament Commentaries. Nashville: Abingdon, 2001.

————. *Israel's Praise: Doxology against Idolatry and Ideology*. Minneapolis: Fortress, 1988.

————. *Spirituality of the Psalms*. Minneapolis: Fortress, 2002.

————. *Theology of the Old Testament: Testimony, Dispute, Advocacy*. Minneapolis: Fortress, 1997.

————. *Worship in Ancient Israel: An Essential Guide*. Nashville: Abingdon, 2005.

Buchanan, Colin, ed. *Anglican Eucharistic Liturgies: 1985–2010; The Authorized Rites of the Anglican Communion*. London: Canterbury Press Norwich, 2011.

Burack, Elmer H. "Spiritually in the Workplace." *Journal of Organizational Change Management* 12, no. 4 (1999): 280–91.

Butland, Cameron. *Work in Worship: A Treasury of Prayers, Readings, and Hymns*. London: Hodder & Stoughton, 1985.

———. *Work in Worship*. Rev. ed. Edited by David Welbourn. London: Industrial Christian Fellowship, 1997.

Calvin, John. *Commentary on the Book of Psalms*. Translated by James Anderson. Vol. 4. Edinburgh: Calvin Translation Society, 1847.

———. *Institutes of the Christian Religion*. Edited by John T. McNeill. Translated by Ford Lewis Battles. Vol. 1. Louisville: Westminster John Knox, 1960.

Cardó, Daniel. *The Cross and the Eucharist in Early Christianity: A Theological and Liturgical Investigation*. Cambridge: Cambridge University Press, 2019.

Carrette, Jeremy, and Richard King. *Selling Spirituality: The Silent Takeover of Religion*. New York: Routledge, 2005.

Catholic Cultural Life. "May: Blessing All Who Work the Land." https://catholicrurallife.org/resources/spiritual/calendar-of-blessings/5-may-blessing-of-all-who-work-the-land.

Cherry, Constance M. *The Worship Architect: A Blueprint for Designing Culturally Relevant and Biblically Faithful Services*. Grand Rapids: Baker Academic, 2010.

Chi, Uli. "God's Call to Create and Serve through Business." September 23, 2014. https://www.youtube.com/watch?v=7W5E3430gGo.

Christensen, Richard L. "Deuteronomy 26:1–11." *Interpretation* 49 (1995): 59–62.

Chrysostom, John. *Baptismal Instructions*. Translated and Annotated by Paul W. Harkins. Ancient Christian Writers. Westminster: The Newman, 1963.

———. *Homilies on First Corinthians*. In *Saint Chrysostom: Homilies on the Epistles of Paul to the Corinthians*, edited by Philip Schaff, 54–58. Nicene and Post-Nicene Fathers of the Christian Church 12. New York: The Christian Literature Company, 1898.

Clapp, Rodney. *A Peculiar People: The Church as Culture in a Post-Christian Society*. Downers Grove, IL: InterVarsity, 1996.

Clement of Alexandria. "Exhortation to the Heathen." In *Ante-Nicene Fathers*, vol. 3, *Fathers of the Second Century: Hermas, Tatian, Theophilus, Athenagoras, and Clement of Alexandria*. Edited by Alexander Roberts, James Donaldson, and Arthur Cleveland Coxe. Translated by William Wilson. New York: Cosimo, 2007.

Clifford, R. J. *Creation Accounts in the Ancient Near East and in the Bible*. Catholic Biblical Quarterly Monograph Series 26. Washington, DC: Catholic University of America Press, 1994.

Coffey, David. "The Equipping Church." Theology of Work Project. https://www.theologyofwork.org/key-topics/the-equipping-church.

Cohen, Abraham. *Everyman's Talmud: The Major Teachings of the Rabbinic Sages.* New York: Schocken, 1949.

Common Worship: Services and Prayers for the Church of England. London: Church House, 2006.

Cone, James H. "Black Spirituals: A Theological Interpretation." *Theology Today* 29, no. 1 (1972): 54–69.

———. *God of the Oppressed.* Rev. ed. Maryknoll, NY: Orbis Books, 1997.

Connolly, R. Hugh. *Didascalia Apostolorum: The Syriac Version Translated and Accompanied by the Verona Latin Fragments.* Ancient Texts and Translations. Eugene, OR: Wipf & Stock, 2009.

Corbon, Jean. *The Wellspring of Worship.* Translated by Matthew J. O'Connell. San Francisco: Ignatius, 2005.

Cotter, Jim. *Out of the Silence . . . Into the Silence: Prayer's Daily Round.* Harlech: Cairns Publications, 2006.

Cox, Harvey. "Christianity." In *Global Religions: An Introduction,* edited by Mark Juergensmeyer, 17–27. New York: Oxford University Press, 2003.

Coxe, A. Cleveland, Alexander Roberts, and James Donaldson, eds. *Ante-Nicene Fathers: Translations of the Writings of the Fathers Down to A.D. 325.* 10 vols. New York: Christian Literature Publishing, 1885–96.

Crainshaw, Jill Y. *When I in Awesome Wonder: Liturgy Distilled from Daily Life.* Collegeville, MN: Liturgical Press, 2017.

Crawford, Matthew B. "The Case for Working with Your Hands." *New York Times Magazine,* May 21, 2009. https://www.nytimes.com/2009/05/24/magazine/24labor-t.html.

Cummings, Owen. *Eucharist and Ecumenism: The Eucharist across the Ages and Traditions.* Eugene, OR: Pickwick, 2013.

Cyprian. "Treaties 8: On Works and Alms." New Advent, 2020. http://www.newadvent.org/fathers/050708.htm.

Dahl, Gordon. *Work, Play, and Worship in a Leisure-Oriented Society.* Minneapolis: Augsburg, 1972.

Daly, Robert J. *Sacrifice Unveiled: The True Meaning of Christian Sacrifice.* New York: T&T Clark, 2009.

Daniels, Denise, and Shannon Vandewarker. *Working in the Presence of God: Spiritual Practices for Everyday Work.* Peabody, MA: Hendrickson, 2019.

Darden, Bob. *People Get Ready! A New History of Black Gospel Music.* New York: Continuum, 2004.

Davies, Eryl W. "Walking in God's Ways: The Concept of *Imitatio Dei* in the Old Testament." In *In Search of True Wisdom: Essays in Old Testament Interpretation in Honour of Ronald E. Clements*, edited by Edward Ball, 99–115. Journal for the Study of the Old Testament Supplement Series 300. Sheffield: Sheffield Academic Press, 1999.

Davis, Ellen F. *Getting Involved with God: Rediscovering the Old Testament*. Lanham, MD: Rowman & Littlefield, 2001.

———. *Scripture, Culture, and Agriculture: An Agrarian Reading of the Bible*. Cambridge: Cambridge University Press, 2009.

Dawson, Gerrit Scott. *Jesus Ascended: The Meaning of Christ's Continuing Incarnation*. New York: T&T Clark, 2004.

Deist, Ferdinand E. *Material Culture of the Bible: An Introduction*. New York: Sheffield Academic Press, 2000.

Del Verme, Marcelle. *Didache and Judaism: Jewish Roots of an Ancient Christian-Jewish Work*. New York: T&T Clark, 2004.

De Vaux, Roland. *Ancient Israel: Its Life and Institutions*. Grand Rapids: Eerdmans, 1997.

Dillard, Cynthia B. "To Address Suffering That the Majority Can't See: Lessons from Black Women's Leadership in the Workplace." *New Directions for Adult and Continuing Education*, 152 (2016): 29–38.

Dix, Dom Gregory. *The Shape of the Liturgy*. New ed. New York: Continuum, 2005.

Dods, Marcus, ed. *The Works of Aurelius Augustine: A New Translation*. 15 vols. Edinburgh: T&T Clark, 1871–76.

Draper, Jonathan A. "First-Fruits and the Support of Prophets, Teachers, and the Poor in Didache 13 in Relation to New Testament Parallels." In *Trajectories through the New Testament and the Apostolic Fathers*, edited by Andrew F. Gregory and Christopher M. Tuckett, 223–43. New York: Oxford University Press, 2005.

Dreyer, Elizabeth. *Earth Crammed with Heaven: A Spirituality of Everyday Life*. New York: Paulist Press, 1994.

Driscoll, Jeremy. "Worship in the Spirit of Logos: Romans 12:1–2 and the Source and Summit of Christian Life." In *Letter and Spirit*, vol. 5, *Liturgy and Empire: Faith in Exile and Political Theology*, 77–101. Steubenville, OH: St. Paul Center for Biblical Theology, 2009.

Dyrness, William. *Poetic Theology: God and the Poetics of Everyday Life*. Grand Rapids: Eerdmans, 2011.

Eastwood, Cyril. *The Royal Priesthood of the Faithful: An Investigation of the Doctrine from Biblical Times to the Reformation*. Minneapolis: Augsburg, 1963.

Éla, Jean-Marc. *My Faith as an African*. Translated by John Pairman Brown and Susan Perry. Eugene, OR: Wipf & Stock, 1988.

English, Leona M., and Paula Cameron. "Social Justice and Spirituality: Educating for a Complicated Workplace." *New Directions for Adult and Continuing Education* 152 (2016): 19–27.

Fagerberg, David. *Consecrating the World: On Mundane Liturgical Theology*. Kettering, OH: Angelico, 2016.

———. *Theologia Prima: What Is Liturgical Theology?* 2nd ed. Chicago: Hillenbrand, 2004.

Fanucci, Laura Kelly. *To Bless Our Callings: Prayers, Poems, and Hymns to Celebrate Vocation*. Eugene, OR: Wipf & Stock, 2017.

Ferguson, Everett. "Sacrifices." In *Encyclopedia of Early Christianity*, edited by Everett Ferguson, 1015–17. 2nd ed. New York: Routledge, 2013.

Fields, Colin. "Jesus the Worker in 'Misa Campesina.'" *Plough Music Series* (blog), May 8, 2014. https://www.plough.com/en/topics/culture/music/jesus-the-worker-in-misa-campesina.

Foley, Edward, John F. Baldovin, Mary Collins, and Joanne M. Pierce, eds. *A Commentary on the Order of Mass of the Roman Missal: A New English Translation Developed under the Auspices of the Catholic Academy of Liturgy*. Collegeville, MN: Liturgical Press, 2011.

Fretheim, Terence E. "The Book of Genesis: Introduction, Commentary, and Reflections." In *The New Interpreter's Bible*, vol. 1, *General Articles on the Bible, General Articles on the Old Testament, the Book of Genesis, Book of Exodus, Book of Leviticus*. Nashville: Abingdon, 1994.

———. *Exodus*. Interpretation: A Bible Commentary for Teaching and Preaching. Louisville: Westminster John Knox, 2010.

Garber, Steven. "Vocation as Integral, Not Incidental." The Washington Institute for Faith, Vocation and Culture, April 25, 2011. http://www.washingtoninst.org/893/vocation-as-integral-not-incidental.

Garnett, Sterling. "Liturgy, Greece and Rome." In *The Encyclopedia of Ancient History*, edited by Roger Bagnall, Kai Brodersen, Craige B. Champion, Andrew Erskine, and Sabine R. Huebner, 4119–21. Malden, MA: Wiley-Blackwell, 2012.

Gebru, Mebratu Kiros. "Liturgical Cosmology: The Theological and Sacramental Dimensions of Creation in the Ethiopian Liturgy." PhD diss., Toronto School of Theology, 2012.

Geoghegan, Arthur T. *The Attitude towards Labor in Early Christianity and Ancient Culture*. Washington, DC: Catholic University of America Press, 1945.

George, Cathy H. *You Are Already Praying: Stories of God at Work*. New York: Morehouse, 2013.

Gerety, Rowan Moore. "Buying the Body of Christ." *Killing the Buddha* (blog), January 3, 2012. http://killingthebuddha.com/mag/dogma/buying-the-body-of-christ.

Giggie, John M. *After Redemption: Jim Crow and the Transformation of African American Religion in the Delta; 1875–1915*. New York: Oxford University Press, 2008.

Godoy, Carlos Mejía. *La misa campesina nicaragüense*. Managua: Ministeria de Cultura, 1980.

Goheen, Michael. *Introducing Christian Mission Today: Scripture, History, and Issues*. Downers Grove, IL: IVP Academic, 2014.

———. "The Missional Calling of Believers in the World: Lesslie Newbigin's Contribution." In *A Scandalous Prophet: The Way of Mission after Newbigin*, edited by Thomas F. Foust, George R. Hunsberger, J. Andrew Kirk, and Werner Ustorf, 37–55. Grand Rapids: Eerdmans, 2002.

Goldingay, John. *Isaiah*. Understanding the Bible Commentary Series. Grand Rapids: Baker Books, 2012.

———. *Israel's Gospel*. Vol. 1 of *Old Testament Theology*. Downers Grove, IL: IVP Academic, 2003.

———. *Israel's Life*. Vol. 3 of *Old Testament Theology*. Downers Grove, IL: IVP Academic, 2009.

———. *Psalms*. Baker Commentary on the Old Testament Wisdom and Psalms. 3 vols. Grand Rapids: Baker Academic, 2006–8.

Grabbe, Lester L. *Judaic Religion in the Second Temple Period: Belief and Practice from the Exile to Yavneh*. New York: Routledge & Kegan Paul, 2000.

"Grand Rapids Drivers Must Give Bikes More Room under New 'Safe-Passing' Law." *Michigan Radio NPR*, September 29, 2015. https://www.michiganradio.org/post /grand-rapids-drivers-must-give-bikes-more-room-under-new-safe-passing-law.

Grumett, David. *Material Eucharist*. New York: Oxford University Press, 2016.

Guardini, Romano. *The Spirit of the Liturgy*. Translated by Ada Lane. New York: Continuum, 1998.

Guerric of Igny. *Liturgical Sermons*. Translated by the monks of Mount Saint Bernard Abbey. Cistercian Fathers Series 32. Spencer, MA: Cistercian Publications, 1970.

Guroian, Vigen. "Seeing Worship as Ethics: An Orthodox Perspective." *Journal of Religious Ethics* 13, no. 2 (1985): 332–59.

Guyton, Morgan. "Worship and Justice in the Feast of First Fruits (Deuteronomy 26)." *Mercy Not Sacrifice (Patheos)* (blog), June 6, 2015. https://www.patheos.com /blogs/mercynotsacrifice/2015/06/06/worship-and-justice-in-the-feast-of-first -fruits-deuteronomy-26/#wIKu2Oeb34sjql79.99.

Haarsma, Deborah B. "The People Had a Mind to Work: A Service for the Sunday before Labor Day." *Reformed Worship*, June 2004. https://www.reformedworship .org/article/june-2004/people-had-mind-work-service-sunday-labor-day.

Halker, Clark. "Jesus Was a Carpenter: Labor Song-Poets, Labor Protest, and True Religion in Gilded Age America." *Labor History* 32, no. 2 (1991): 273–89.

Hall, Joseph. *The Works of the Right Reverend Joseph Hall*. Edited by Philip Wynter. Rev. ed. 10 vols. Oxford: Oxford University Press, 1863.

Hamburger, Jeffrey F. *Nuns as Artists: The Visual Culture of a Medieval Convent*. Berkeley: University of California Press, 1997.

Hauerwas, Stanley, and Samuel Wells. "How the Church Managed before There Was Ethics." In *The Blackwell Companion to Christian Ethics*, edited by Stanley Hauerwas and Samuel Wells, 39–51. 2nd ed. Malden, MA: Wiley-Blackwell, 2011.

Hauerwas, Stanley, and William Willimon. *The Truth about God: The Ten Commandments in Christian Life*. Nashville: Abingdon, 1999.

Haughey, John C. *Converting 9 to 5: Bringing Spirituality to Your Daily Work*. Eugene, OR: Wipf & Stock, 1989.

Heidel, Alexander. *The Babylonian Genesis*. Chicago: University of Chicago Press, 1942.

Heilbroner, Robert L. *The Act of Work*. Washington, DC: Library of Congress, 1985.

Henderson, J. Frank, Kathleen Quinn, and Stephen Larson. *Liturgy, Justice, and the Reign of God: Integrating Vision and Practice*. New York: Paulist Press, 1989.

Hicks, Douglas A. *Religion and the Workplace: Pluralism, Spirituality, Leadership*. New York: Cambridge University Press, 2003.

Hicks, Frederick C. N. *The Fullness of Sacrifice: An Essay in Reconciliation*. London: SPCK, 1953.

Hill, Peter C., and Bryan J. Dik, eds. *Psychology of Religion and Workplace Spirituality*. Charlotte, NC: Information Age, 2012.

Hoffman, Frederick. *Days and Nights with Jesus, or Words for the Faithful*. New York: James Pott, 1883.

Holman, Susan. *The Hungry Are Dying: Beggars and Bishops in Roman Cappadocia*. Oxford Studies in Historical Theology. Oxford: Oxford University Press, 2001.

Holmgren, Frederick. "The Pharisee and the Tax Collector: Luke 18:9–14 and Deuteronomy 26:1–15." *Interpretation* 48 (1994): 252–61.

Howard, Richard. "Is There a Place for Eucharistic Sacrifice in Reformed Worship?" In *Reforming Worship: English Reformed Principles and Practice*, edited by Julian Templeton and Keith Riglin, 113–28. Eugene, OR: Wipf & Stock, 2012.

Hughes, John. *The End of Work: Theological Critiques of Capitalism*. Malden, MA: Blackwell, 2007.

Humphris, Ben. "Has the Body of Christ Been Made into a Commodity." *Expository Times* 127 (2016): 225–29.

Hymns of the Rural Spirit. New York: Commission of Worship, Federal Council of the Churches of Christ in America, 1947.

Irenaeus. *Against Heresies*." In *Ante-Nicene Fathers*, edited by A. Cleveland Coxe, James Donaldson, and Alexander Roberts, translated by Alexander Roberts and William Rambaut, Vol. 1. New York: Christian Literature Publishing Co., 1885.

———. *Fragments from the Lost Writings of Irenaeus*. Whitefish: Kessinger, 2010.

Irwin, John. "O God, Thy Rain and Sun and Soil." In *Hymns of the Rural Spirit*. New York: Commission of Worship, Federal Council of the Churches of Christ in America, 1947.

Janzen, Waldemar. *Old Testament Ethics: A Paradigmatic Approach*. Louisville: Westminster John Knox, 1994.

Jensen, David H. *Responsive Labor: A Theology of Work*. Louisville: Westminster John Knox, 2006.

Jethani, Skye, and Luke Bobo. *Discipleship with Monday in Mind: How Churches across the Country Are Helping Their People Connect Faith and Work*. Overland Park, KS: Made to Flourish, 2016.

Johnson, Maxwell E. *Praying and Believing in Early Christianity: The Interplay between Christian Worship and Doctrine*. Collegeville, MN: Liturgical Press, 2013.

Jungmann, Josef A. *The Early Liturgy, to the Time of Gregory the Great*. Translated by Francis A. Brunner. Notre Dame, IN: University of Notre Dame Press, 1959.

———. *The Mass of the Roman Rite: Its Origins and Development (Missarum Sollemnia)*. Translated by Francis A. Brunner. 2 vols. Notre Dame, IN: Christian Classics, 2012.

———. *The Sacrifice of the Church: The Meaning of the Mass*. Translated by Clifford Howell. Collegeville, MN: Liturgical Press, 1956.

Junker, Tércio Brethanha. *Prophetic Liturgy: Toward a Transforming Christian Praxis*. Eugene, OR: Pickwick, 2014.

Kaemingk, Matthew. "Lesslie Newbigin's Missional Approach to the Modern Workplace." *Missiology* 39, no. 3 (2011): 323–33.

Kaiser, Walter C., Jr. *Toward Old Testament Ethics*. Grand Rapids: Zondervan, 1991.

Keller, Timothy, with Katherine Leary Alsdorf. *Every Good Endeavor: Connecting Your Work to God's Work*. New York: Penguin, 2016.

Kent, Matthew. "A Theology of Work." *Theology on the Ground* (blog), June 15, 2016. http://theologyontheground.com/a-theology-of-work.

"Kenya's Prayer Train: A Commute of Prayers and Songs." *BBC News*, May 28, 2017. https://www.bbc.com/news/world-africa-39950150.

Kidner, Derek. *Psalms 1–72*. Downers Grove, IL: IVP Academic, 2014.

Kidwell, Jeremy. "Drawn into Worship: A Biblical Ethics of Work." PhD diss., University of Edinburgh, 2013.

———. *The Theology of Craft and the Craft of Work: From Tabernacle to Eucharist*. New York: Routledge & Kegan Paul, 2016.

Kilmartin, Edward J. "Offerings." In *Encyclopedia of Early Christianity*, edited by Everett Ferguson, 827–28. 2nd ed. New York: Routledge & Kegan Paul, 2013.

Kim, Young Sung. "Tongsung Kido." ARMYBARMY. http://www.armybarmy.com/JAC/article2-84.html.

Kimelman, Reuven. "Abraham Joshua Heschel: Our Generation's Teacher in Honor of the Tenth Yahrzeit." *Religion and Intellectual Life* 2 (Winter 1985): 9–18.

Kittel, Gerhard, ed. *Theological Dictionary of the New Testament*. Translated by Geoffrey W. Bromiley. 10 vols. Grand Rapids: Eerdmans, 1964–76.

Klawans, Jonathan. *Purity, Sacrifice, and the Temple: Symbolism and Supersessionism in the Study of Ancient Judaism*. New York: Oxford University Press, 2006.

Kline, Meredith. *Kingdom Prologue: Genesis Foundations for a Covenantal Worldview*. Eugene, OR: Wipf & Stock, 2006.

Knight, Frederick C. *Working the Diaspora: The Impact of African Labor on the Anglo-American World, 1650–1850*. New York: New York University Press, 2010.

Konieczny, Stanley J., and Gregory Pierce. *For Those Who Work: Stations of the Cross Ordinary Mysteries of the Rosary*. Chicago: ACTA Publications, 1991.

Kraemer, Hendrik. *A Theology of the Laity*. 1958. Reprint, Vancouver: Regent College Publishing, 2005.

Krispenz, Jutta. "Idolatry, Apostasy, Prostitution: Hosea's Struggle against the Cult." In *Priests & Cults in the Book of the Twelve*, edited by Lena-Sofia Tiemeyer, 9–29. Ancient Near East Monographs 14. Atlanta: SBL Press, 2016.

Kuyper, Abraham. *The Exalted Nature of Christ's Kingship*. Vol. 1 of *Pro Rege: Living under Christ the King*. Translated by Albert Gootjes. Bellingham, WA: Lexham, 2016.

Lambert, Lake. *Spirituality, Inc.: Religion in the American Workplace*. New York: New York University Press, 2009.

Lang, Bernhard. *Sacred Games: A History of Christian Worship*. New Haven: Yale University Press, 1997.

Lazor, Paul. "Father Alexander Schmemann—A Personal Memoir." *St Vladimir's Orthodox Theological Seminary* (blog), January 14, 2007. https://www.svots.edu/content/father-alexander-schmemann-personal-memoir.

Leech, Kenneth. *The Eye of the Storm: Living Spiritually in the Real World*. San Francisco: HarperSanFrancisco, 1992.

Leithart, Peter J. "The Ecology of the Tribute Offering." *Theopolis Institute* (blog), March 13, 1992. https://theopolisinstitute.com/the-ecology-of-the-tribute-offering.

———. *1 & 2 Kings*. Brazos Theological Commentary on the Bible. Grand Rapids: Brazos, 2016.

LeMon, Joel M. "Psalms." In *The Old Testament and Ethics: A Book-by-Book Survey*, edited by Joel B. Green and Jacqueline E. Lapsley, 97–100. Grand Rapids: Baker Academic, 2013.

Limburg, James. *Hosea–Micah*. Interpretation. Louisville: Westminster John Knox, 1988.

Linzey, Andrew. *Animal Theology*. Champaign: University of Illinois Press, 1994.

Lips-Wiersma, Marjolein. "Theorizing the Dark Side of the Workplace Spirituality Movement." *Journal of Management Inquiry* 18, no. 4 (2009): 288–300.

Livius, "The Epic of Atrahasis," trans. B. R. Foster, May 6, 2019. https://www.livius.org/sources/content/anet/104–106-the-epic-of-atrahasis.

Loh, I-to. *Hymnal Companion to "Sound the Bamboo": Asian Hymns in their Cultural and Liturgical Contexts*. Chicago: GIA Publications, 2011.

LoRusso, James Dennis. *Spirituality, Corporate Culture, and American Business: The Neoliberal Ethic and the Spirit of Global Capital*. New York: Bloomsbury Academic, 2017.

Lowe, Fletcher, Jr. "A Commissioning to Vocation in Daily Life." Theology of Work Project. https://www.theologyofwork.org/resources/a-commissioning-to-vocation-in-daily-life.

Lowe, Kevin M. *Baptized with the Soil: Christian Agrarians and the Crusade for Rural America*. New York: Oxford University Press, 2016.

Maertens, Thierry, and Kathryn Sullivan. *A Feast in Honor of Yahweh*. Notre Dame, IN: Fides, 1965.

Malesic, Jonathan. "'Nothing Is to Be Preferred to the Work of God': Cultivating Monastic Detachment for a Postindustrial Work Ethic." *Journal of the Society of Christian Ethics* 35, no. 1 (2015): 45–61.

Marques, Joan, and Satinder Dhiman, eds. *Leading Spiritually: Ten Effective Approaches to Workplace Spirituality*. New York: Palgrave Macmillan, 2014.

Marrs, Rick R. "Micah and a Theological Critique of Worship." In *Worship and the Hebrew Bible: Essays in Honour of John T. Willis*, edited by M. Patrick Graham, Rick R. Marrs, and Steven L. McKenzie, 184–203. Journal for the Study of the Old Testament: Supplement Series 284. Sheffield: Sheffield Academic, 1999.

Martin, Joan. "By Perseverance and Unwearied Industry." In *Cut Loose Your Stammering Tongue: Black Theology in the Slave Narratives*, edited by Dwight N. Hopkins and George C. L. Cummings, 107–30. Louisville: Westminster John Knox, 2003.

Marx, Karl. "A Contribution to the Critique of Hegel's Philosophy of Right. Introduction." In *Early Writings*, translated by Rodney Livingstone and Gregor Benton, 243–58. New York: Penguin Books, 1992.

Matthews, Victor H., and Don C. Benjamin. *Social World of Ancient Israel: 1250–587 BCE*. Peabody, MA: Hendrickson, 1993.

Mays, James Luther. *Amos: A Commentary*. Old Testament Library. Philadelphia: Westminster, 1969.

Mazza, Enrico. *The Eucharistic Prayers of the Roman Rite*. Translated by Matthew J. O'Connell. New York: Pueblo, 1986.

———. *Mystagogy: A Theology of Liturgy in the Patristic Age*. Translated by Matthew J. O'Connell. New York: Pueblo, 1989.

McCann, J. Clinton, Jr. "The Hope of the Poor: The Psalms in Worship and Our Search for Justice." In *Touching the Altar: The Old Testament for Christian Worship*, edited by Carol M. Bechtel, 155–78. Grand Rapids: Eerdmans, 2008.

———. *A Theological Introduction to the Book of Psalms: The Psalms as Torah*. Nashville: Abingdon, 1993.

McConville, J. Gordon. *Being Human in God's World: An Old Testament Theology of Humanity*. Grand Rapids: Baker Academic, 2016.

McFarland, Beverly, and Micki Reaman, eds. *Cracking the Earth: A 25th Anniversary Anthology from CALYX*. St. Paul: CALYX, 2001.

McGowan, Andrew B. *Ancient Christian Worship: Early Church Practices in Social, Historical, and Theological Perspective*. Grand Rapids: Baker Academic, 2014.

———. *Ascetic Eucharists: Food and Drink in Early Christian Ritual Meals*. New York: Oxford University Press, 1999.

McKelvey, Douglas Kaine. *Every Moment Holy*. Nashville: Rabbit Room Press, 2017.

McLarney, Gerard. *St. Augustine's Interpretation of the Psalms of Ascent*. Washington, DC: Catholic University of America Press, 2014.

Meeks, Wayne A. *The First Urban Christians: The Social World of the Apostle Paul*. New Haven: Yale University Press, 2003.

Metropolitan Kallistos (Ware) of Diokleia. "Through Creation to the Creator." In *Toward an Ecology of Transfiguration: Orthodox Christian Perspectives on Environment, Nature, and Creation*, edited by John Chryssavgis and Bruce V. Foltz, 86–105. New York: Fordham University Press, 2013.

Meyers, Ruth. *Missional Worship, Worshipful Mission: Gathering as God's People, Going Out in God's Name*. Grand Rapids: Eerdmans, 2014.

Middleton, Richard J. *The Liberating Image: The* Imago Dei *in Genesis 1*. Grand Rapids: Brazos, 2005.

Milavec, Aaron. *The Didache: Faith, Hope, and Life of the Earliest Christian Communities, 50–70 C.E.* New York: Newman, 2003.

———. "When, Why, and for Whom Was the Didache Created? Insights into the Social and Historical Setting of the Didache Communities." In *Matthew and the Didache: Two Documents from the Same Jewish-Christian Milieu?*, edited by Huub van de Sandt, 63–84. Minneapolis: Fortress, 2005.

Milgrom, Jacob. *Leviticus: A Book of Ritual and Ethics*. Minneapolis: Fortress, 2004.

Miller, David. *God at Work: The History and Promise of the Faith at Work Movement*. Oxford: Oxford University Press, 2007.

Mitchell, Nathan. "The Spirituality of Christian Worship." *Spirituality Today* 34, no. 1 (1982). http://opcentral.org/resources/2015/01/12/nathan-mitchell-the-spirituality-of-christian-worship.

Mitroff, Ian I., and Elizabeth A. Denton. *A Spiritual Audit of Corporate America: A Hard Look at Spirituality, Religion, and Values in the Workplace*. San Francisco: Jossey-Bass, 1999.

Möller, K. "Prophets and Prophecy." In *Dictionary of the Old Testament: Historical Books*, edited by Bill T. Arnold and H. G. M. Williamson, 825–29. Downers Grove, IL: InterVarsity, 2005.

Morgan, Reuben. "Still." Hillsong Worship. Australia: Hillsong, 2003.

Morrow, Jeffrey. "Creation as Temple-Building and Work as Liturgy in Genesis 1–31." *Journal of the Orthodox Center for the Advancement of Biblical Studies* 2, no. 1 (2009): 159–78.

———. "Work as Worship in the Garden and the Workshop: Genesis 1–3, the Feast of St. Joseph the Worker, and Liturgical Hermeneutics." *Logos* 15, no. 4 (2012): 159–78.

Mott, Stephen Charles. *A Christian Perspective on Political Thought*. New York: Oxford University Press, 1993.

Mouw, Richard J. *Called to Holy Worldliness*. Philadelphia: Fortress, 1980.

———. *When the Kings Come Marching In: Isaiah and the New Jerusalem*. Rev. ed. Grand Rapids: Eerdmans, 2002.

Muir, Edward. *Ritual in Early Modern Europe*. New York: Cambridge University Press, 2005.

Muirhead, Russell. *Just Work*. Cambridge: Harvard University Press, 2004.

Neal, Judi, ed. *Handbook of Faith and Spirituality in the Workplace: Emerging Research and Practice*. New York: Springer, 2013.

Nedungatt, George, and Michael Featherstone, eds. *The Council in Trullo Revisited*. Rome: Pontificium Institutum Orientalium Studiorum, 1995.

Newbigin, Lesslie. "The Christian Layman in the World and in the Church." *National Christian Council Review* 72 (1952): 185–89.

———. *Foolishness to the Greeks: The Gospel and Western Culture*. Grand Rapids: Eerdmans, 1986.

———. "The Form and Structure of the Visible Unity of the Church (Part 1)." *National Christian Council Review* 92 (1972): 444–51.

———. "The Form and Structure of the Visible Unity of the Church (Part 2)." *National Christian Council Review* 93 (1973): 4–18.

———. *The Good Shepherd: Meditations on Christian Ministry in Today's World*. Grand Rapids: Eerdmans, 1977.

———. "Ministry and Laity." *National Christian Council Review* 85 (1965): 479–83.

———. *Sign of the Kingdom*. Grand Rapids: Eerdmans, 1981.

———. *Unfinished Agenda: An Updated Autobiography*. Eugene, OR: Wipf & Stock, 1993.

Niederwimmer, Kurt. *The Didache: A Commentary*. Translated by Linda M. Maloney. Edited by Harold W. Attridge. Hermeneia. Minneapolis: Fortress, 1998.

Norris, Kathleen. *The Quotidian Mysteries: Laundry, Liturgy, and "Women's Work."* New York: Paulist Press, 1998.

Origen. *Homilies on Numbers*. Translated by Thomas P. Scheck. Edited by Christopher A. Hall. Ancient Christian Texts. Downers Grove, IL: IVP Academic, 2009.

Osiek, Carolyn. *The Shepherd of Hermas: A Commentary*. Edited by Helmut Koester. Minneapolis: Augsburg Fortress, 1999.

Pak, Su Yon, Unzu Lee, Jung Ha Kim, and Myung Ji Cho. *Singing the Lord's Song in a New Land: Korean American Practices of Faith*. Louisville: Westminster John Knox, 2005.

Park, Andrew S. *The Wounded Heart of God: The Asian Concept of Han and the Christian Doctrine of Sin*. Nashville: Abingdon, 1993.

Parker, Kenneth L., and Eric J. Carlson, eds. *Practical Divinity: The Works and Life of Revd Richard Greenham*. London: Routledge & Kegan Paul, 2016.

Patterson, Ben. *Serving God: The Grand Essentials of Work and Worship*. Downers Grove, IL: InterVarsity, 1994.

Pearson, Andrew. *Making Creation Visible: God's Earth in Christian Worship*. Cambridge: Grove, 1996.

Pecklers, Keith F. *The Unread Vision: The Liturgical Movement in the United States of America, 1926–1955*. Collegeville, MN: Liturgical Press, 1998.

Penner, Jeremy. *Patterns of Daily Prayer in Second Temple Period Judaism*. Boston: Brill, 2012.

Perkins, Sharon K. "Blessing Fields and Repelling Grasshoppers." In *God, Grace, and Creation*, edited by Philip J. Rossi, 201–21. College Theology Society Annual Volume 55. Maryknoll, NY: Orbis Books, 2009.

Peterson, Eugene. *Reversed Thunder: The Revelation of John and the Praying Imagination*. New York: HarperCollins, 1991.

Phelan, Thomas. "Offertory." In *The New Westminster Dictionary of Liturgy and Worship*, edited by J. G. Davies, 393–95. Philadelphia: Westminster Press, 1986.

Phillips, L. Edward. "Liturgy and Ethics." In *Liturgy in Dialogue: Essays in Memory of Ronald Jasper*, edited by Paul Bradshaw and Bryan Spinks, 86–99. London: SPCK, 1993.

Philo. *The Works of Philo: Complete and Unabridged*. Translated by C. D. Yonge. Updated ed. Peabody, MA: Hendrickson, 1993.

Pierce, Charles P., and Louis Weil. *Liturgy for Living*. Rev. ed. Harrisburg, PA: Morehouse, 2000.

Pierce, Gregory F. A. *Spirituality at Work: 10 Ways to Balance Your Life on the Job*. Chicago: Loyola, 2001.

Porter's Gate Worship Project. "Day by Day." Written by Lowana Wallace and Isaac Wardell. Featuring Joy Ike. *Work Songs*. New York: The Fuel Music, 2017.

Price, Charles P., and Louis Weil. *Liturgy for Living*. Rev. ed. Harrisburg, PA: Morehouse, 2000.

Radner, Ephraim. *Leviticus*. Brazos Theological Commentary on the Bible. Grand Rapids: Brazos, 2008.

Ramírez, Daniel. "Migrating Faiths: A Social and Cultural History of Pentecostalism in the U.S.–Mexico Borderlands." PhD diss., Duke University, 2005.

Ranft, Patricia. *The Theology of Work: Peter Damian and the Medieval Religious Renewal Movement*. New York: Palgrave Macmillan, 2006.

Reed, Esther D. *Work, For God's Sake*. London: Darton, Longman, and Todd, 2010.

Rhodes, Michael. "'Follow Us as We Follow Moses': Learning Biblical Economics from the New Testament's Appropriation of Old Testament Narratives, Practices and Liturgies." In *Ecclesia and Ethics: Moral Formation and the Church*, edited by E. Allen Jones III, John Frederick, John Anthony Dunne, Eric Lewellen, and Janghoon Park, 179–92. T&T Clark Biblical Studies. London: Bloomsbury T&T Clark, 2016.

Richards, William, and James Richardson. *Prayers for Today*. Nairobi: Uzima, 1977.

Richardson, Alan. *The Biblical Doctrine of Work*. London: SCM Press, 1954.

Rigsby, R. O. "Firstfruits." In *Dictionary of the Old Testament: Pentateuch*, edited by T. Desmond Alexander and David W. Baker, 303–15. Downers Grove, IL: InterVarsity, 2003.

Rivard, Derek A. *Blessing the World: Ritual and Lay Piety in Medieval Religion*. Washington, DC: Catholic University of America Press, 2009.

Robertson, Whitney Wherrett. *Life and Livelihood: A Handbook for Spirituality at Work*. Harrisburg, PA: Morehouse, 2004.

Roldán, Alberto Fernando. "The Priesthood of All Believers & Integral Mission." In *The Local Church, Agent of Transformation: An Ecclesiology for Integral Mission*, edited by C. René Padilla and Tetsunao Yamamori, 151–77. Buenos Airés: Ediciones Kairós, 2004.

Romero, Oscar. *The Violence of Love*. Translated by James R. Brockman. Maryknoll, NY: Orbis Books, 2004.

Roseberry, David. "How to Bless Your Business." *Anglican Pastor* (blog), May 2, 2016. https://anglicanpastor.com/blessing-a-business.

Rowthorn, Anne. *The Liberation of the Laity*. Eugene, OR: Wipf & Stock, 2000.

Roy, Christian. *Traditional Festivals: A Multicultural Encyclopedia*. 2 vols. Santa Barbara, CA: ABC-CLIO, 2005.

Rozenfeld, Ben Tsiyon. *Markets and Marketing in Roman Palestine*. Leiden: Brill, 2005.

Sadler, Rodney S., Jr. "Singing a Subversive Song: Psalm 137 and 'Colored Pompey.'" In *The Oxford Handbook of the Psalms*, edited by William P. Brown, 447–58. New York: Oxford University Press, 2014.

Safrai, S., and M. Stern, eds. *The Jewish People in the First Century: Historical Geography, Political History, Social, Cultural and Religious Life and Institutions*. Vol. 2. Philadelphia: Fortress, 1987.

Sanders, Scott Russell. *Writing from the Center*. Bloomington: Indiana University Press, 1997.

"Savior of the Apple Feast Day Is Celebrated in Ukraine." *112 Ukraine*, August 19, 2018. https://112.international/ukraine-top-news/savior-of-the-apple-feast-day -is-celebrated-in-ukraine-31269.html.

Saxton, Jo. *Real God, Real Life: Finding a Spirituality That Works*. London: Hodder & Stoughton, 2010.

Sayers, Dorothy L. *Creed or Chaos? And Other Essays in Popular Theology*. London: Methuen, 1947.

Scheller, Christine A. "Faith at Work, Part 2: Avodah and the Faith at Work Movement." Theology of Work Project. https://www.theologyofwork.org/the-high-calling/blog/faith-work-part-2-avodah-and-faith-work-movement.

Schlesinger, Eugene R. *Missa Est!: A Missional Liturgical Ecclesiology*. Minneapolis: Fortress, 2017.

Schmemann, Alexander. *For the Life of the World: Sacraments and Orthodoxy*. Crestwood, NY: St. Vladimir's Seminary Press, 1963.

Schmit, Clayton J. *Sent and Gathered: A Worship Manual for the Missional Church*. Grand Rapids: Baker Academic, 2009.

Scholes, Jeffrey. *Vocation and the Politics of Work: Popular Theology in a Consumer Culture*. Lanham, MA: Lexington Books, 2013.

Schumacher, Christopher. *God in Work: Discovering the Divine Pattern for Work in the New Millennium*. Oxford: Lion Publishing, 1998.

Scott, Margaret. *The Eucharist and Social Justice*. New York: Paulist Press, 2009.

Searle, Mark. "Ritual." In *The Study of Liturgy*, edited by Cheslyn Jones, Geoffrey Wainwright, Edward Yarnold, and Paul Bradshaw, 51–60. New York: Oxford University Press, 1992.

Shann, G. V. *Book of Needs of the Holy Orthodox Church with an Appendix Containing Offices for the Laying on of Hands*. London: David Nutt, 1894.

Sherman, Doug, and William Hendricks. *Your Work Matters to God*. Colorado Springs: NavPress, 1987.

Sinclair, John. *Un Esocés Con Alma Latina*. Mexico: CUP, 1990.

Skarsaune, Oskar. *In the Shadow of the Temple: Jewish Influences on Early Christianity*. Downers Grove, IL: InterVarsity, 2002.

Sklar, Jay. *Leviticus: An Introduction and Commentary*. Tyndale Old Testament Commentaries. Downers Grove, IL: IVP Academic, 2014.

Smith, James K. A. *Desiring the Kingdom: Worship, Worldview, and Cultural Formation*. Grand Rapids: Baker Academic, 2009.

———. "Sanctification for Ordinary Life." *Reformed Worship* 103, March 2012. https://www.reformedworship.org/article/march-2012/sanctification-ordinary-life.

———. *You Are What You Love: The Spiritual Power of Habit*. Grand Rapids: Brazos, 2016.

Smith, Thérèse. *"Let the Church Sing!": Music and Worship in a Black Mississippi Community*. Rochester: University of Rochester Press, 2004.

Smith, Yolanda Y. *Reclaiming the Spirituals: New Possibilities for African American Christian Education*. Eugene, OR: Wipf & Stock, 2004.

Sound the Bamboo. Christian Conference of Asia Hymnal. Taiwan: GIA Publications, 2000.

Staley, Vernon, ed. *Ordo Romanus Primus.* London: De La More, 1905.

Steele, Richard. *The Religious Tradesman; Or, Plain and Serious Hints of Advice for the Tradesman's Prudent and Pious Conduct, from His Entrance into Business, to His Leaving It Off.* Trenton, NJ: Francis S. Wiggins, 1823.

Stevenson, J., ed. *A New Eusebius: Documents Illustrating the History of the Church to AD 337.* Revised by W. H. C. Frend. 3rd ed. Grand Rapids: Baker Academic, 2013.

Stilgoe, John R. "Jack-o-Lanterns to Surveyors: The Secularization of Landscape Boundaries." *Environmental History Review* 1, no. 1 (1976): 14–30.

Stone, Darwell. *A History of the Doctrine of the Holy Eucharist.* London: Longmans, Green, 1909.

Strassfeld, Michael. "Avodah: Vocation, Calling, Service." *My Jewish Learning* (blog). https://www.myjewishlearning.com/article/avodah-vocation-calling-service.

Swen, E. Julu, Urs Schweizer, Gladys Mangiduyos, and Priscilla Muzerengwa. "Celebrating God's Bounty." *Interpreter,* August 2014. http://www.interpretermagazine.org/topics/celebrating-gods-bounty.

Taft, Robert F. *The Great Entrance: A History of the Transfer of Gifts and Other Pre-Anaphoral Rites of the Liturgy of St. John Chrysostom.* Orientalia Christiana Analecta 200. Rome: Pontifical Oriental Institute, 1975.

Teilhard de Chardin, Pierre. *The Divine Milieu: An Essay on the Interior Life.* New York: Harper & Brothers, 1960.

Terkel, Studs. *Working: People Talk about What They Do All Day and How They Feel about What They Do.* New York: New Press, 1972.

Theokritoff, George. "The Cosmology of the Eucharist." In *Toward an Ecology of Transfiguration: Orthodox Christian Perspectives on Environment, Nature, and Creation,* edited by John Chryssavgis and Bruce V. Foltz, 131–35. New York: Fordham University Press, 2013.

Theology of Work Project, and Peter Challen. "Instill in Each of Us at Our Work New Attitudes to Your Economy (Prayer)." Theology of Work Project. https://www.theologyofwork.org/work-in-worship/prayer-material-for-services/intercessions/instill-in-each-of-us-at-our-work-new-attitudes-to-your-economy-prayer.

Theology of Work Project, and Alistair Mackenzie. "The Equipping Church." Theology of Work Project. https://www.theologyofwork.org/key-topics/the-equipping-church.

Theology of Work Project, and Tim Meadowcroft and William Messenger. "Work, Worship and the Environment (Haggai 1:1–2:19; Zechariah 7:8–14)." Theology of Work Project. https://www.theologyofwork.org/old-testament/the-twelve-prophets/faithful-work-after-the-exilehaggai-zechariah-malachi/work-worship-and-the-environment-haggai-11-219-zechariah-78-14.

Theology of Work Project, and James Siddons. "God, Inspire All Decision Makers to Be Responsible to Stakeholders (Prayer)." Theology of Work Project. https://www.theologyofwork.org/work-in-worship/prayer-material-for-services/inter cessions/god-inspire-all-decision-makers-to-be-responsible-to-stakeholders -prayer.

Theology of Work Project, compiled by David Welbourn. "The Blessing of a Ship." Theology of Work Project. https://www.theologyofwork.org/work-in-worship /sample-services/the-blessing-of-a-ship.

———. "Intercessions about Work." Theology of Work Project. https://www.theolo gyofwork.org/work-in-worship/prayer-material-for-services/intercessions.

———. "From Ruthlessness in Making Money and Irresponsibility Spending It, Lord, Deliver Us (Prayer)." Theology of Work Project. https://www.theologyofwork.org /work-in-worship/prayer-material-for-services/intercessions/from-ruthlessness-in -making-money-and-irresponsibility-spending-it-lord-del.

T'Ofori-Atta, Ndugu. *ChristKwanza: An African American Church Liturgy, Derived from Traditional African Communal Celebration of the Harvest of the First Fruit; Matunda Ya Kwanza*. Clinton, NY: Struggler's Community, 1991.

Toryough, Godwin N. "The Biblical Ethics of Work: A Model for African Nations." *Verbum et Ecclesia* 31, no. 1 (2010). https://verbumetecclesia.org.za/index.php/ve /article/view/363.

Underhill, Evelyn. *Collected Papers of Evelyn Underhill*. Edited by Lucy Menzies. New York: Longmans, Green, 1946.

———. *The Mystery of Sacrifice: A Meditation on the Liturgy*. London: Aeterna, 1938.

Van der Kolk, Bessel A. *The Body Keeps the Score: Brain, Mind, and Body Healing of Trauma*. New York: Viking, 2014.

Vargas, Lena. "Auto Angels Repair Cars for Qualifying Low-Income Families," December 8, 2018. https://q13fox.com/2018/12/08/auto-angels-repair-cars-for-low -income-families.

Vest, Norvene. *Friend of the Soul: A Benedictine Spirituality of Work*. Lanham, MD: Cowley, 1997.

Von Allmen, J.-J. *Worship: Its Theology and Practice*. New York: Oxford University Press, 1965.

Vondey, Wolfgang. "The Making of a Black Liturgy: Pentecostal Worship and Spirituality from African Slave Narratives to American Cityscapes." *Black Theology* 10, no. 2 (2012): 147–68.

Walton, John. *The Lost World of Genesis One: Ancient Cosmology and the Origins Debate*. Downers Grove, IL: IVP Academic, 2009.

Wang, Caroline C., and Mary Ann Burris. "Photovoice: Concept, Methodology, and Use for Participatory Needs Assessment." *Health Education and Behavior* 24, no. 3 (1997): 369–87.

Wannenwetsch, Bernd. "Eucharist and the Ethics of Sacrifice and Self-Giving: Offertory Exemplified." In *Liturgy and Ethics: New Contributions from Reformed Perspectives*, edited by Pieter Vos, 131–48. Studies in Reformed Theology 33. Leiden: Brill, 2018.

———. *Political Worship: Ethics for Christian Citizens*. Oxford Studies in Theological Ethics. New York: Oxford University Press, 2004.

Ward, Graham. *The Politics of Discipleship: Becoming Postmaterial Citizens*. Grand Rapids: Baker Academic, 2009.

Ward, Hannah, and Jennifer Wild, eds. *Human Rites: Worship Resources for an Age of Change*. London: Mowbray, 1995.

Warren, Frederick E. *The Liturgy and Ritual of the Ante-Nicene Church*. 2nd ed. London: SPCK, 1912.

Warren, Tish Harrison. *Liturgy of the Ordinary: Sacred Practices in Everyday Life*. Downers Grove, IL: IVP Books, 2016.

Weil, Louis, and Charles P. Price. *Liturgy for Living*. Rev. ed. Harrisburg, PA: Morehouse, 2000.

Welch, Lawrence J. *Christology and Eucharist in the Early Thought of Cyril of Alexandria*. San Francisco: Catholic Scholars Press, 1994.

Wenham, Gordon J. *The Book of Leviticus*. New International Commentary on the Old Testament. Grand Rapids: Eerdmans, 1979.

———. *Genesis 1–15*. Word Biblical Commentary. Vol. 1. Grand Rapids: Zondervan, 2017.

———. *Psalms as Torah: Reading Biblical Song Ethically*. Grand Rapids: Baker Academic, 2012.

Wesley, John. "Privilege of Those That Are Born of God." In *The Works of John Wesley*. Vol. 5. Grand Rapids: Zondervan, 1958.

Westermann, Claus. *Isaiah 40–66: A Commentary*. Translated by D. M. G. Stalker. Old Testament Library. Philadelphia: Westminster, 1969.

Whelan, Matthew Philipp. "Prefiguring the Salvation of the World: The Eucharist and Agriculture." In *God, Grace, and Creation*, edited by Philip J. Rossi, 187–201. Annual Publication of the College Theology Society 55. Maryknoll, NY: Orbis Books, 2009.

White, Shane, and Graham White. *The Sounds of Slavery: Discovering African American History through Songs, Sermons, and Speech*. Boston: Beacon, 2005.

Wiles, Maurice, and Mark Santer, eds. *Documents in Early Christian Thought*. Cambridge: Cambridge University Press, 1975.

Williams, Roman R. "Engaging and Researching Congregations Visually: Photovoice in a Mid-Sized Church." *Ecclesial Practices* 6, no. 1 (2019): 5–27.

Williams, Rowan D. *Eucharistic Sacrifice: The Roots of a Metaphor*. Bramcote, UK: Grove Books, 1982.

Willimon, William H. *The Service of God: Christian Work and Worship*. Nashville: Abingdon, 1983.

Willis, Timothy M. "Eat and Rejoice before the Lord: The Optimism of Worship in the Deuteronomic Code." In *Worship and the Hebrew Bible: Essays in Honour of John T. Willis*, edited by M. Patrick Graham, Rick R. Marrs, and Steven L. McKenzie, 276–94. Journal for the Study of the Old Testament: Supplement Series 284. Sheffield: Sheffield Academic Press, 1999.

Willson, Cory. "Between Two Worlds: How Two Pastors Are Helping People Integrate Their Faith and Work." *Leadership Journal*, April 1, 2014. https://www.christianitytoday.com/pastors/2014/april/between-two-worlds.html.

———. "Putting Business on the Mission Map: How Churches Can Serve Businesspeople." *Comment*, October 19, 2012. https://www.cardus.ca/comment/article/putting-business-on-the-mission-map-how-churches-can-serve-businesspeople/#.

———. "Shaping the Lenses on Everyday Work: A Neo-Calvinist Understanding of the Poetics of Work and Vocational Discipleship." PhD diss., Vrije Universiteit Amsterdam, 2016.

Winkworth, Susanna. *The History and Life of the Reverend Doctor John Tauler of Strasburgh: With Twenty-Five of His Sermons; Translated from the German, with Additional Notices of Tauler's Life and Times*. London: Smith, Elder, and Company, 1857.

Winner, Lauren F. "Dislocated Exegesis: Reading the Bible in Unexpected Places." *Christian Century*, March 17, 2011. https://www.christiancentury.org/article/2011–03/dislocated-exegesis.

Witherington, Ben, III. *Work: A Kingdom Perspective on Labor*. Grand Rapids: Eerdmans, 2011.

Witt, Tom. "Singing with the Earth and the Global Church." *Liturgy* 27, no. 2 (2012): 17–30.

Wolterstorff, Nicholas. *Acting Liturgically: Philosophical Reflections on Religious Practice*. New York: Oxford University Press, 2018.

———. "More on Vocation: A Reply to Eller." *Reformed Journal* (May 1979): 20–23.

———. "The Reformed Liturgy." In *Major Themes in the Reformed Tradition*, edited by Donald K. McKim, 273–304. Eugene, OR: Wipf & Stock, 1998.

"Worship during the Agricultural Year." *Gloucestershire Churches Environmental Justice Network* (blog). https://www.greengloucestershire.org.uk/resources/worship-resources-prayers-hymns-and-songs-creation-time-.

Wright, Christopher J. H. *The Mission of God: Unlocking the Bible's Grand Narrative*. Downers Grove, IL: InterVarsity, 2006.

———. *Old Testament Ethics for the People of God*. Downers Grove, IL: InterVarsity, 2004.

Wright, N. T. *After You Believe: Why Christian Character Matters*. New York: Harper-One, 2010.

———. *The New Testament and the People of God*. Vol. 1 of *Christian Origins and the Question of God*. London: SPCK, 1992.

Yilpet, Yoilah. "Joel." In *Africa Bible Commentary: A One-Volume Commentary Written by 70 African Scholars*, edited by Tokunboh Adeyemo, 1053–58. Grand Rapids: Zondervan, 2006.

Young, Robin Darling. *In Procession before the World: Martyrdom as Public Liturgy in Early Christianity*. The Père Marquette Lecture in Theology, 2001. Milwaukee: Marquette University Press, 2001.

Yu, Debi. "Tongsung Kido." *Fuller Studio 8: Reading Scripture Globally*, 2017. https://fullerstudio.fuller.edu/voices-on-prayer.

Zahnd, Brian. "Grain and Grape," July 10, 2014. https://brianzahnd.com/2014/07/grain-grape.

Zell, Katharina Schütz. *Church Mother: The Writings of a Protestant Reformer in Sixteenth-Century Germany*. Edited and translated by Elsie McKee. Chicago: University of Chicago Press, 2006.

Zika, Charles. "Hosts, Processions and Pilgrimages." *Past and Present* 118 (February 1988): 25–64.

Zizioulas, John D. *Being as Communion: Studies in Personhood and the Church*. Crestwood, NY: St. Vladimir's Seminary Press, 1985.

———. "Proprietors or Priests of Creation?" *The Orthodox Fellowship of the Transfiguration*. http://www.orth-transfiguration.org/proprietors-or-priests-of-creation.

Scripture Index

Proverbs

Isaiah

Subject Index

Allmen, J.-J., von, 17–18, 20
Apostolic Tradition, 173–74
Augustine of Hippo, 152–53, 163, 186, 188
Averbeck, R. E., 81n25

Baal/Baalism, 119, 121, 130–34
Baldovin, John, 155, 158
Bayly, Lewis, 56–57, 151
Beale, G. K., 53nn39–40
Browning, Elizabeth Barrett, 147
Brueggemann, Walter, 65, 73, 86, 88, 99n17, 111

Calvin, John, 40, 207
Cherry, Constance, 22, 249–50
Christ's Table, 197, 199. *See also* Lord's Supper, Lord's Table
church
   institutional, 28–29, 243, 253
   organic, 28–29, 243
Clapp, Rodney, 24
Communion, 24, 138, 141, 178, 183, 184, 193, 195. *See also* Eucharist; Lord's Supper; Lord's Table
Crainshaw, Jill, 147
Cyril of Alexandria, 186–87

Daniels, Denise, 46–47
Davis, Ellen, 65n1, 70–72, 121, 130, 132, 133
Didache, 151, 168–69, 168n10
Didascalia, 151–52, 164n4, 169–70

economy, 32–33, 69–73, 79, 103, 112, 119–21, 123, 126, 155, 177, 200, 204–6, 233, 238
   of Christ, 182, 243
   divine, 207
   of Egypt, 136
   eucharistic, 205
   global, 206–7, 229
   of God, 24, 45, 57, 70–73, 71n5, 81, 83–86, 110, 111n36, 112–14, 121, 126, 131–32, 176–80, 185, 194, 200, 202–4, 208, 213, 225–26, 246, 254
   of Pharaoh, 69–72, 86, 136
   Sabbath, 204
   of the world, 24, 110, 126, 200, 204, 242
   of Yahweh
Eucharist, 80, 144n5, 153, 164n2, 165, 182, 183, 193, 195. *See also* Lord's Supper; Lord's Table

Fagerberg, David, 17, 57, 117, 155, 197
feasts, 64, 82–88, 208, 215, 222
   harvest, 83–85, 125
   liturgy of, 85
   of Tabernacles, 84,
   of the Transfiguration, 148
   in worship, 86

garden priests, 53, 212. *See also* priest: workers as
Gnostics/Gnosticism, 180, 182